AI Application Programming

AI APPLICATION PROGRAMMING

M. TIM JONES

CHARLES RIVER MEDIA, INC.
Hingham, Massachusetts

Publisher: David Pallai
Production: Publishers' Design and Production Services, Inc.
Cover Design: The Printed Image

CHARLES RIVER MEDIA, INC.
10 Downer Avenue
Hingham, Massachusetts 02043
781-740-0400
781-740-8816 (FAX)
info@charlesriver.com
www.charlesriver.com

This book is printed on acid-free paper.

M. Tim Jones. *AI Application Programming.*
ISBN: 1-58450-278-9

All brand names and product names mentioned in this book are trademarks or service marks of their respective companies. Any omission or misuse (of any kind) of service marks or trademarks should not be regarded as intent to infringe on the property of others. The publisher recognizes and respects all marks used by companies, manufacturers, and developers as a means to distinguish their products.

Library of Congress Cataloging-in-Publication Data

Jones, M. Tim.
    AI application programming / M. Tim Jones.
        p.   cm.
Includes bibliographical references.
    ISBN 1-58450-278-9 (pbk. w. CD-ROM : acid-free paper)
    1. Artificial intelligence—Data processing.   2. Artificial
intelligence—Mathematical models. I. Title.
    Q336. J67 2003
    006.3'0285—dc21
                            2003001207

Printed in the United States of America
03 7 6 5 4 3 2

CHARLES RIVER MEDIA titles are available for site license or bulk purchase by institutions, user groups, corporations, etc. For additional information, please contact the Special Sales Department at 781-740-0400.

Requests for replacement of a defective CD-ROM must be accompanied by the original disc, your mailing address, telephone number, date of purchase and purchase price. Please state the nature of the problem, and send the information to CHARLES RIVER MEDIA, INC., 10 Downer Avenue, Hingham, Massachusetts 02043. CRM's sole obligation to the purchaser is to replace the disc, based on defective materials or faulty workmanship, but not on the operation or functionality of the product.

This book is dedicated to my wife Jill and my kids Megan, Elise, and Marc. Their patience, support, and encouragement made this book possible.

Contents

Acknowledgments

This book owes much to many people. While I wrote the software for this book, the algorithms were created and evolved by a large group of researchers and practitioners. These include (in no particular order) Alan Turing, John McCarthy, Arthur Samuel, N. Metropolis, Gail Carpenter, Stephen Grossberg, Marco Dorigo, David Rumelhart, Geoffrey Hinton, John Von Neumann, Donald Hebbs, Teuvo Kohonen, John Hopfield, Warren McCulloch, Walter Pitts, Marvin Minsky, Seymour Papert, John Holland, John Koza, Thomas Back, Bruce MacLennan, Patrick Winston, Charles Forgy, Lotfi Zadeh, Rodney Brooks, Andrei Markov, James Baker, Doug Lenat, Claud Shannon, and Alan Kay. Thanks also to Dan Klein for helpful reviews on the early revisions of this book.

Preface

This book is about AI, particularly what is known as Weak AI, or the methods and techniques that can help make software smarter and more useful. While early AI concentrated on building intelligent machines that mimicked human behavior (otherwise known as Strong AI), much of AI research and practice today concentrates on goals that are more practical. These include embedding AI algorithms and techniques into software to provide them with the ability to learn, optimize, and reason.

The focus of this book is to illustrate a number of AI algorithms, and provide detailed explanations of their inner workings. Some of the algorithms and methods included are neural networks, genetic algorithms, forward-chaining rules-systems, fuzzy logic, ant algorithms, and intelligent agents. Additionally, sample applications are provided for each algorithm, some very practical in nature, others more theoretical. My goal in writing this book was to demystify some of the more interesting AI algorithms so that a wider audience can use them. It's my hope that through the detailed discussions of the algorithms in this book, AI methods and techniques can find their way into more traditional software domains. Only when AI is applied in practice can it truly grow—my desire is that this book helps developers apply AI techniques to make better and smarter software. I can be reached at mtj@mtjones.com.

1 History of AI

In this initial chapter, we'll begin with a short discussion of artificial intelligence (AI) and a brief history of modern AI. Some of the more prominent researchers will also be discussed, identifying their contributions to the field. Finally, the structure of the book is provided at the end of this chapter, identifying the methods and techniques detailed within this text.

WHAT IS AI?

Artificial intelligence is the process of creating machines that can act in a manner that could be considered by humans to be intelligent. This could be exhibiting human characteristics, or much simpler behaviors such as the ability to survive in dynamic environments.

To some, the result of this process is to gain a better understanding of ourselves. To others, it will be the base from which we engineer systems that act intelligently. In either case, AI has the potential to change our world like no other technology.

In its infancy, researchers of AI over-promised and under-delivered. The development of intelligent systems in the early days was seen as a goal just in reach, though this never materialized. Today, the claims of AI are much more practical. AI has been divided into branches, each with different goals and applications.

The problem with AI is that technologies that are researched under the umbrella of AI become common once they're introduced into mainstream products and become standard tools. For example, building a machine that could understand human speech was once considered an AI task. Now the process that includes technologies such as neural networks and Hidden

Markov Models are commonplace. It's no longer considered AI. Rodney Brooks describes this as "the AI effect." Once an AI technology becomes utilized, it's no longer AI. For this reason, the AI acronym has also been coined "Almost Implemented," as once it's done it's no longer magic, it's just common practice.

STRONG AND WEAK AI

Since artificial intelligence means so many things to so many people, another classification is in common use. *Strong AI* represents the field of making computers think at a level equal to humans. In addition to the ability to think, the computer is also considered a conscious entity.

Weak AI represents the wider domain of AI technologies. These features can be added to systems to give them intelligent qualities. This book focuses on weak AI and the methods that can be installed into other systems.

THE RESULT OF AI

Research in AI has resulted in many commonplace technologies that we now take for granted. Recall that in the early 1960s, research into miniaturization for the Apollo space program resulted in the development of integrated circuits that play such a crucial role in technology today. AI has yielded similar benefits such as voice recognition and optical character recognition.

Many commercial products today include AI technologies. Video cameras include fuzzy logic firmware that provides the ability to steady the image from a mobile operator. Fuzzy logic has also found its way into dishwashers and other devices. No mention is made of these technologies because people want products that work, but they don't really care how they work. There may also be the component of fear that some buyers may experience. Noting that a product includes an AI technology may simply not sit well with some consumers.

 Fuzzy logic is discussed in detail in Chapter 9.

NOTE

AI'S MODERN TIMELINE

While volumes could be written about the history and progression of AI, this section will attempt to focus on some of the important epochs of AI's advance as well as the pioneers that shaped it. In order to put the progression into perspective, we'll focus on a short list of some of the modern ideas of AI beginning in the 1940s [Stottler Henke 2002].

1940s—Birth of the Computer

The era of intelligent machines came soon after the development of early computing machines. Many of the early computers were built to crack World War II enemy ciphers, which were used to encrypt communications. In 1940, Robinson was constructed as the first operational computer using electromagnetic relays. Its purpose was the decoding of German military communications encrypted by the Enigma machine. Robinson was named after the designer of cartoon contraptions, Heath Robinson. Three years later, vacuum tubes replaced the electromechanical relays to build the Colossus. This faster computer was built to decipher increasingly complex codes. In 1945, the more commonly known ENIAC was created at the University of Pennsylvania by Dr. John W. Mauchly and J. P. Eckert, Jr. The goal of this computer was to compute World War II ballistic firing tables.

Neural networks with feedback loops were constructed by Walter Pitts and Warren McCulloch in 1945 to show how they could be used to compute. These early neural networks were electronic in their embodiment and helped fuel enthusiasm for the technique. Around the same time, Norbert Wiener created the field of cybernetics, which included a mathematical theory of feedback in biological and engineered systems. An important aspect of this discovery was the concept that intelligence is the process of receiving and processing information to achieve goals.

Finally, in 1949, Donald Hebbs introduced a way to provide learning capabilities to artificial neural networks. Called Hebbian learning, the process adjusts the weights of the neural network such that its output reflects its familiarity with an input. While problems existed with the method, almost all unsupervised learning procedures are Hebbian in nature.

1950s—The Birth of AI

The 1950s began the modern birth of AI. Alan Turing proposed the "Turing Test" as a way to recognize machine intelligence. In the test, one or more people would pose questions to two hidden entities, and based upon the responses determine which entity was human and which was not. If the panel could not correctly identify the machine imitating the human, it could be considered intelligent. While controversial, a form of the Turing Test called the "Loebner Prize" exists as a contest to find the best imitator of human conversation.

AI in the 1950s was primarily symbolic in nature. It was discovered that computers during this era could manipulate symbols as well as numerical data. This led to the construction of a number of programs such as the Logic Theorist (by Newell, Simon, and Shaw) for theorem proving and the General Problem Solver (Newell and Simon) for means-end analysis. Perhaps the biggest application development in the 1950s was a checkers-playing program (by Arthur Samuel) that eventually learned how to beat its creator.

Two AI languages were also developed in the 1950s. The first, Information Processing Language (or IPL) was developed by Newell, Simon, and Shaw for the construction of the Logic Theorist. IPL was a list processing language and led to the development of the more commonly known language, LISP. LISP was developed in the late 1950s and soon replaced IPL as the language of choice for AI applications. LISP was developed at the MIT AI lab by John McCarthy, who was one of the early pioneers of AI.

John McCarthy coined the name AI as part of a proposal for the Dartmouth conference on AI. In 1956, researchers of early AI met at Dartmouth College to discuss thinking machines. As part of McCarthy's proposal, he wrote:

> The study is to proceed on the basis of the conjecture that every aspect of learning or any other feature of intelligence can be in principle be so precisely described that a machine can be made to simulate it. An attempt will be made to find how to make machines use language, form abstractions and concepts, solve kinds of problems now reserved for humans, and improve themselves. [McCarthy et al. 1955]

The Dartmouth conference brought together early AI researchers for the first time, but did not reach a common view of AI.

In the late 1950s, John McCarthy and Marvin Minsky founded the Artificial Intelligence Lab at MIT, still in operation today.

1960s—The Rise of AI

In the 1960s, an expansion of AI occurred due to advancements in computer technology and an increasing number of researchers focusing on the area. Perhaps the greatest indicator that AI had reached a level of acceptability was the emergence of critics. Two books written during this period included Mortimer Taube's *Computers and Common Sense: The Myth of Thinking Machines*, and Hubert and Stuart Dreyfus's *Alchemy and AI* (RAND corporation study).

Knowledge representation was a strong theme during the 1960s, as strong AI continued to be a primary theme in AI research. Toy worlds were built, such as Minsky and Papert's "Blocks Microworld Project" at MIT and Terry Winograd's SHRDLU to provide small confined environments to test ideas on computer vision, robotics, and natural language processing.

John McCarthy founded Stanford University's AI Laboratory in the early 1960s, which, among other things, resulted in the mobile robot Shakey that could navigate a block world and follow simple instructions.

Neural network research flourished until the late 1960s following the publication of Minsky and Papert's *Perceptrons: An Introduction to Computational Geometry*. The authors identified limitations of simple, single-layer perceptrons, which resulted in a severe reduction of funding in neural network research for over a decade.

Perhaps the most interesting aspect of AI in the 1960s was the portrayal of AI in the future in Arthur C. Clarke's book, and Stanley Kubrick's film based upon the book, *2001: A Space Odyssey*. HAL, an intelligent computer onboard a Jupiter-bound spacecraft, murdered most of the crew out of paranoia over its own survival.

1970s—The Fall of AI

The 1970s represented the fall of AI after an inability to meet irrational expectations. Practical applications of AI were still rare, which compounded funding problems for AI at MIT, Stanford, and Carnegie Mellon. Funding for AI research was also minimized in Britain around the same time. Fortunately, research continued with a number of important developments.

Doug Lenet of Stanford University created the Automated Mathematician (AM) and later EURISKO to discover new theories within mathematics. AM successfully rediscovered number theory, but based upon a limited amount of encoded heuristics, reached a ceiling in its discovering ability. EURISKO, Lenet's follow-up effort, was built with AM's limitations in mind and could identify its own heuristics as well as determine which were useful and which were not [Wagman 2000].

The first practical applications of fuzzy logic appeared in the early 1970s (though Lotfi Zadeh created the concept in the 1960s). Fuzzy control was applied to the operation of a steam engine at Queen Mary College and was the first among numerous applications of fuzzy logic to process control.

The creation of languages for AI continued in the 1970s with the development of Prolog (PROgrammation en LOGique, or Programming in Logic). Prolog was well suited for the development of programs that manipulate symbols (rather than perform numerical computation) and operates with rules and facts. While Prolog proliferated outside of the United States, LISP retained its stature as the language of choice for AI applications.

The development of AI for games continued in the 1970s with the creation of a backgammon program at Carnegie Mellon. The program played so well that it defeated the world champion backgammon player, Luigi Villa of Italy. This was the first time that a computer had defeated a human in a complex board game.

1980s—An AI Boom and Bust

The 1980s showed promise for AI as the sales of AI-based hardware and software exceeded $400 million in 1986. Much of this revenue was the sale of LISP computers or expert systems that were gradually getting better and cheaper.

Expert systems were used by a variety of companies and a number of scenarios such as mineral prospecting, investment portfolio advisement, and a number of specialized applications such as electric locomotive diagnosis at GE. The limits of expert systems were also identified, as their knowledge bases grew larger and more complex. For example, Digital Equipment Corporation's XCON (system configurator) reached 10,000 rules and proved to be very difficult to maintain.

Neural networks also experienced a revival in the 1980s. Neural networks found applications for a variety of different problems such as speech recognition and other problems requiring learning.

Unfortunately, the 1980s saw both a rise and a fall of AI. This was primarily because of expert systems' failings. However, many other AI applications improved greatly during the 1980s. For example, speech recognition systems could operate in a speaker-independent manner (used by more than one speaker without explicit training), support a large vocabulary, and operate in a continuous manner (allowing the speaker to talk in a normal manner instead of word starts and stops).

1990s to Today—AI Rises Again, Quietly

The 1990s introduced a new era in weak AI applications (see Table 1.1). It was found that building a product that integrates AI isn't sought after because it includes an AI technology, but because it solves a problem more efficiently or effectively than with traditional methods. Therefore, AI found integration within a greater number of applications, but without fanfare.

TABLE 1.1 AI Applications in the 1990s (adapted from Stottler Henke, 2002)

Credit Card Fraud Detection Systems

Face Recognition Systems

Automated Scheduling Systems

Business Revenue and Staffing Requirements Prediction Systems

Configurable Data Mining Systems for Databases

Personalization Systems

A notable event for game-playing AI occurring in 1997 was the development of IBM's chess-playing program *Deep Blue* (originally developed at Carnegie Mellon). This program, running on a highly parallel supercomputer, was able to beat Gary Kasparov, the world chess champion.

Another interesting AI event in the late 1990s occurred over 60 million miles from Earth. The Deep Space 1 (DS1) was created to test 12 high-risk technologies, including a comet flyby and testing methods for future space missions. DS1 included an artificial intelligence system called the Remote Agent, which was handed control of the spacecraft for a short duration. This job was commonly done by a team of scientists through a set of ground control terminals. The goal of the Remote Agent was to demonstrate that an intelligent system could provide control capabilities for a complex spacecraft, allowing scientists and spacecraft control teams to concentrate on mission-specific elements.

BRANCHES OF AI

While it's difficult to define a set of unique branches of AI techniques and methods, a standard taxonomy is provided in Table 1.2. Some of the items represent problems, while others represent solutions, but the list represents a good starting point to better understand the domain of AI.

TABLE 1.2   Branches of Artificial Intelligence (adapted from "The AI FAQ" [Kantrowitz 2002])

Automatic Programming	Specify behavior, allow AI system to write the program
Bayesian Networks	Building networks with probabilistic information
Constraint Satisfaction	Solving NP-complete problems using a variety of techniques
Knowledge Engineering	Transforming human knowledge into a form that a computer can understand
Machine Learning	Programs that learn from past experience
Neural Networks	Modeling programs that are structured like mammalian brains
Planning	Systems that identify the best sequence of actions to reach a given goal
Search	Finding a path from a start state to a goal state

We'll touch on all of these topics within this book, illustrating not only the technology, but providing C language source code that illustrates the technique to solve a sample problem.

KEY RESEARCHERS

While many researchers have evolved AI into the field that it is today, this section will attempt to discuss a small cross-section of those pioneers and their contributions.

Alan Turing

The British mathematician Alan Turing first introduced the idea that all human-solvable problems can be reduced to a set of algorithms. This opened the door to the idea that thought itself might be algorithmically reducible, and therefore machines could be programmed to mimic humans in thought and perhaps consciousness. In coming to this conclusion, Alan Turing created the Turing Machine, which could mimic the operation of any other computing machine. Later, Alan Turing proposed the Turing Test to provide the means to recognize machine intelligence.

John McCarthy

John McCarthy is not only one of the earliest AI researchers, but he continues his research today as a Hoover Institution Senior Fellow at Stanford University. He co-founded the MIT AI Laboratory, founded the Stanford AI Lab, and organized the first conference on AI in 1956 (Dartmouth Conference). His research has brought us the LISP language, considered the primary choice of symbolic AI software development today. Time-sharing computer systems, including the ability to mathematically prove the correctness of computer programs, were an early invention of John McCarthy.

Marvin Minsky

Marvin Minsky has been one of the most prolific researchers in the field of AI as well as many others. He is currently the Toshiba Professor of Media Arts and Sciences at MIT where, with John McCarthy, he founded MIT's AI Lab in 1958. Marvin Minsky has written seminal papers in a variety of fields including neural networks, knowledge representation, and cognitive psychology. He created the AI concept of frames that modeled phenomena in cognition, language understanding, and visual perception. Professor Minsky also built the first hardware neural network-learning machine and built the first LOGO turtle.

Arthur Samuel

Arthur Samuel (1901–1990) was an early pioneer in machine learning and artificial intelligence. He had a long and illustrious career as an educator and an engineer, and was known as being helpful and modest of his achievements. Samuel is most well known for his checkers-playing program, developed in

1957. This was one of the first examples of an intelligent program playing a complex game. Not only did the program result in beating Samuel, it defeated the fourth-rated checkers player in the nation. Samuel's papers on machine learning are still noted as worthwhile reading.

PHILOSOPHICAL, MORAL, AND SOCIAL ISSUES

Many philosophical questions followed the idea of creating an artificial intelligence. For example, is it actually possible to create a machine that can think when we don't really understand the process of thought ourselves? How would we classify a machine being intelligent? If it simply acts intelligent, is it conscious? In other words, if an intelligent machine were created, would it be intelligent or simply mimic what we perceive as being intelligent?

Many believe now that emotions play a part in intelligence, and therefore it would be impossible to create an intelligent machine without also giving it emotion. Since we blame many of our poor decisions on emotions, could we knowingly impart affect on our intelligent machine knowing the effect that it could have? Would we provide all emotions, mimicking our own plight, or be more selective? Arthur C. Clarke's *2001: A Space Odyssey* provides an interesting example of this problem.

Beyond the fears of creating an artificial intelligence that turns us into its servants, many other moral issues must be answered if an intelligent machine is created. For example, if scientists did succeed in building an intelligent machine that mimicked human thought and was considered conscious, could we turn it off?

STRUCTURE OF THIS BOOK

The purpose of this book is to provide discussions of a variety of AI methods and techniques along with source code applications to demonstrate them. Each method is discussed at a high level, as well as the low level, detailing the properties and flow of the algorithms. In many cases, practical and useful applications are selected to demonstrate the algorithms. In others, applications that are more theoretical are chosen to identify the usefulness of the algorithms.

Chapter 2 introduces simulated annealing, the modeling of problem solving after the physical process of annealing (cooling of a molten substance to a solid). The constraint problem of N-Queens was chosen to illustrate the algorithm's capabilities.

Chapter 3 discusses adaptive resonance theory (or ART) and its clustering capabilities. The modern problem of personalization was chosen to demonstrate its properties.

Chapter 4 details the newer technique of ant algorithms and their pathfinding properties. The traveling salesman problem was chosen to illustrate how simulated ants could navigate a graph and identify Hamiltonian paths.

In Chapter 5, neural networks using the back propagation learning algorithm are discussed. To illustrate the generalization capabilities of the trained networks, the problem of creating game AI behaviors is detailed.

Chapter 6 introduces genetic algorithms and its subfield of genetic programming. The optimization capabilities of the genetic algorithm are demonstrated through the creation of instruction sequences to solve specific numeric problems.

In Chapter 7, the field of artificial life is discussed through the evolution of winner-takes-all neural networks. Simple organisms are evolved within a closed environment to demonstrate food webs and the evolution of survival skills within the organism's neural network controller.

Chapter 8 discusses an older technique from symbolic AI of rules-based systems. A simple forward-chaining, rules-based system is constructed and a fault-tolerant subsystem is encoded within rules and facts to manage sensors.

Chapter 9 introduces fuzzy logic and its strengths in building control systems. A number of examples are provided, detailing a simple battery charge control system using fuzzy control.

In Chapter 10, hidden Markov models are discussed along with other probabilistic graph methods. The technique is used to mimic existing literary works using them as a model for text generation.

Chapter 11 introduces the newer field of intelligent agents along with a discussion of the different types and their characteristics. A simple web-filtering agent is constructed that autonomously collects news items of interest based upon predefined search criteria.

Finally, in Chapter 12, some of the new AI methods and future of AI are discussed.

REFERENCES

[Kantrowitz 2002] Kantrowitz, Mark. (2002). "The AI Frequently Asked Questions," maintained by Ric Crabbe and Amit Dubey. Available online at *http://www.faqs.org/faqs/ai-faq/general/* (accessed January 17, 2003)

[McCarthy et al. 1955] McCarthy, J., M. Minsky, N. Rochester, and C.E. Shannon. (1955). "A Proposal for the Dartmouth Summer Research Project on Artificial Intelligence," August 31, 1955. Available online at *http://www-formal.stanford.edu/jmc/history/dartmouth/dartmouth.html* (accessed January 17, 2003)

[Stottler Henke 2002] Stottler Henke. (2002). "History of AI" available online at *http://www.shai.com/ai_general/history.htm* (accessed January 17, 2003)

[Wagman 2000] Wagman, Morton. (2000). *Scientific Discovery Processes in Humans and Computers: Theory and Research in Psychology and Artificial Intelligence.* Westport, Conn.:Praeger Publishers.

RESOURCES

Clarke, Arthur C. *2001: A Space Odyssey.* Roc, 1968.

Crevier, Daniel. *AI: The Tumultuous History of the Search for Artificial Intelligence.* New York: Basic Books, 1993.

Kurzweil, Ray. *The Age of Spiritual Machines: When Computers Exceed Human Intelligence.* New York: Viking, 1999.

McCarthy, John. "Arthur Samuel, Pioneer in Machine Learning," available online at *http://www-db.stanford.edu/pub/voy/museum/samuel.html* (accessed January 17, 2003)

McCarthy, John. "Home Page at Stanford University," available online at *http://www-formal.stanford.edu/jmc/* (accessed January 17, 2003)

Minsky, Marvin; Papert, Seymour. *Perceptrons: An Introduction to Computational Geometry.* Cambridge, Mass.: MIT Press, 1969.

Minksy, Marvin. "Home Page at MIT," available online at *http://web.media.mit.edu/~minsky/* (accessed January 17, 2003)

Taube, Mortimer. *Computers and Common Sense: The Myth of Thinking Machines.* Columbia University Press, 1961.

2 Simulated Annealing

In this chapter, we'll investigate an optimization method called simulated annealing. As the name implies, the search method mimics the process of annealing. Annealing is the physical process of heating and then cooling a substance in a controlled manner. The desired result is a strong crystalline structure, compared to fast untempered cooling which results in a brittle defective structure. The structure in question is our encoded solution, and the temperature is used to determine how and when new solutions are accepted.

NATURAL MOTIVATION

The structural properties of a solid depend upon the rate of cooling after the solid has been heated beyond its melting point. If the solid is cooled slowly, large crystals can be formed that are beneficial to the composition of the solid. If the solid is cooled in a less controlled way, the result is a fragile solid with undesirable properties.

When the solid has reached its melting point, a large amount of energy is present within the material. As the temperature is reduced, the energy within the material decreases as well. Another way of looking at annealing is as a process of "shaking," where at higher temperatures there exists higher molecular activity within a physical system. Consider the shaking of a box containing a physical landscape, where a marble is moved around randomly searching for the global minimum [Gallant 1994]. At higher temperatures, the marble is able to move freely around the landscape, while at lower temperatures the shaking is reduced, leading to less movement of the marble. The goal is to encounter the global minimum while shaking violently. As the temperature is reduced, it is less likely that the marble will be moved from the minimum. This is the search process as borrowed from annealing.

SIMULATED ANNEALING ALGORITHM

Let's now look at how the metaphor of cooling a molten substance can be used to solve a problem. The simulated annealing algorithm is very simple and can be defined in five steps (see Figure 2.1).

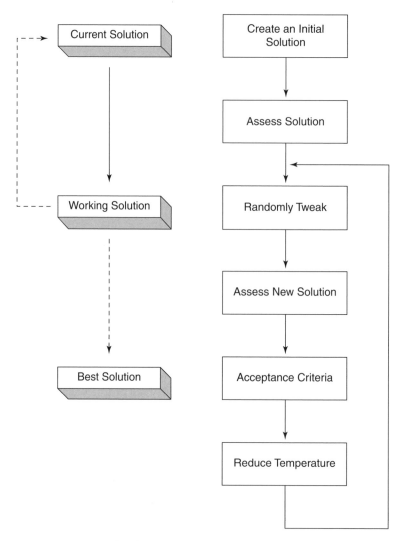

FIGURE 2.1   Simulated annealing algorithm.

Initial Solution

For most problems, the initial solution will be a random one. This is loaded into what is called the *current solution*. Another alternative is to load the initial solution with an existing solution, possibly one found in a previous run. This gives the algorithm a base from which to search for a more optimal solution to the problem.

Assess Solution

Assessing the solution consists of decoding the current solution and then performing whatever action is necessary to evaluate it against the given problem. Note that the encoded solution may simply consist of a set of variables. These variables would be decoded from the current solution and the *energy* of the solution assessed based upon how well it solved the given problem.

Randomly Tweak Solution

Tweaking the solution begins by copying the current solution into what is called the *working solution*. We then randomly modify the working solution. How the working solution is modified depends upon the encoding. Consider an encoding of the Traveling Salesman Problem (TSP), where each element represents a unique city. To tweak this working solution, we pick two elements and swap them. This keeps the solution consistent by not allowing duplicates of cities or any cities from being removed from the solution.

Once the working solution has been tweaked, we assess the solution as defined in the previous step. This random trial is based upon the Metropolis algorithm (discussed later in detail).

Acceptance Criteria

At this point in the algorithm, we have two solutions. The first is our original solution called the current solution and the second is the tweaked version called the working solution. Each has an associated energy, which is the strength of the solution (let's say that the lower the energy, the better the solution).

Our working solution is then compared to the current solution. If the working solution has less energy than the current solution (i.e., is a better solution), then we copy the working solution to the current solution and move on to temperature reduction.

However, if the working solution is worse than the current solution, we evaluate the acceptance criteria to figure out what to do with the current working solution. The probability of acceptance is based on Equation 2.1 (which is based upon the law of thermodynamics).

$$P(\delta E) = \exp\left(-\frac{\delta E}{T}\right) \qquad (2.1)$$

What this means is more easily visualized in Figure 2.2. At high temperatures (> 60 degrees Celsius), worse solutions are accepted more often than they are rejected. If the delta energy is lower, the probability is even higher for acceptance. As the temperature decreases, so does the probability for accepting a worse solution. With decreasing temperature, higher delta energies contribute to lower acceptance probabilities.

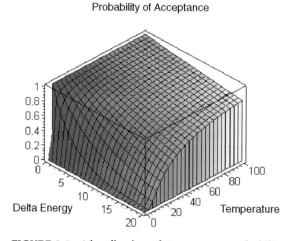

FIGURE 2.2 Visualization of Acceptance Probability.

At higher temperatures, simulated annealing permits acceptance of worse solutions in order to search more of the available solution landscape. As the temperature decreases, the search allowable also decreases until equilibrium is reached when the temperature reaches 0 degrees C.

Reduce Temperature

After some number of iterations through the algorithm at this temperature, we reduce the temperature by a small amount. Large varieties of cooling schedules exist, but in this example we'll use a simple geometric function (see Equation 2.2):

$$T_{i+1} = \alpha T_i \tag{2.2}$$

Constant α is less than one. Many other cooling strategies are possible, including linear and non-linear functions.

Repeat

A number of iterations will be performed at a single temperature. When that set of iterations is complete, the temperature is reduced and the process continues until the temperature reaches zero.

SAMPLE ITERATION

To help illustrate the algorithm, let's run through a couple of iterations to see how it works. Note that when the working solution has a lower energy (representing a better solution) than the current solution, it's always used. Only when the working solution is worse than the current solution does the acceptance probability equation come into play.

Let's say in our current environment that the temperature is 50 C and the current solution has an energy of 10. We copy the current solution to the working solution and tweak it. After assessing the energy, the new working solution has an energy of 20. In this case, the energy for the working solution is worse (higher) than the original solution and therefore we use the acceptance criteria.

| current solution energy | 10 |
| working solution energy | 20 |

The delta energy for this sample is (working solution energy − current solution energy), or 10. Plugging this delta, and our temperature of 50, into Equation 2.1, we get a probability:

$$P = \exp\left(\frac{-10}{50}\right) = 0.818731$$

Therefore, for this sample we see that it's very likely that the worse solution will be propagated forward.

Let's now look at an example near the end of the temperature schedule. Our temperature is now 2 and the energies for the current and working solutions are:

current solution energy   3
working solution energy   7

The delta energy for this sample is four. Using this delta and the temperature, we again use Equation 2.1 to find the probability of acceptance:

$$P = \exp\left(\frac{-4}{2}\right) = 0.135335$$

Given the low probability result of this sample, it's very unlikely that the working solution will be propagated on to the subsequent iterations.

That's the basic flow of the algorithm. Let's now apply simulated annealing to a problem and see how well it actually works.

SAMPLE PROBLEM

For this algorithm, we'll look at a very famous problem that has been attacked by a wide variety of search algorithms. The N-Queens problem (or NQP) is defined as the placement of N queens on an N-by-N board such that no queen threatens any other queen using the standard rules of chess (see Figure 2.3).

The 8-Queens problem was first solved in 1850 by Carl Friedrich Gauß. The search algorithm, as can be inferred by the date of the solution, was trial and error. The N-Queens problem has since been solved using depth-first search (1987), divide and conquer (1989), genetic algorithms (1992), and a variety of other methods. In 1990, Rok Sosic and Jun Gu solved the 3,000,000-Queens problem using local search and conflict minimization [Schaller 2001].

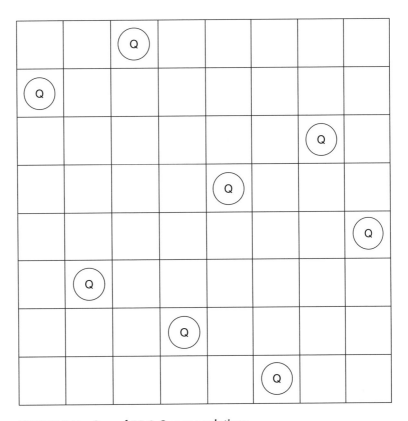

FIGURE 2.3   One of 92 8-Queens solutions.

Solution Encoding

The encoding for the N-Queens solution is a standard one that takes into account the final solution, and thus reduces the search space. Note from Figure 2.3 that only one queen can be found in each row and in each column. This constraint makes it much easier to create an encoding that will be manipulated by the simulated annealing algorithm.

Since each column contains only one queen, an N-element array will be used to represent the solution (see Figure 2.4).

The N-element array represents the row indices of queen placement. For example, in Figure 2.4, column 1 contains the value 5, which represents the row for which the queen will be placed.

Creating a random solution is also a very simple process. We initialize our solution with each queen occupying the same row as its column. We then

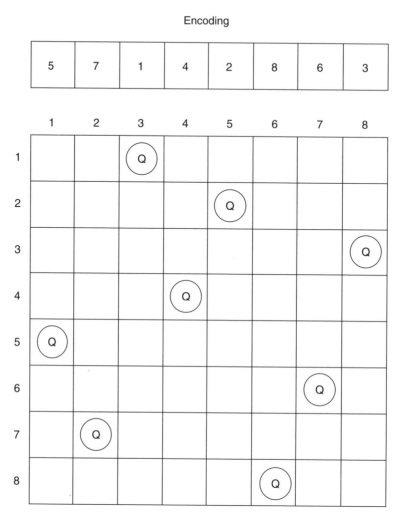

FIGURE 2.4 N-Queens solution encoding.

walk through each column and pick a random number from 1 to N for each. The two elements are then swapped (the current column with the randomly selected column). When we reach the end, the solution will be randomly perturbed.

Finally, given the encoding, there are never horizontal or vertical conflicts on the board. Therefore, only diagonal conflicts need to be checked when assessing the energy of the solution.

Energy

The energy of a solution is defined as the number of conflicts that arise given an encoding. The goal is to find an encoding that exhibits energy of zero, or no conflicts on the board.

Temperature Schedule

For this problem, we'll begin with a temperature of 30 degrees C and step down to zero using a geometric schedule (as defined in Equation 2.2). Our source will utilize 0.98 as α. As we'll see later, the temperature schedule shows a fast decline and slow convergence to the final temperature of zero.

At each temperature change, we'll perform 100 steps. This permits the algorithm a number of search steps at this plateau.

The source for the simulated annealing algorithm to solve the N-Queens problem can be found on the CD-ROM at ./software/ch2/emsa/. Also on the CD-ROM is an experimental population-based simulated annealing algorithm that has been used to solve the NQP for N of up to 80. This is on the CD-ROM at ./software/ch2/emsapop/.

ON THE CD

SOURCE DISCUSSION

Let's now look at the source that implements the simulated annealing algorithm to solve the N-queens problem.

First, we'll look at the symbolic constants and types that are used by the algorithm. See Listing 2.1.

Listing 2.1   Types and Symbolic Constants.

```
#define MAX_LENGTH 30

typedef int solutionType[MAX_LENGTH];

typedef struct {
  solutionType solution;
  float energy;
} memberType;

/* Annealing Schedule */
```

```
#define INITIAL_TEMPERATURE      30.0
#define FINAL_TEMPERATURE        0.5
#define ALPHA                    0.99
#define STEPS_PER_CHANGE         100
```

The solutionType is our encoding for the N-Queens problem. The MAX_LENGTH symbolic defines the size of the board (in this case, we're solving the 30-Queens problem). The MAX_LENGTH can be increased (to 50 or more), though some changes to the cooling schedule may be necessary for larger solutions.

We encapsulate the solution within another type called memberType, which also includes the energy assessed for the solution.

The remainder of Listing 2.1 defines the cooling schedule. The INITIAL_TEMPERATURE and FINAL_TEMPERATURE define the bounds of the schedule and ALPHA is the constant used for geometric cooling. STEPS_PER_CHANGE defines the number of iterations that we'll perform at each temperature change (plateau).

Next, we'll look at the support functions for the algorithm. Listing 2.2 contains the encoding initialization and tweaking functions. These are used to create an initial solution and to randomly perturb it.

Listing 2.2   Initialization and Tweaking Functions.

```
void tweakSolution( memberType *member )
{
  int temp, x, y;

  x = getRand(MAX_LENGTH);
  do {
    y = getRand(MAX_LENGTH);
  } while (x == y);

  temp = member->solution[x];
  member->solution[x] = member->solution[y];
  member->solution[y] = temp;
}


void initializeSolution( memberType *member )
{
  int i;
```

```
/* Initial setup of the solution */
for (i = 0 ; i < MAX_LENGTH ; i++) {
  member->solution[i] = i;
}

/* Randomly perturb the solution */
for (i = 0 ; i < MAX_LENGTH ; i++) {
  tweakSolution( member );
}

}
```

In `initializeSolution`, we create a solution where each of the N queens is placed on the board. Each queen has identical row and column indices, thereby ensuring that no horizontal or vertical conflicts exist. The solution is then perturbed using the `tweakSolution` function. The `tweakSolution` function is used later in the algorithm to perturb the working solution as derived from the current solution.

Assessing a solution is the job of `computeEnergy`. This function identifies any conflicts that exist with the current solution (see Listing 2.3).

Listing 2.3   Assessing the Solution.

```
void computeEnergy( memberType *member )
{
  int  i, j, x, y, tempx, tempy;
  char board[MAX_LENGTH][MAX_LENGTH];
  int conflicts;
  const int dx[4] = {-1,  1, -1,  1};
  const int dy[4] = {-1,  1,  1, -1};

  /* Standard library function to clear memory */
  bzero( (void *)board, MAX_LENGTH * MAX_LENGTH );

  for (i = 0 ; i < MAX_LENGTH ; i++) {
    board[i][member->solution[i]] = 'Q';
  }

  /* Walk through each of the Queens, and compute the number
   * of conflicts
   */
```

```
        conflicts = 0;

        for (i = 0 ; i < MAX_LENGTH ; i++) {

          x = i; y = member->solution[i];

          /* NOTE: Based upon the encoding, horizontal and vertical
           * conflicts will never occur!
           */

          /* Check diagonals */
          for (j = 0 ; j < 4 ; j++) {

            tempx = x ; tempy = y;
            while(1) {
              tempx += dx[j]; tempy += dy[j];
              if ((tempx < 0) || (tempx >= MAX_LENGTH) ||
                    (tempy < 0) || (tempy >= MAX_LENGTH)) break;
              if (board[tempx][tempy] == 'Q') conflicts++;
            }

          }

        }

      member->energy = (float)conflicts;
    }
```

For demonstration purposes, we'll actually build the chessboard. This isn't necessary, but it makes the resulting solution much simpler to visualize. Note the dx and dy arrays. These delta arrays are used to calculate the next position on the board for each queen that we've found. In the first case, dx = -1 and dy = -1. This corresponds to movement in the northwest direction. The final case, dx = 1, dy = -1, corresponds to movement in the northeast direction.

We select each queen on the board (denoted by the x and y pair) and then walk each of the four diagonals looking for conflicts (other queens in the path). Each time one is found, we increment the conflicts variable. At the end of this routine, we load the conflicts into the member structure as the energy component.

The next support function is used to copy one solution to another. Recall from Listing 2.1 that a solution is encoded and stored within memberType. The copySolution routine copies the contents of one memberType to another (see Listing 2.4).

Listing 2.4   Copying One Solution to Another.

```
void copySolution( memberType *dest, memberType *src )
{
  int i;

  for (i = 0 ; i < MAX_LENGTH ; i++) {
    dest->solution[i] = src->solution[i];
  }
  dest->energy = src->energy;
}
```

The final support function that we'll investigate is emitSolution. This function quite simply creates a chessboard representation from an encoded solution and emits it to standard out. The solution to be emitted is passed as an argument to the function. See Listing 2.5.

Listing 2.5   Emitting a Solution in Chessboard Format.

```
void emitSolution( memberType *member )
{
  char board[MAX_LENGTH][MAX_LENGTH];
  int x, y;

  bzero( (void *)board, MAX_LENGTH * MAX_LENGTH );

  for (x = 0 ; x < MAX_LENGTH ; x++) {
    board[x][member->solution[x]] = 'Q';
  }

  printf("board:\n");
  for (y = 0 ; y < MAX_LENGTH ; y++) {
    for (x = 0 ; x < MAX_LENGTH ; x++) {
      if (board[x][y] == 'Q') printf("Q ");
      else printf(". ");
    }
    printf("\n");
  }
  printf("\n\n");
}
```

Within emitSolution, the board is constructed based upon the encoding (row = index, contents = column). The board is then emitted with "Q" as a location with a queen and a "." as an empty location.

Now that we've looked at all of the support functions, we'll look at the actual simulated annealing algorithm (coded within the main() function in Listing 2.6).

Listing 2.6   Simulated Annealing Algorithm.

```
int main()
{
  int  timer=0, step, solution=0, useNew, accepted;
  float temperature = INITIAL_TEMPERATURE;
  memberType current, working, best;
  FILE *fp;

  fp = fopen("stats.txt", "w");

  srand(time(NULL));

  initializeSolution( &current );
  computeEnergy( &current );
  best.energy = 100.0;

  copySolution( &working, &current);

  while (temperature > FINAL_TEMPERATURE) {

    printf("Temperature : %f\n", temperature);

    accepted = 0;

    /* Monte Carlo Step */
    for (step = 0 ; step < STEPS_PER_CHANGE ; step++) {

      useNew = 0;

      tweakSolution( &working );
      computeEnergy( &working );

      if (working.energy <= current.energy) {

        useNew = 1;
```

```
    } else {

      float test = getSRand();
      float delta = working.energy - current.energy;
      float calc = exp(-delta/temperature);

      if (calc > test) {
        accepted++;
        useNew = 1;
      }

    }

    if (useNew) {
      useNew = 0;
      copySolution( &current, &working );

      if (current.energy < best.energy) {
        copySolution( &best, &current );
        solution = 1;
      }

    } else {

      copySolution( &working, &current);

    }

  }

  fprintf(fp, "%d %f %f %d\n",
            timer++, temperature, best.energy, accepted);

  printf("Best energy = %f\n", best.energy);

  temperature *= ALPHA;
}

fclose(fp);

if (solution) {
  emitSolution( &best );
}
```

```
    return 0;
}
```

The simulated annealing algorithm shown in Listing 2.6 follows very closely the summarized algorithm in Figure 2.1. After two ancillary steps (opening a file for plot data and seeding the random number generator), we initialize our current solution named `current` and assess the energy of the solution with `computeEnergy`. We then copy the current solution to the working solution and start the algorithm.

The outer loop of the algorithm tests the current temperature against the final temperature. Note that we exit the loop once the current temperature is less than or equal to the `FINAL_TEMPERATURE`. This avoids us having to use a zero temperature in the acceptance probability equation.

The inner loop of the algorithm is called the Metropolis Monte Carlo simulation [Metropolis et al. 1953]. This loop is performed for a number of iterations at the current temperature to fully exploit the search capabilities of the temperature.

The first step in the Monte Carlo simulation is to tweak the working solution using the `tweakSolution` function. We then compute the energy of the working solution and compare it against our current solution. If the energy of the new working solution is less than (or equal to) the current solution, we accept it by default. Otherwise, we perform Equation 2.1 (acceptance probability equation) to determine if this worse solution should propagate. The delta is calculated as the difference of the `working` energy and the `current` energy. Note that to get here, the `working` energy is always greater than the `current`. We calculate a random number between 0 and 1 for our probability and then compare it with the result of Equation 2.1. If we've met the acceptance criteria (the result of Equation 2.1 is greater than our random number), we accept the working solution. This entails copying the working solution to `current`, since the working solution will again be tweaked at the next iteration of the Monte Carlo inner loop.

If the working solution is not accepted, we copy the current solution over the working solution. At the next iteration, the older working solution is lost and we tweak the existing current solution and try again.

After emitting some information to our statistics file, we reduce the temperature after performing the required number of iterations of the inner loop. Recall from Equation 2.2 that our temperature schedule is a simple geometric function. We multiply our current temperature by ALPHA, and repeat our outer loop.

At the end of the algorithm, we emit the best solution that was found (as long as one was actually found, as indicated by the solution variable). This variable is set within the inner loop after determining that a solution with less energy was found than the current best solution.

SAMPLE RUN

Let's look at the result of a sample run. In this run, we'll start the temperature at 100, though it's really only necessary to start at about 30 to solve the problem. We start from 100 to illustrate the algorithm (as shown in Figure 2.5).

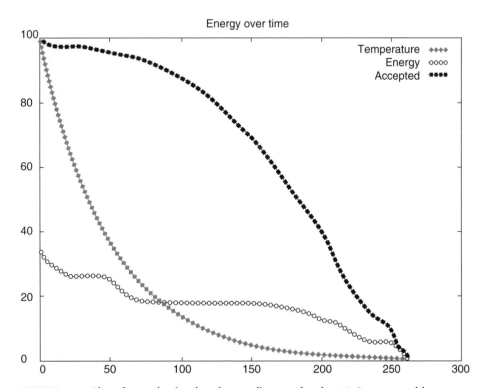

FIGURE 2.5 Plot of sample simulated annealing run for the 40-Queens problem.

The element falling sharply from 100 to 0 is the temperature. The cooling schedule uses Equation 2.2. The element falling less sharply is the number of accepted worse solutions (based upon the acceptance probability Equation 2.1). Since the acceptance probability is a function of the temperature, a correlation is easily seen. Finally, the line interspersed with '+' symbols is the best solution energy. As this graph shows, the perfect solution is not found until very near the end. This is true in all runs because of the acceptance criteria equation. The sharp drop of the "Accepted" graph element at the end of the plot is indicative of this—a sharp reduction in the acceptance of worse solutions can be seen.

The actual 40-Queens solution, as represented by Figure 2.5, is shown in Figure 2.6.

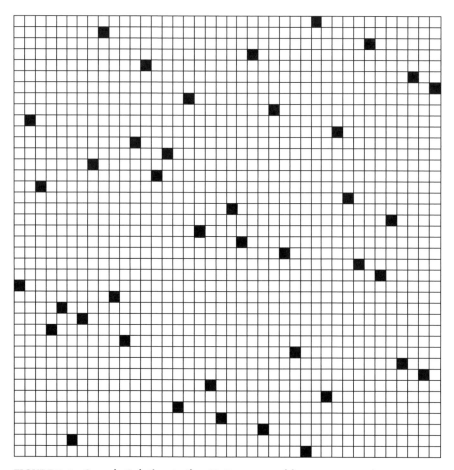

FIGURE 2.6 Sample Solution to the 40-Queens problem.

ADJUSTING THE ALGORITHM PARAMETERS

The parameters for the algorithm can be adjusted depending upon the complexity of the problem to be solved. This section will define some of these parameters along with the effects that can be realized.

Initial Temperature

The initial temperature must be high enough to permit movement of solutions to other parts of the solution landscape. Graham Kendall shows that knowing the maximum distance between one neighbor (solution) and another permits the calculation of the initial temperature [Kendall 2002].

The initial temperature can also be dynamically defined. Given statistics on the rate of acceptance of worse solutions and discovery of new better solutions, the temperature can be raised until a sufficient number of acceptances/discoveries have occurred. This is similar to heating a solid until it is liquid, after this there is no point in further increasing the temperature [Dowsland 1995].

Final Temperature

While zero is a good symbolic final temperature, the geometric function used within this example means that the algorithm will run far longer than practically useful. Therefore, the final temperature from Listing 2.1 shows 0.5 degrees. Depending upon the temperature function used, this value may vary.

Temperature Function

The actual temperature function used can be varied depending upon the problem to be solved. Figure 2.5 shows the temperature over time using a geometric function. A large variety of other temperature cooling functions can be used. These functions may result in a steep reduction in the first half of the temperature schedule, or a slow reduction followed by a steep loss in temperature. A very nice illustration of sample cooling schedules can be found at Brian Luke's Web site "Simulated Annealing Cooling Schedules" [Luke 2001].

Iterations at Temperature

At higher temperatures, the simulated annealing algorithm looks for the global optimum over the entire solution landscape. As cooling occurs, there is less movement and the algorithm searches the local optimum to optimize it. The number of iterations to perform at each temperature step is therefore important. In our sample problem (see Listing 2.1) we specified that 100 iterations are performed. It's useful to manually experiment with the number of iterations to find what's optimal for the problem at hand.

OTHER APPLICATIONS

Simulated annealing can be effective in solving a wide range of combinatorial optimization problems. A short list is provided below.

- Path Generation
- Image Reconstruction
- Task Assignment and Scheduling
- Circuit Layout
- Global Routing
- Visual Object Detection and Recognition
- Design Specialized Digital Filters

It should be noted that since simulated annealing is a random process, finding a solution using the algorithm can take time, and in some cases, it may never converge on a solution at all.

SUMMARY

In this chapter, we've looked at the simulated annealing algorithm as a way to perform search and optimization procedures. Simulated annealing follows a physical metaphor of a solid heated to its melting point and then cooled slowly to form a uniform solid. At high temperatures, the search process is permitted to search over the entire landscape. As the temperature is reduced, the search space decreases to the local area around the current solution. To illustrate the algorithm, we solved the classic N-Queens problem up to N=50. Finally, we investigated the parameters of simulated annealing and how they could be manipulated to help solve more complex problems, or simpler problems with greater speed.

REFERENCES

[Carpenter and Grossberg 1987] Carpenter, G. and S. Grossberg. (1987). "A Massively Parallel Architecture for a Self-Organizing Neural Pattern Recognition Machine." *Computer Vision, Graphics and Image Processing 37.*

[Dowsland 1995] Dowsland, Kathryn. (1995). "Simulated Annealing,"in *Modern Heuristic Techniques for Combinatorial Problems*, Colin Reeves (ed.). New York: McGraw-Hill.

[Gallant 1994] Gallant, Stephen. (1994). *Neural Network Learning.* Cambridge, Mass.: MIT Press.

Kendall, Graham. (2002). "Simulated Annealing," available online at *http://www.cs.nott.ac.uk/~gxk/aim/notes/simulatedannealing.doc* (accessed January 17, 2003)

[Luke 2001] Luke, Brian T. (2001). "Simulated Annealing Cooling Schedules," available online at *http://members.aol.com/btluke/simanf1.htm* (accessed January 17, 2003)

[Metropolis et al. 1953] Metropolis, N. et al. (1953)."Equation of State Calculation by Fast Computing Machines." *Journal of Chem. Phys.* 21:1087–1091.

[Schaller 2001] Schaller, H. Nikolaus. (2001). "The N-Queens Problem (NQP)," available online at *http://www.dsitri.de/projects/NQP/* (accessed January 17, 2003).

3 | Introduction to Adaptive Resonance Theory (ART1)

In this chapter, Grossberg and Carpenter's famous ART1 algorithm will be presented. ART1 is the first algorithm in the family of adaptive resonance theory algorithms. It is a very simple, unsupervised learning algorithm with biological motivations. Following a discussion of the theory of ART1, the algorithm will be demonstrated in the application of personalization, otherwise known as a recommender system.

CLUSTERING ALGORITHMS

A clustering algorithm is a method by which a set of data is separated and grouped into smaller sets (or clusters) of similar data. It also separates out dissimilar elements. One purpose of clustering data into separate groups is for classification. While classification has many uses, one common use exploits the similarities in the clusters by analyzing any differences that exist. We'll look more at this specific use in a later section.

BIOLOGICAL MOTIVATIONS

Clustering algorithms are motivated by biology in that they offer the ability for learning through classification. We routinely learn new concepts by relating them to existing knowledge. We classify the new knowledge by initially trying to cluster it with something we already know (as a basis for our understanding). If we cannot relate it to something we already know, then we must create a new structure for understanding that is different from our existing patterns. This new pattern may then form the basis for understanding new knowledge.

By clustering new concepts together with analogous old ones, and creating new clusters when we encounter new knowledge, we solve what Grossberg coined the *stability-plasticity dilemma*. The problem is how to adapt (learn new things) without the new knowledge destroying what we've already learned. The ART1 algorithm includes the necessary elements to not only create new clusters when sufficiently different data is encountered, but also to reorganize clusters based upon the changes.

THE ART1 ALGORITHM

The ART1 algorithm works with objects called *feature vectors*. A feature vector is nothing more than a collection of binary values that represent some type of information. An example of a feature vector is the purchase history of a customer (see Figure 3.1). Each element in the feature vector identifies whether the customer has purchased an item (represented as a 1 if the item has been purchased by the customer, otherwise 0). The sample feature vector shown in Figure 3.1 illustrates a customer that has purchased a hammer and a wrench.

Hammer	Paper	Snickers®	Screwdriver	Pen	Kit-Kat®	Wrench	Pencil	Heath Bar®	Tape Measure	Binder
1	0	0	0	0	0	1	0	0	0	0

Customer Feature Vector

FIGURE 3.1   Example feature vector containing customer purchase data.

This feature vector describes the customer in terms of his purchase habit by identifying items that he's purchased (for which we have knowledge). We collect and apply the ART1 algorithm to the set of customer feature vectors to separate them into clusters. The idea is that a collection of similar customers (contained within a cluster) will yield interesting information about the common attributes of the customer set.

ART1 in Detail

We begin with a set of feature vectors (we'll call these examples $E_{1..K}$) and a set of initialized prototype vectors ($P_{1..N}$). The prototype vector is the "center" of the cluster. The number of prototype vectors, N, is the maximum number of clusters that can be supported. The d parameter represents the length of the vector. We initialize a vigilance parameter (ρ, or rho) to a small value between 0 and 1.0, and a beta parameter to a small positive integer. We'll discuss these in more detail shortly. See Figure 3.2 for a list of the working parameters.

Some of the operations shown in Figure 3.2 may be foreign to some readers. The vector bitwise AND is a simple binary AND of the two vectors. The result is a new vector such that if an element is set to one in the result, then

$P_i \cap E$	Vector bitwise AND
$\|v\|$	Magnitude of v (number of 1s set).
N	Number of Prototype Vectors
ρ	Vigilance parameter (0 < p <= 1)
P	Prototype Vector
E	Example Vector
d	Dimension of Vectors (length)
B	Beta parameter

FIGURE 3.2   ART1 algorithm parameters.

each element of the two original vectors is set. The magnitude is the count of the non-zero elements of the vector.

The ART1 algorithm flow is shown in Figure 3.3.

The equations used in this flow are shown as Equations 3.1 through 3.4.

Initially, no prototype vectors exist, so at the start of the algorithm an initial prototype vector is created with the first example vector (Equation 3.1). We then check all subsequent example feature vectors against each existing prototype vector for their proximity (how close the example feature vector is to the current prototype vector).

$$P_0 = E_0 \tag{3.1}$$

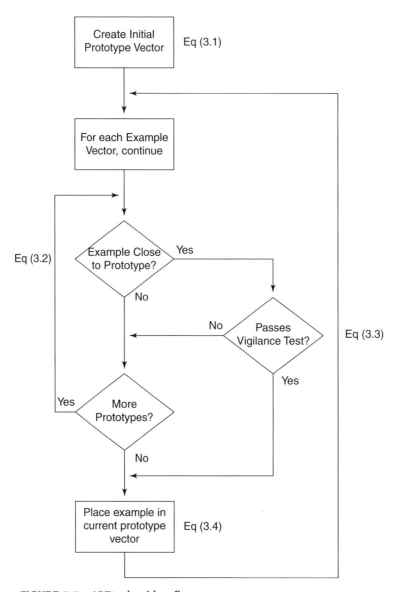

FIGURE 3.3 ART1 algorithm flow.

The beta parameter used in the proximity equation (Equation 3.2) is a "tie-breaker" that favors prototypes with more 1's over those with fewer 1's when all of the 1's in the prototype vector are also in the example feature vector being tested [Gallant 1994].

$$\frac{\left\|P_i \cap E\right\|}{\beta + \left\|P_i\right\|} > \frac{\left\|E\right\|}{\beta + d} \tag{3.2}$$

If the proximity test is satisfied, the next test is to check the example feature vector and the prototype vector against the vigilance parameter (Equation 3.3). The purpose of the vigilance parameter is to define the class size. If vigilance is large, larger classes result (clusters with larger numbers of members). Decreasing the vigilance parameter will result in clusters with fewer members. If the vigilance parameter is set low enough (< 0.1), the feature vectors must match the prototype vectors for acceptance.

$$\frac{\left\|P_i \cap E\right\|}{\left\|E\right\|} < \rho \tag{3.3}$$

Finally, if we pass the vigilance test, we incorporate the current example feature vector into the current prototype vector (Equation 3.4). This process is simply a bitwise AND of the example vector and the prototype vector. If we don't pass the vigilance test (or the proximity test) we check the next prototype vector. If we exhaust all of the prototype vectors without clustering the example vector, we create a new prototype vector from the feature vector. This results in a new cluster since none of the existing clusters passed any of the similarity tests.

$$P_i = P_i \cap E \tag{3.4}$$

Finally, we walk through all of the example feature vectors and compare them to the entire set of prototype vectors (per the flow diagram in Figure 3.3). Although we've already clustered all of the examples, we're now checking to make sure that all example feature vectors are in the correct cluster. This is because subsequent feature vector checks could have created new clusters, so further checks are necessary to make sure that clustered feature vectors don't need to be moved to another cluster.

Once we've run through all of the example vectors without making any changes, we've converged on a clustering solution and the process is complete. To avoid the possibility of oscillations of a feature vector moving between two prototype vectors, we cap the number of iterations to force a

convergence. This is set sufficiently high to avoid prematurely converging on
a solution.

Running through the Algorithm

Let's look at the algorithm at work with a simple example. Let's say that we
have two clusters represented by prototype vectors P_0 and P_1 (as shown in Figure 3.4). Also shown are the example feature vector and the working parameters for the algorithm.

$$P_0 = \{1,0,0,1,1,0,1\} \qquad \beta = 1.0$$
$$P_1 = \{1,1,0,0,0,1,0\} \qquad \rho = 0.9$$
$$E = \{1,1,1,0,0,1,0\} \qquad d = 7$$

FIGURE 3.4 Sample prototype and
example vectors.

*The beta and rho parameters in Figure 3.4 were chosen after some experi-
mentation. For any given problem, it's advisable to try some number of combinations to find the parameter pair that yields the best results.*

Now let's run the tests of the ART1 algorithm to see where the example
vector will be clustered (see Figure 3.5).

Proximity Test P_0/E_x (Eq2) $\frac{1}{5} > \frac{4}{8}$ (False)
Proximity Test P_1/E_x (Eq1) $\frac{3}{5} > \frac{4}{8}$ (True)
Vigilance Test P_1/E_x (Eq3) $\frac{3}{4} < 0.9$ (True)
P1 AND Ex   (Eq4) $\{1,1,0,0,0,1,0\}$ AND $\{1,1,1,0,0,1,0\} = \{1,1,0,0,0,1,0\}$

FIGURE 3.5 ART1 algorithm check on sample data from Figure 3.4.

In the first test (Figure 3.5), we perform the proximity test for prototype
vector P_0. Using Equation 3.2, we find that the test fails (0.2 is not greater than
0.5). Next, we check the example feature vector against P_1. In this case, the test
succeeds, so we try the vigilance test. The vigilance test also succeeds, so the example vector is associated with the cluster represented by P_1. We finally modify the prototype vector by performing a bitwise AND of P_1 with the example

vector (Equation 3.4). After updating a prototype vector, all of the feature vectors are then checked against all of the available prototype vectors to ensure they are in the correct cluster. Once new changes occur, clustering is complete.

Learning in ART1

As example feature vectors are tested against the prototype vectors, new clusters are created or existing clusters are modified at the inclusion of an example. This is known as "resonance" and indicates the process of learning within the algorithm. When the algorithm reaches equilibrium (i.e., no further changes occur with the prototype vectors), learning is complete and the data set is classified.

Advantages of ART1 over other Clustering Algorithms

ART1 is both conceptually simple and easy to implement. Earlier algorithms, such as McQueen's k-means clustering algorithm, while much simpler, have some significant drawbacks. For example, k-means does not allow the creation of new clusters (the clusters are statically defined at the start). There is also no parameter within k-means to adjust the class size of the resulting clusters. A drawback to both algorithms (ART1 and k-means) is that the final set of clusters (and prototype vectors) can be influenced based upon the order in which training is performed.

The ART Family of Algorithms

Large varieties of ART algorithms have been created as variations on the original or to solve a different class of problems. While ART1 operates on discrete data, the ART2 algorithm was created for clustering continuous data (such as waveforms). ARTMAP is a supervised version of ART that can learn arbitrary mappings of binary patterns. Fuzzy ARTMAP is a synthesis of ARTMAP and fuzzy logic.

Other varieties of ART models exist. For more information, see the Resources section at the end of this chapter.

USING ART1 FOR PERSONALIZATION

Let's now look at the application of the ART1 algorithm to the problem of personalization. First, let's define and better understand personalization.

What Is Personalization?

The idea of personalization is not new, traditional companies have been doing it for quite some time. The rise in popularity of personalization is due primarily to the advantages of using it in Web environments. Commercial Web sites permit near real-time personalization—before a consumer makes a purchase, the site can recommend other items that are likely to appeal to the customer. This time is critical to the seller since they can alter buying behavior of the customer prior to the purchase in the hopes of increasing their revenue.

Achieving Personalization

Personalization involves taking some set of inputs and returning one or more recommendations to the user through some type of computation. The method by which personalization is performed varies depending upon the type of data available for input, the required representation of the output, and in some cases the speed and accuracy by which the output must be computed.

Many companies use a variety of methods to achieve personalization. Most algorithms (or methods for tuning existing algorithms) are kept secret since they represent strategic importance to the owner. Amazon.com uses a method called "Collaborative Filtering," which provides recommendations based upon the similarity of a customer's purchases to the purchases of others. A similarity metric is used to extract a subgroup of customers from the stored population. Given this sub-population, recommendations are made based upon differences identified between the members.

Personalization Using ART1

Using ART1 for personalization involves two steps. First, we perform the standard ART1 algorithm on our feature vectors (customer data). Next, to make a recommendation, we analyze the feature vector (representing the customer to which we're going to make a recommendation) as well as a new element called the *sum vector*. The sum vector, not part of ART1, represents the sums of the columns of the feature vectors within the cluster (see Figure 3.6).

Let's look at the process of recommendation by way of an example. Let's say the customer to whom we're going to make a recommendation is represented by feature vector u, which is a member of cluster A. The contents of the

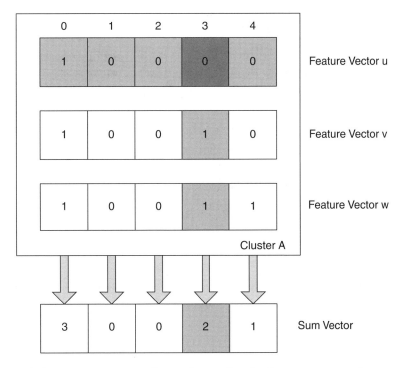

FIGURE 3.6   Recommending an item using the feature vector and sum vector.

feature vector follow the example given in Figure 3.1 (purchase history of customer). We first look at the sum vector to identify which items (columns) are represented by the cluster (those with non-zero values). We then find the largest value item in the sum vector that corresponds with an element in the customer's feature vector of value zero. This represents an item that the customer has not purchased that is popular within the cluster. This intersection is the basis for the recommendation. The assumption (or statistical prediction) is that since 66% of the customers within this cluster have purchased this item (given item three within the example), it's likely that the current customer might purchase it as well.

The source code for the ART1 algorithm can be found on the CD-ROM at ./software/ch3/.

SOURCE CODE DISCUSSION

ON THE CD

The ART1 source code includes the recommendation algorithm as discussed above. The complete source is available on the CD-ROM at ./software/ch3. The ART1 source can be compiled on Linux or on Windows using the Cygwin UNIX environment.

The source includes a sample data set within a structure at the head of the file. The data set is a set of feature vectors that represent the customer purchase records. Per the notation in the algorithm discussion, a one value represents a purchase of the item by the customer; a zero represents no purchase. The feature vectors (customer database) and other relevant structures are shown in Listing 3.1.

Listing 3.1   ART1 Data Structures for Personalization.

```
#define MAX_ITEMS                       (11)
#define MAX_CUSTOMERS                   (10)
#define TOTAL_PROTOTYPE_VECTORS         (5)

const float beta = 1.0;        /* Small positive number */
const float vigilance = 0.9;   /* 0 <= vigilance < 1 */

int numPrototypeVectors = 0;   /* Total prototype vectors */

int prototypeVector[TOTAL_PROTOTYPE_VECTORS][MAX_ITEMS];

/* sumVector supports making recommendations. */
int sumVector[TOTAL_PROTOTYPE_VECTORS][MAX_ITEMS];

/* Number of occupants of the cluster */
int members[TOTAL_PROTOTYPE_VECTORS];

/* Identifies the cluster to which a particular customer belongs */
int membership[MAX_CUSTOMERS];

/*
 * Feature vectors are contained within the database array. A one
     in
 * the field represents a product that the customer has purchased.
   A
 * zero represents a product not purchased by the customer.
```

```
*/

/*        Hmr  Ppr  Snk  Scr  Pen  Kkt  Wrn  Pcl  Hth  Tpm  Bdr */
int database[MAX_CUSTOMERS][MAX_ITEMS] = {
        { 0,   0,   0,   0,   0,   1,   0,   0,   1,   0,   0},
        { 0,   1,   0,   0,   0,   0,   0,   1,   0,   0,   1},
        { 0,   0,   0,   1,   0,   0,   1,   0,   0,   1,   0},
        { 0,   0,   0,   0,   1,   0,   0,   1,   0,   0,   1},
        { 1,   0,   0,   1,   0,   0,   0,   0,   0,   1,   0},
        { 0,   0,   0,   0,   1,   0,   0,   0,   0,   0,   1},
        { 1,   0,   0,   1,   0,   0,   0,   0,   0,   0,   0},
        { 0,   0,   1,   0,   0,   0,   0,   0,   1,   0,   0},
        { 0,   0,   0,   0,   1,   0,   0,   1,   0,   0,   0},
        { 0,   0,   1,   0,   0,   1,   0,   0,   1,   0,   0}
};
```

The `prototypeVector` represents the prototype vectors for each of the clusters. The `sumVector` is used solely for recommendation, and is not part of the standard ART1 algorithm. The `members` array specifies the number of members for a particular cluster and the `membership` array identifies to which particular cluster a customer feature vector belongs. Finally, the `database` structure defines the unique feature vectors for the customers.

The `main` routine performs the ART1 processing and then makes recommendations based upon the ART1 results. The `main` function is shown in Listing 3.2.

Listing 3.2 ART1 Personalization `main` Function.

```
int main()
{
  int customer;

  srand( time( NULL ) );

  initialize();

  performART1();

  displayCustomerDatabase();

  for (customer = 0 ; customer < MAX_CUSTOMERS ; customer++) {
    makeRecommendation( customer );
```

```
   }

   return 0;
}
```

After setting the random seed using srand, the initialize function is called to clear and initialize the structures used by the ART1 and recommendation algorithm. The ART1 algorithm is represented by the performART1 function and recommendations are made using the makeRecommendation function. The function displayCustomerDatabase is used to show prototype vectors for each cluster created and the feature vector occupants of the clusters. This function can be viewed on the CD-ROM.

ON THE CD

Listing 3.3   Initializing the Algorithm Structures.

```
void initialize( void )
{
  int i, j;

  /* Clear out prototype vectors */
  for (i = 0 ; i < TOTAL_PROTOTYPE_VECTORS ; i++) {
    for (j = 0 ; j < MAX_ITEMS ; j++) {
      prototypeVector[i][j] = 0;
      sumVector[i][j] = 0;
    }
    members[i] = 0;
  }

  /* Initialize example vectors to no membership to any cluster */
  for (j = 0 ; j < MAX_CUSTOMERS ; j++) {
    membership[j] = -1;
  }

}
```

The initialize function in Listing 3.3 clears out the prototype vectors, sum vector as well as the members and membership arrays.

Two support functions are shown in Listing 3.4. These are the vectorMagnitude and vectorBitwiseAnd functions.

Listing 3.4   Support Functions for the ART1 Algorithm.

```
int vectorMagnitude( int *vector )
{
  int j, total = 0;

  for (j = 0 ; j < MAX_ITEMS ; j++) {
    if (vector[j] == 1) total++;
  }

  return total;
}

void vectorBitwiseAnd( int *result, int *v, int *w )
{
  int i;
  for (i = 0 ; i < MAX_ITEMS ; i++) {
    result[i] = (v[i] && w[i]);
  }

  return;
}
```

The `vectorMagnitude` function simply counts the number of elements within the vector that are set (value of 1) and returns the total. The `vectorBitwiseAnd` performs a bitwise AND of two vectors, resulting in a new vector.

Two prototype vector routines are also provided to create a new cluster and update a cluster based upon changes that have occurred within it (occupant moving in or out of the cluster). These functions are shown in Listing 3.5

Listing 3.5   Prototype Vector Manipulation Functions.

```
int createNewPrototypeVector( int *example )
{
  int i, cluster;

  for (cluster = 0 ; cluster < TOTAL_PROTOTYPE_VECTORS ;
    cluster++) {
    if (members[cluster] == 0) break;
  }
```

```
    if (cluster == TOTAL_PROTOTYPE_VECTORS) assert(0);

  numPrototypeVectors++;

  for (i = 0 ; i < MAX_ITEMS ; i++) {
    prototypeVector[cluster][i] = example[i];
  }

  members[cluster] = 1;

  return cluster;
}


void updatePrototypeVectors( int cluster )
{
  int item, customer, first = 1;

  assert( cluster >= 0);

  for (item = 0 ; item < MAX_ITEMS ; item++) {
    prototypeVector[cluster][item] = 0;
    sumVector[cluster][item] = 0;
  }

  for (customer = 0 ; customer < MAX_CUSTOMERS ; customer++) {
    if (membership[customer] == cluster) {
      if (first) {
        for (item = 0 ; item < MAX_ITEMS ; item++) {
          prototypeVector[cluster][item] =
              database[customer][item];
          sumVector[cluster][item] = database[customer][item];
        }
        first = 0;
      } else {
        for (item = 0 ; item < MAX_ITEMS ; item++) {
          prototypeVector[cluster][item] =
            prototypeVector[cluster][item] &&
              database[customer][item];
         sumVector[cluster][item] += database[customer][item];
        }
      }
    }
```

```
   }

   return;
}
```

The first function, `createNewPrototypeVector`, takes an example feature vector and creates a new cluster with it. The example feature vector is simply copied to the prototype vector for the cluster. The number of members for the cluster is automatically initialized to one. Function `updatePrototypeVectors` recalculates the prototype vector based upon the occupants contained within it. Recall from Equation 3.4, that the prototype vector is nothing more than a bitwise AND of all of the feature vectors. The function in Listing 3.5 loads the first feature vector into the prototype vector and then performs the AND operation on the subsequent feature vectors within the cluster. The `sumVector` is also computed here, which is used solely for making recommendations and plays no part in the ART1 algorithm.

The ART1 algorithm is shown in Listing 3.6. The implementation includes debug output, though these portions have been removed from the listing. To enable the debug feature to watch the ART1 process, change the `#undef` to `#define` at the top of the source for DEBUG.

Listing 3.6   ART1 Algorithm.

```
int performART1( void )
{
  int andresult[MAX_ITEMS];
  int pvec, magPE, magP, magE;
  float result, test;
  int index, done = 0;
  int count = 50;

  while (!done) {

    done = 1;

    /* Walk through each of the customers */
    for (index = 0 ; index < MAX_CUSTOMERS ; index++) {

      /* Step 3 */
      for (pvec = 0 ; pvec < TOTAL_PROTOTYPE_VECTORS ; pvec++) {
```

```
/* Does this vector have any members? */
if (members[pvec]) {

  vectorBitwiseAnd( andresult,
                    &database[index][0],
                    &prototypeVector[pvec][0] );

  magPE = vectorMagnitude( andresult );
  magP  = vectorMagnitude( &prototypeVector[pvec][0] );
  magE  = vectorMagnitude( &database[index][0] );

  result = (float)magPE / (beta + (float)magP);

  test = (float)magE / (beta + (float)MAX_ITEMS);

  /* Equation 2 */
  if (result > test) {

    /* Test for vigilance acceptability (Equation 3)*/
    if (((float)magPE/(float)magE) < vigilance) {

      int old;

      /* Ensure this is a different cluster */
      if (membership[index] != pvec) {

        /* Move the customer to the new cluster */

        old = membership[index];
        membership[index] = pvec;

        if (old >= 0) {
          members[old]--;
          if (members[old] == 0) numPrototypeVectors--;
        }
        members[pvec]++;

        /* Recalculate the prototype vectors for the old
         * and new clusters.
         */
        if ((old >= 0) && (old < TOTAL_PROTOTYPE_VECTORS))
        {
          updatePrototypeVectors( old );
        }
```

```
                    updatePrototypeVectors( pvec );

                    done = 0;
                    break;

                  } else {
                    /* Already in this cluster */
                  }

                } /* vigilance test */

              }

            }

          } /* for vector loop */

          /* Check to see if the current vector was processed */
          if (membership[index] == -1) {

            /* No prototype vector was found to be close to the example
             * vector.  Create a new prototype vector for this example.
             */
            membership[index] =
              createNewPrototypeVector( &database[index][0] );
            done = 0;

          }

        } /* for customers loop */

      if (!count–) break;

    } /* !done */

    return 0;
}
```

The ART1 algorithm is a very simple nested loop where all customer feature vectors are compared against all cluster prototype vectors. When no further changes occur in the clusters (it's no longer resonating), the algorithm
is complete and we return to the main function. The source is a simple

implementation of Equations 3.1 through 3.4. The mag* variables are the magnitudes of the vectors and are calculated once for efficiency. The algorithm also includes a number of optimizations to ignore prototype vectors that have no members (empty clusters are not considered). If the example feature vector is not classified during the cluster loop, a new cluster is automatically created. This handles Equation 3.1 in a clean fashion.

The final function, makeRecommendation, provides the recommendation service for a given customer (represented by their feature vector). See Listing 3.7.

Listing 3.7 Recommendation Algorithm.

```
void makeRecommendation ( int customer )
{
  int bestItem = -1;
  int val = 0;
  int item;

  for (item = 0 ; item < MAX_ITEMS ; item++) {

    if ((database[customer][item] == 0) &&
        (sumVector[membership[customer]][item] > val)) {
      bestItem = item;
      val = sumVector[membership[customer]][item];
    }

  }

  printf("For Customer %d, ", customer);

  if (bestItem >= 0) {
    printf("The best recommendation is %d (%s)\n",
            bestItem, itemName[bestItem]);
    printf("Owned by %d out of %d members of this cluster\n",
            sumVector[membership[customer]][bestItem],
            members[membership[customer]]);
  } else {
    printf("No recommendation can be made.\n");
  }

  printf("Already owns: ");
  for (item = 0 ; item < MAX_ITEMS ; item++) {
```

```
      if (database[customer][item]) printf("%s ", itemName[item]);
    }
    printf("\n\n");
}
```

Per Figure 3.6, the algorithm looks for the intersection of the most purchased item in the cluster that was also not purchased by the current customer. The initial loop in `makeRecommendation` finds this intersection by keeping track of the most purchased item and recording the item number (column of the `sumVector`). The remaining code simply emits textual information defining the recommendation (if one could be made). The function also emits all items that the customer has purchased as a check of the result.

Tweaking the Algorithm

Three important parameters can be tuned for the algorithm. The maximum number of clusters possible (defined as `TOTAL_PROTOTYPE_VECTORS`), should be set high enough so that the algorithm can create a new cluster if it needs to. Since the ability to create new clusters is a major advantage for ART1, sufficient clusters should be available.

The beta and vigilance parameters are very important to the proper operation of ART1. The vigilance parameter is of considerable importance because it determines the quality of the recommendations that can be made. If the clusters are too large, recommendations might not be suitable because of the large variance of the feature vectors contained within the cluster. If the clusters are too small, the recommendations again might not be relevant because not enough feature vectors are present to find interesting similarities. The beta parameter, as defined in by Stephen Gallant [Gallant 1994] is a tiebreaker that favors prototypes that are more similar over those that have fewer similarities.

SAMPLE OUTPUT

Let's now look at the sample output that is emitted from the recommender utility (per the source discussed above). The source was compiled with DEBUG disabled, so the inner workings of the ART1 algorithm are not shown.

The first element emitted in the output is the actual clustering of the feature vectors. This shows each of the prototype vectors (that represent the clusters) along with the member feature vectors (see Listing 3.8). From this data set, four clusters were created, even though five were available.

Listing 3.8   Clustering Output from the Recommender Utility.

```
ProtoVector  0 : 0 0 0 0 0 0 0 0 1 0 0

Customer  0    : 0 0 0 0 0 1 0 0 1 0 0    : 0 :
Customer  7    : 0 0 1 0 0 0 0 0 1 0 0    : 0 :
Customer  9    : 0 0 1 0 0 1 0 0 1 0 0    : 0 :

ProtoVector  1 : 0 0 0 0 1 0 0 1 0 0 0

Customer  3    : 0 0 0 0 1 0 0 1 0 0 1    : 1 :
Customer  8    : 0 0 0 0 1 0 0 1 0 0 0    : 1 :

ProtoVector  2 : 0 0 0 1 0 0 0 0 0 0 0

Customer  2    : 0 0 0 1 0 0 1 0 0 1 0    : 2 :
Customer  4    : 1 0 0 1 0 0 0 0 0 1 0    : 2 :
Customer  6    : 1 0 0 1 0 0 0 0 0 0 0    : 2 :

ProtoVector  3 : 0 0 0 0 0 0 0 0 0 0 1

Customer  1    : 0 1 0 0 0 0 0 1 0 0 1    : 3 :
Customer  5    : 0 0 0 0 1 0 0 0 0 0 1    : 3 :

ProtoVector  4 : 0 0 0 0 0 0 0 0 0 0 0
```

Listing 3.9 provides a portion of the output of the recommendation utility. This applies textual names to the items represented by the feature vector as well as the resulting recommendation choice.

Listing 3.9   Output of the Recommendation Algorithm.

```
For Customer 0, The best recommendation is 2 (Snickers)
Owned by 2 out of 3 members of this cluster
Already owns: Kit-Kat Heath-Bar

For Customer 1, The best recommendation is 4 (Pen)
```

```
Owned by 1 out of 2 members of this cluster
Already owns: Paper Pencil Binder

For Customer 2, The best recommendation is O (Hammer)
Owned by 2 out of 3 members of this cluster
Already owns: Screwdriver Wrench Tape-Measure

For Customer 3, No recommendation can be made.
Already owns: Pen Pencil Binder
```

In each case, the ART1 algorithm correctly segmented the customers into groups based upon the items that they've purchased. Customer 0 was placed into the "candy" cluster, Customer 1 into an "office supplies" cluster and Customer 2 into a "tools" cluster. Recommendations follow the groupings that should be a good prediction of the customer's buying habits. Note that no recommendations could be made for Customer 3. This is because this customer's feature vector was the same as the prototype vector (no dissimilar elements), which meant that it had purchased all items that were represented by this cluster.

PRIVACY ISSUES

Another interesting application of this algorithm is for book recommendations. Consider a recommender system for library users. Each library user is encoded as a feature vector. The feature vector represents the books checked out by the user. Each element of the feature vector represents a small range of books within the spectrum of the Dewey Decimal Classification System (such as 100 – 103). This range represents books within the genre of philosophy. Upon application of the ART1 algorithm, clusters of feature vectors would be further refined to identify the percentage for which a particular book was checked out within the group. This data could be used to then recommend a book to a library user who may not be familiar with it.

This application actually works well with test data, but could never work practically due to privacy issues. Most libraries claim that they don't keep historical records of texts that a particular library user checks out. Without a historical data set, the ART1 algorithm in this application is useless.

There is also quite a bit of fear associated with personalization algorithms. When they work well, they have the ability to predict a user's actions. This can create an uneasy feeling for some as they realize that their behavior is being predicted solely upon external observations. While in this application, the result could be helpful to the user, other applications exist which can invade an individual's privacy. To combat the fear involved in these types of applications, most companies introduce privacy policies to define to customers what data is collected, what is done with it, and who is able to see or utilize it.

OTHER APPLICATIONS

ART1 generally provides the ability to cluster data into independent segments. The clustering can be of use by itself to understand the classes (types) of clusters that result. Additionally, as we saw in the personalization algorithm, looking at the members of an individual cluster can provide interesting information. Additional applications include:

- Statistics
- Pattern recognition
- Reducing the dimensionality of search spaces
- Biology
- Web search engines
- Spatial data mining
- many others

SUMMARY

This chapter has illustrated a simple algorithm that clusters sets of data into groups for use as a recommender system. While originally defined as an off-line processing tool that could be used for data mining, the efficiency of the algorithm lends itself to real-time processing of data within a commercial Web environment.

The example application shown here was very simple and represented a very small data set. For Web site personalization, the data set could include not only a representation of the Web content, but also time spent viewing a particular piece of content. The types and representation of the data ultimately depend upon the algorithm providing the personalization service. With proper encoding within feature vectors, the ART1 algorithm can work with a wide variety of data representing many aspects of a consumer's behavior in a Web setting.

Despite the harmful applications that exist for personalization engines, they can be beneficial timesaving devices and therefore should not be overlooked.

REFERENCES

[Gallant 1994] Gallant, Stephen. 1994. *Neural Network Learning*. Cambridge, Mass.: MIT Press.

RESOURCES

Carpenter, G. and S. Grossberg. 1987. "A Massively Parallel Architecture for a Self-Organizing Neural Pattern Recognition Machine," *Computer Vision, Graphics and Image Processing 37*: 54–115.

Wolfram Research. "Eric Weisstein's World of Mathematics," available online at *http://mathworld.wolfram.com/* (accessed January 17, 2003)

4 Ant Algorithms

In this chapter, we'll look into an interesting multi-agent simulation that's useful in solving a wide variety of problems. Ant algorithms, or Ant Colony Optimization (the name coined by its inventor Marco Dorigo), uses the natural metaphor of ants and stigmergy to solve problems over a physical space [Dorigo 1996]. Nature has provided a number of different methods and ideas in the space of optimization (as illustrated by other chapters in this book such as "Simulated Annealing" and "Introduction to Genetic Algorithms"). Ant algorithms are particularly interesting in that they can be used to solve not only static problems, but also highly dynamic problems such as routing problems in changing networks.

NATURAL MOTIVATION

Although ants are blind, they navigate complex environments and can find food some distance from their nest and return to their nest successfully. They do this by laying pheromones while they navigate their environment. This process, known as stigmergy, modifies their environment to permit communication between the ants and the colony as well as memory for the return trip to the nest.

What is most surprising about this process is that ants tend to take the best route between their nest and some external landmark. This natural optimization is again part of stigmergy. As more ants use a particular trail to an external landmark, the trail becomes higher in pheromone concentration. The closer the landmark is to the nest, the higher the number of round-trips made by each ant. For a landmark that's farther away, a lesser number of round-trips are made, and a higher concentration of pheromones is applied.

The higher the concentration of pheromones, the more ants will choose this route over others that might be available. This iterative process achieves suboptimal to optimal trails between the endpoints.

Ant algorithms are interesting because they share some of the fundamental qualities of ants themselves. Ants are altruistic, cooperative, and work collectively toward a common goal. Ant algorithms share these traits in that the simulated ants within the environment work in parallel to solve a problem, and through stigmergy, help others to further optimize the solution.

Consider the example in Figure 4.1. Two ants at their nest must reach the food on the other side of the obstacle. While the ants travel, each ant deposits a small amount of pheromone along the route as a marker.

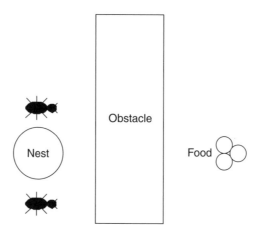

FIGURE 4.1   Initial configuration (T_0).

With equal probability, each ant takes a different route. One ant takes the upper route and the other the lower route. Since the lower route is half the distance to the food, the lower ant has reached the destination at time T_1. The ant taking the higher route has only reached the halfway mark (see Figure 4.2).

Once an ant reaches the food, it takes one of the objects and returns back to the nest using the same path. At time T_2, the lower ant has returned to the nest with the food while the upper ant has finally reached the food landmark (see Figure 4.3).

Recall that as each ant travels, a small amount of pheromone is deposited along the trail. In the case of the upper ant, the trail has been covered only

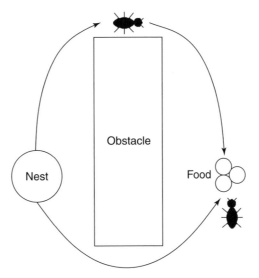

FIGURE 4.2 One unit of time has passed (T_1).

once during the period T_0-T_2. The lower ant has covered its trail twice during the same period. Therefore, twice the amount of pheromone has been deposited along the lower trail compared to the upper trail. At time T_4, the upper ant will have returned to the nest while the lower ant will have completed another run to the food landmark and back. At this point, the

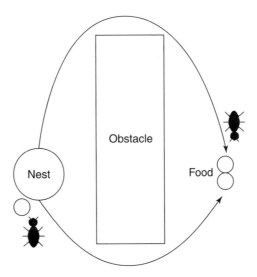

FIGURE 4.3 Two units of time have passed (T_2).

concentration of pheromone on the lower trail will be twice that of the upper trail. The upper ant will then likely decide to use the lower trail, based solely on the concentration of pheromone detected.

This is the basic idea behind ant algorithms—optimization through indirect communication between autonomous agents.

ANT ALGORITHM

Let's now look at the ant algorithm in detail to better understand how it functions for a specific problem.

Network

For this discussion, the environment in which our ants will exist is a fully connected bidirectional graph. Recall that a graph is a set of nodes (or vertices) connected via edges (or lines). Each edge has an associated weight, which we'll identify as the distance between the two nodes connected by the edge. The graph is bidirectional so that an ant can traverse the edge in either direction (see Figure 4.4).

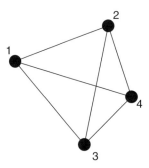

Graph with Vertex set V = {1,2,3,4}

Edge set E ={{1,2},{1,4},{1,3},{2,3},{2,4},{3,4}}

FIGURE 4.4 Example of fully-connected bidirectional graph V with edge set E.

The Ant

An ant is a single agent within the ant algorithm, commonly part of a larger population (colony) used to solve a given problem. The ant is endowed with a set of simple rules that define how it chooses its path through the graph. The ant maintains a *tabu* list, which is simply a list of nodes that it has visited. This list is kept so that the ant moves through each node only once. A path between two vertices on a graph where each vertex is visited only once is known as a Hamiltonian path (first proposed by mathematician Sir William Hamilton).

The ant also maintains the list of nodes in its current tour in the order in which the ant has traveled. This is used later to identify the tour length through the nodes.

While in nature an ant will lay pheromone along the trail as it travels, in the ant algorithm the ant distributes pheromone on the edges of the graph once the tour is complete. The reason for this will be discussed in the section titled "Ant Tour."

Initial Population

A population of ants is created and then uniformly distributed across the nodes of the graph. Distributing the ants equally across the nodes is important because we want all nodes to have an equal chance as a starting point. Starting each ant in the same place would assume that the particular node was the optimal starting node—something we simply don't know.

Ant Movement

Ant movement is based upon a single, very simple, probability equation. While an ant has not yet completed a tour (visited all nodes within the graph, otherwise known as a *path*), the following equation is used to identify the next edge to take (Equation 4.1).

$$P = \frac{\tau(r,u)^{\alpha} * \eta(r,u)^{\beta}}{\sum_{k} \tau(r,u)^{\alpha} * \eta(r,u)^{\beta}} \qquad (4.1)$$

where $\tau(r,u)$ is the intensity of pheromone on the edge between nodes r and u, $\tau(r,u)$ is a heuristic function that represents the inverse of the distance measure of the edge, α represents a weight for the pheromone, and β a weight for the heuristic. The α and β parameters define the relative importance of the two terms and how much they factor in to the probability equation. Recall that an ant travels only to nodes that have not yet been visited (as defined by *tabu*). Therefore, the probability is calculated only for those edges that lead to nodes not yet visited. Variable k represents the edges that have not yet been visited.

Ant Tour

An ant tour exists when an ant has completed its visit to each of the nodes on the graph. Note that no cycles are permitted, based upon the existence of the *tabu* list. Once the ant tour is complete, the length of the entire tour can be computed. This is simply the sum of all distances of edges traveled by the ant. Equation 4.2 shows the amount of pheromone that is left on each edge of the tour for ant k. Variable Q is a constant.

$$\Delta\tau_{ij}^{k}(t) = \frac{Q}{L^{k}(t)} \tag{4.2}$$

This quantity is a measure of the trail—smaller trail lengths represent higher pheromone levels while higher tour lengths represent smaller pheromone levels. This quantity is then used in Equation 4.3 to increase the pheromone along each edge of the tour.

$$\tau_{ij}(t) = \tau_{ij}(t) + (\Delta\tau_{ij}^{k}(t) * \rho) \tag{4.3}$$

Note that this is applied to the entire path, so that each edge is provided with pheromone at a level proportional to the shortness of the path. This is why we must wait until the tour is complete before updating the pheromone levels, otherwise the actual tour length would not be known. Constant ρ is a value between 0 and 1.

Pheromone Evaporation

On the initial tour, each edge has the same probability of being taken. In order to slowly remove edges that are part of poor paths through the network, pheromone evaporation takes place throughout all edges of the network. Using constant ρ from Equation 4.3, we get the evaporation Equation 4.4.

$$\tau_{ij}(t) = \tau_{ij}(t) \,{}^{\star}\, (1 - \rho) \tag{4.4}$$

Therefore, we use the inverse coefficient of trail updates for pheromone evaporation.

Restart

When the ant tour is complete, the edges updated based upon the tour lengths, and evaporation on all edges has been performed, the algorithm is restarted. The *tabu* list is cleared and the tour length zeroed. The ants are permitted to migrate through the network using Equation 4.1 as a guide to the next edge to be investigated.

This process can be performed for a constant number of tours, or until no changes have been seen for some number of tours. The best path is then emitted as the solution.

SAMPLE ITERATION

Now that we have the basic algorithm under our belt, let's walk through a simple iteration of the algorithm to see the equations in action. Recall from Figure 4.1 the simple scenario of two ants taking two paths to reach the same destination. Figure 4.5 provides a simplified view of this with two edges between the two nodes (V_0 and V_1). Each edge is initialized so that each is given equal probability of being selected.

Two ants are started at node V_0, and are labeled A_0 and A_1. Since the probability is equal that a path will be taken, we'll ignore the path equation in this cycle. In Figure 4.6, each ant takes a separate path (ant A_0 takes the upper path and ant A_1 takes the lower path).

Using the table provided in Figure 4.6, we can see that ant A_0 traveled 20 steps while ant A_1 only traveled 10 steps. Using Equation 4.2, we calculate the pheromone level that should be applied.

TIP

We can alter the way the algorithm works by tweaking the parameters (such as ρ, α, and β). We can give more weight to the pheromone levels, or more to the actual distance between the nodes. Information on adjusting the parameters will be outlined after the source discussion.

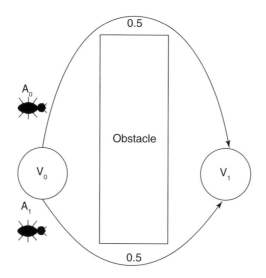

FIGURE 4.5 Initial configuration of the sample problem.

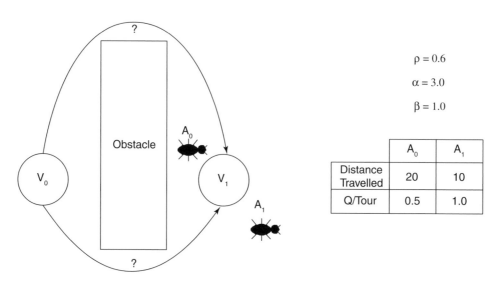

FIGURE 4.6 Simple ant tour completed.

Next, we use Equation 4.3 to calculate how much pheromone will actually be deposited. For ant A_0, this results in:

$$= 0.1 + (0.5*0.6) = 0.4$$

For ant A_1, the pheromone result is:

$$= 0.1 + (1.0*0.6) = 0.7$$

Next, we use Equation 4.4 to evaporate the pheromone on the trail. This results (for each trail) in:

$$= 0.4*(1.0 - 0.6) = 0.16$$
$$= 0.7*(1.0 - 0.6) = 0.28$$

These values represent the new pheromone levels for each trail (upper and lower, correspondingly). Now let's move our ants back to node V_0 and use the probability Equation 4.1 to determine which path the ants should now take.

The probability that an ant will take the upper path (given a pheromone level of 0.16) is:

$$\frac{(0.16)^{3.0} * (0.5)^{1.0}}{\left((0.16)^{3.0} * (0.5)^{1.0}\right) + \left((0.28)^{3.0} * (1.0)^{1.0}\right)} = \frac{0.002048}{0.024} = P(0.085)$$

The probability that the ant will take the lower path (given a pheromone level of 0.28) is:

$$\frac{(0.28)^{3.0} * (1.0)^{1.0}}{\left((0.16)^{3.0} * (0.5)^{1.0}\right) + \left((0.28)^{3.0} * (1.0)^{1.0}\right)} = \frac{0.021952}{0.024} = P(0.915)$$

Given the two probabilities, with a very high likelihood, both ants will take the lower path, which also represents the most optimal path to the destination.

SAMPLE PROBLEM

For a sample problem to apply the ant algorithm, we'll look at the Traveling Salesman Problem (or TSP). The goal of the TSP is to find the shortest tour through a graph using a Hamiltonian path (a path that visits each node only once). Mathematicians first studied the general TSP in the 1930s (such as Karl Menger in Vienna), though problems related to it were treated in the 1800s, particular by Irish mathematician Sir William Rowan Hamilton.

In the next section, we'll review the code to solve the TSP and then look at some sample solutions of varying sizes.

 The source code for the Ant Simulator for TSP can be found on the CD-

ON THE CD ROM at ./software/ch4.

SOURCE CODE DISCUSSION

The following listings will illustrate the ant algorithm to find good to optimal solutions for the Traveling Salesman Problem.

First we'll look at the data structures for both the cities on the plane and the ants that will traverse the cities. Listing 4.1 contains the types and symbolic constants used to represent the cities and ants.

Listing 4.1   Types and Symbolic Constants for City/Ant Representation.

```
#define MAX_CITIES        30

#define MAX_DISTANCE      100

#define MAX_TOUR    (MAX_CITIES * MAX_DISTANCE)

typedef struct {
    int x;
    int y;
} cityType;


#define MAX_ANTS    30

typedef struct {
    int curCity;
    int nextCity;
    unsigned char tabu[MAX_CITIES];
    int pathIndex;
    unsigned char path[MAX_CITIES];
    double tourLength;
```

```
} antType;
```

Type `cityType` is used to represent a city within the `MAX_DISTANCE` by `MAX_DISTANCE` grid. `antType` represents a single ant within the simulation. In addition to keeping track of the current and next city on the tour (`curCity` and `nextCity`), each ant must also keep track of the cities that have already been visited via the `tabu` array and the actual tour that was taken through `path`. Finally, the total length of the tour is stored within `tourLength`.

For a given size TSP, it's sometimes important to change the parameters of the equations. Here are the defaults for a 30 city TSP (see Listing 4.2). Adjusting the parameters will be discussed in a later section.

Listing 4.2   Ant Algorithm Problem Parameters.

```
#define ALPHA        1.0
#define BETA         5.0      /* Favor Distance over Pheromone */
#define RHO          0.5      /* Intensity / Evaporation */
#define QVAL         100

#define MAX_TOURS         20

#define MAX_TIME     (MAX_TOURS * MAX_CITIES)

#define INIT_PHEROMONE     (1.0 / MAX_CITIES)
```

The `ALPHA` parameter (α) defines the relative importance of the trail (pheromone level on the trail). `BETA` (β) defines the relative importance of visibility (reciprocal of distance). `RHO` (ρ) is used as a coefficient of the amount of pheromone an ant deposits on the trail (otherwise known as trail persistence), where (1.0-ρ) specifies the rate of evaporation of the trail after a tour is complete. `QVAL` (or simply Q in Equation 4.2) is a constant related to the quantity of pheromone deposited on the trail. The remaining constants will be reviewed in the source.

The data structures used by the algorithm include the array of `cities` and `ants`. Another special structure, `distance`, pre-calculates the distance of each city to every other. The pheromone levels are stored within the `pheromone` array. Each two-dimensional array within the simulation uses the first dimension as the departure city and the second dimension as the destination. See Listing 4.3 for all globals used in the simulation, and Listing 4.4 for the initialization function.

Listing 4.3 Globals and Runtime Structures.

```
cityType cities[MAX_CITIES];

antType ants[MAX_ANTS];

            /* From      To    */
double  distance[MAX_CITIES][MAX_CITIES];

            /* From      To    */
double  pheromone[MAX_CITIES][MAX_CITIES];

double  best=(double)MAX_TOUR;
int     bestIndex;
```

The first function to review is initialization (`init`) as shown in Listing 4.4.

Listing 4.4 Initialization Function.

```
void init( void )
{
  int from, to, ant;

  /* Create the cities and their locations */
  for (from = 0 ; from < MAX_CITIES ; from++) {

    /* Randomly place cities around the grid */
    cities[from].x = getRand( MAX_DISTANCE );
    cities[from].y = getRand( MAX_DISTANCE );

    for (to = 0 ; to < MAX_CITIES ; to++) {
      distance[from][to] = 0.0;
      pheromone[from][to] = INIT_PHEROMONE;
    }

  }

  /* Compute the distances for each of the cities on the map */
  for ( from = 0 ; from < MAX_CITIES ; from++) {

    for ( to = 0 ; to < MAX_CITIES ; to++) {

      if ((to != from) && (distance[from][to] == 0.0)) {
```

```
        int xd = abs(cities[from].x - cities[to].x);
        int yd = abs(cities[from].y - cities[to].y);

        distance[from][to] = sqrt( (xd * xd) + (yd * yd) );
        distance[to][from] = distance[from][to];
    }

  }

}

/* Initialize the ants */
to = 0;
for ( ant = 0 ; ant < MAX_ANTS ; ant++ ) {

  /* Distribute the ants to each of the cities uniformly */
  if (to == MAX_CITIES) to = 0;
  ants[ant].curCity = to++;

  for ( from = 0 ; from < MAX_CITIES ; from++ ) {
    ants[ant].tabu[from] = 0;
    ants[ant].path[from] = -1;
  }

  ants[ant].pathIndex = 1;
  ants[ant].path[0] = ants[ant].curCity;
  ants[ant].nextCity = -1;
  ants[ant].tourLength = 0.0;

  /* Load the ant's current city into tabu */
  ants[ant].tabu[ants[ant].curCity] = 1;

  }
}
```

Function `init` performs three basic functions to prepare for execution of the ant algorithm. The first is creation of the cities. For each city that must be created (defined by MAX_CITIES), we generate a random number for the two x,y coordinates and store them into the current city record. Additionally, while in the loop of initializing `cities`, we use the opportunity to clear out the `distance` and `pheromone` arrays at the same time.

Next, as an optimization step, we pre-calculate the distances between all cities created within the `cities` structure. The distance measure is calculated using simple 2-dimensional coordinate geometry (Pythagorean theorem).

Finally, the `ant` structure is initialized. Recall that the ants must be uniformly distributed across all of the cities. To do this, the `to` variable is initialized and simply cycles through each city as an ant is associated with it. Once `to` reaches the end of the cities, it restarts to the first city (city 0) and the process begins again. The `curCity` field within the `ant` structure is loaded with the current city (the starting city for the ant). The `tabu` and `path` lists are cleared next. A zero within the `tabu` array denotes that the city has not yet been visited; otherwise, a one identifies it as a city already in the ant's path. The `path` is loaded with the current city for the ant and the `tourLength` is cleared.

Once a tour is complete, each ant must be reinitialized and then distributed across the graph. This is provided by the `restartAnts` function (see Listing 4.5).

Listing 4.5   restartAnts Function to Reinitialize All Ants.

```
void restartAnts( void )
{
  int ant, i, to=0;

  for ( ant = 0 ; ant < MAX_ANTS ; ant++ ) {

    if (ants[ant].tourLength < best) {
      best = ants[ant].tourLength;
      bestIndex = ant;
    }

    ants[ant].nextCity = -1;
    ants[ant].tourLength = 0.0;

    for (i = 0 ; i < MAX_CITIES ; i++) {
      ants[ant].tabu[i] = 0;
      ants[ant].path[i] = -1;
    }

    if (to == MAX_CITIES) to = 0;
    ants[ant].curCity = to++;
```

```
        ants[ant].pathIndex = 1;
        ants[ant].path[0] = ants[ant].curCity;

        ants[ant].tabu[ants[ant].curCity] = 1;

    }

}
```

During reinitialization, the best tour length is stored so that we can keep track of the progress of the ants. The ant structure is then cleared and reinitialized to begin the next tour.

The `selectNextCity` function provides for selection of the next city to visit in the tour. Also included is the function `antProduct`, which is used in Equation 4.1. See Listing 4.6. The pow function (power, x^y) is part of standard math libraries.

Listing 4.6   Functions `antProduct` and `selectNextCity`.

```
double antProduct( int from, int to )
{
  return (( pow( pheromone[from][to], ALPHA ) *
            pow( (1.0 / distance[from][to]), BETA ) ));
}


int selectNextCity( int ant )
{
  int from, to;
  double denom=0.0;

  /* Choose the next city to visit */
  from = ants[ant].curCity;

  /* Compute denom */
  for (to = 0 ; to < MAX_CITIES ; to++) {
    if (ants[ant].tabu[to] == 0) {
      denom += antProduct( from, to );
    }
  }

  assert(denom != 0.0);
```

```
      do {

        double p;

        to++;
        if (to >= MAX_CITIES) to = 0;

        if ( ants[ant].tabu[to] == 0 ) {

          p = antProduct(from, to)/denom;

          if (getSRand() < p ) break;

        }

      } while (1);

      return to;
    }
```

Function `selectNextCity` is called for a given ant to identify which particular edge to take given the `tabu` list. The edge to take is based upon the probability Equation 4.1. This equation is essentially a ratio of a given path over the sum of the other paths. The first part of `selectNextcity` is to calculate the denominator of the function. Upon doing this, all edges not yet taken are checked using Equation 4.1 to identify which path to choose. When this edge is found, the city to which the ant will move is returned by the function.

The next higher function within the simulation is `simulateAnts`. This function provides the ant movement simulation over the graph (see Listing 4.7).

Listing 4.7 Function `simulateAnts`.

```
    int simulateAnts( void )
    {
      int k;
      int moving = 0;

      for (k = 0 ; k < MAX_ANTS ; k++) {

        /* Ensure this ant still has cities to visit */
```

```
        if (ants[k].pathIndex < MAX_CITIES) {

          ants[k].nextCity = selectNextCity( k );

          ants[k].tabu[ants[k].nextCity] = 1;

          ants[k].path[ants[k].pathIndex++] = ants[k].nextCity;

          ants[k].tourLength +=
                  distance[ants[k].curCity][ants[k].nextCity];

          /* Handle the final case (last city to first) */
          if (ants[k].pathIndex == MAX_CITIES) {
            ants[k].tourLength +=
              distance[ants[k].path[MAX_CITIES-1]][ants[k].path[0]];
          }

          ants[k].curCity = ants[k].nextCity;

          moving++;

        }

      }

    return moving;
  }
```

Function simulateAnts walks through the ant structure and moves ants from their current city to a new city given probability Equation 4.1. The pathIndex field is checked to ensure that the ant has not yet completed its tour, and upon confirming this, a call is made to selectNextCity to choose the next edge. The next city selected is then loaded into the ant structure (nextCity field) as well as the path and tabu. The tourLength is also calculated to keep a running total thus far in the tour. Finally, if we've reached the end of the path, we add into the tourLength the distance to the initial city. This completes the path from the initial city through all other cities and back.

One call to simulateAnts allows each ant to move from one city to the next. Function simulateAnts returns zero when the tour is complete, otherwise a non-zero value is returned.

Once a tour is complete, the process of updating the trails is performed. This includes not only updating the trails for pheromone deposited by ants, but also existing pheromone that has evaporated in time. Function update-Trails provides this part of the simulation (see Listing 4.8).

Listing 4.8   Evaporating and Depositing Pheromone with updateTrails.

```
void updateTrails( void )
{
  int from, to, i, ant;

  /* Pheromone Evaporation */
  for (from = 0 ; from < MAX_CITIES ; from++) {

    for (to = 0 ; to < MAX_CITIES ; to++) {

      if (from != to) {

        pheromone[from][to] *= (1.0 - RHO);

        if (pheromone[from][to] < 0.0)
          pheromone[from][to] = INIT_PHEROMONE;

      }

    }

  }

  /* Add new pheromone to the trails */

  /* Look at the tours of each ant */
  for (ant = 0 ; ant < MAX_ANTS ; ant++) {

    /* Update each leg of the tour given the tour length */
    for (i = 0 ; i < MAX_CITIES ; i++) {

      if (i < MAX_CITIES-1) {
        from = ants[ant].path[i];
        to = ants[ant].path[i+1];
      } else {
        from = ants[ant].path[i];
        to = ants[ant].path[0];
      }

      pheromone[from][to] += (QVAL / ants[ant].tourLength);
```

```
        pheromone[to][from] = pheromone[from][to];

    }

  }

  for (from = 0 ; from < MAX_CITIES ; from++) {
    for (to = 0 ; to < MAX_CITIES ; to++) {
      pheromone[from][to] *= RHO;
    }
  }

}
```

The first task of updateTrails is to evaporate some portion of the pheromone that already exists on the trail. This is performed on all edges using Equation 4.4. The next step is accumulation of new pheromone on the trails from the last tours of all ants. For this step, we walk through each ant and utilize the path array to identify which edge to accumulate the pheromone on as defined by Equation 4.2. Once the accumulation is complete, we apply the _ parameter to reduce the intensity of the pheromone deposited by all ants.

Finally, the main function is very simple, acting as a simulator loop (see Listing 4.9). After seeding the random number generator and initializing the simulation, we run the simulator for the number of steps defined by MAX_TIME. As the ants complete a tour (through the simulateAnts function), the update-Trails function is called to modify the environment.

Listing 4.9   Main Function for the Ant Algorithm Simulation.

```
int main()
{
  int curTime = 0;

  srand( time(NULL) );

  init();

  while (curTime++ < MAX_TIME) {

    if ( simulateAnts() == 0 ) {
```

```
        updateTrails();

        if (curTime != MAX_TIME)
          restartAnts();

        printf("Time is %d (%g)\n", curTime, best);

      }

    }

    printf("best tour %g\n", best);
    printf("\n\n");

    emitDataFile( bestIndex );

    return 0;
  }
```

Note also that each time a tour is completed, the restartAnts function is called to make ready for the next tour through the graph. Only if we're at the end of the simulation do we not call restartAnts. This is because the function destroys the path information for the ant, which we want to retain at the end to emit the best path.

Not shown here is function emitDataFile, used to generate the plots shown in "Sample Runs." Please see the source on the CD-ROM for more information on this function.

ON THE CD

SAMPLE RUNS

Let's now look at a couple of sample runs of the ant algorithm for TSP.

The first run provides a solution for a 30-city TSP (see Figure 4.7). The parameters for this problem were $\alpha = 1.0$, $\beta = 5.0$, $\rho = 0.5$, and $Q = 100$.

The second run presents a 50-city TSP solution (see Figure 4.8). The parameters used for this solution were identical to the 30-city TSP.

Each of these solutions was found in less than five tours. The number of ants in each run was equal to the number of cities.

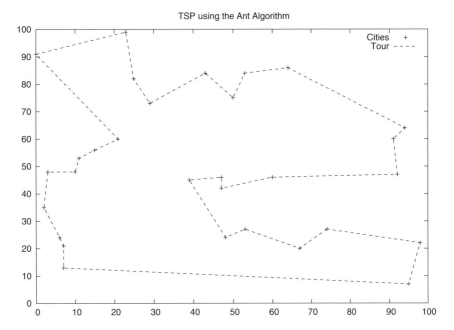

FIGURE 4.7   Sample solution for the 30-city TSP.

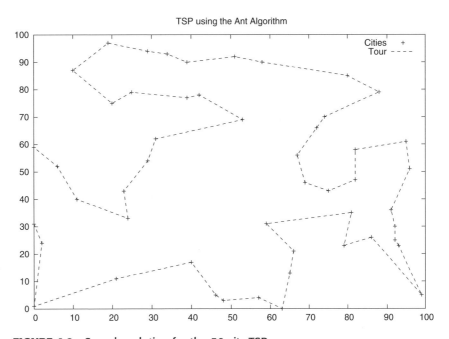

FIGURE 4.8   Sample solution for the 50-city TSP.

ADJUSTING THE ALGORITHM PARAMETERS

Marco Dorigo (inventor of Ant Colony Optimization) provides a very useful discussion of the problem parameters in his article "The Ant System: Optimization by a Colony of Cooperating Agents" [Dorigo et al. 1996]. This section will summarize his findings for the most common adjustable parameters.

Alpha (α) / Beta (β)

A number of α/β combinations were found to yield good solutions in a reasonable amount of time. These are found in Table 4.1.

TABLE 4.1 α/β Parameter Combinations.

α	β
0.5	5.0
1.0	1.0
1.0	2.0
1.0	5.0

The α parameter is associated with pheromone levels (from Equation 4.1), where the β parameter is associated with visibility (distance for the edge). Therefore, whichever value is higher indicates the importance of the parameter within the edge selection probability equation. Note that in one case, the parameters are of equal importance. In all other cases, the visibility of the path is a greater determinant of the path to take.

Rho (ρ)

Recall that while ρ represents the coefficient applied to new pheromone on a path, $(1.0 - \rho)$ represents the coefficient of evaporation of existing pheromone on the trail. Tests were run with $\rho > 0.5$, all of which yielded interesting solutions. Setting ρ to a value less than 0.5 resulted in less than satisfactory results.

This parameter primarily determines the concentration of pheromone that will remain on the edges over time.

Number of Ants

The quantity of ants in the simulation had an effect on the quality of solutions that resulted. While more ants may sound like a reasonable idea, setting the number of ants in the simulation to the number of cities yields the best result.

OTHER APPLICATIONS

The ant algorithm can be applied to a variety of other problems. These include Quadratic Assignment Problems (QAP) and Job-shop Scheduling Problems (JSP).

In QAP, the problem is assigning a set of n resources to a set of m locations, while minimizing the cost of the assignment (a function of the way resources are assigned to the locations). The ant algorithm was found to produce the same quality as other standard approaches.

JSP is a much harder problem to solve. In JSP, a set of M machines and a set of J jobs (consisting of a sequence of activities associated with the machines) must be scheduled so that the jobs are completed in a minimal amount of time. While the solutions found with ant algorithms were not optimal, their application to the problem proves that it can be applied to a variety of different problems successfully.

The ant algorithm has been applied to other problems, such as vehicle routing, graph coloring, and network routing. For a detailed list of ant algorithm applications and the results see Dorigo et al.'s "Ant Algorithms for Discrete Optimization" [Dorigo et al. 1999].

SUMMARY

In this chapter, we've looked at another naturally-inspired method of optimizing routes in a variety of disciplines. The ant algorithm models the behavior of ants within their natural domain to identify optimal paths through landscapes (graphs). The ant algorithm was discussed in terms of the Traveling Salesman Problem (TSP) and an implementation discussed that provides a simple simulation of ants for the TSP. Finally, the parameters of the ant algorithm equations were discussed and combinations that have been shown to yield good results were presented.

REFERENCES

[Dorigo 1996] Dorigo, Marco. (1996). "Ant Colonies for the Traveling Salesman Problem," *BioSystems* 43:73–81.

[Dorigo et al.1996] Dorigo, Marco, et al. (1996). "The Ant System: Optimization by a Colony of Cooperating Agents," *IEEE Transactions on Systems, Man and Cybernetics-Part B* 26, (1):1–13.

[Dorigo et al. 1999] Dorigo, Marco, et al.(1999). "Ant Algorithms for Discrete Optimization," available online at *http://citeseer.nj.nec.com/420280.html* (accessed January 17, 2003)

RESOURCES

Applegate, David et al."History of the Traveling Salesman Problem," available online at
http://www.math.princeton.edu/tsp/histmain.html (accessed January 17, 2003)

Dorigo, Marc. "Marc Dorigo's Ant Colony Optimization Home Page," available online at *http://iridia.ulb.ac.be/~mdorigo/ACO/ACO.html* (accessed January 17, 2003)

Wolfram Reasearch. "Hamiltonian Path," available online at
http://mathworld.wolfram.com/HamiltonianPath.html (accessed January 17, 2003)

5　Introduction to Neural Networks and the Backpropagation Algorithm

This chapter introduces feed-forward, multi-layer neural network architectures with learning provided by the backpropagation algorithm. Backpropagation is likely the most important learning algorithm for neural networks and has contributed to a resurgence of biologically-inspired methods for computation. After detailing neural networks and backpropagation, we'll look at the resulting network's application in game character AI.

While a large variety of neural network topologies and learning algorithms exist, this chapter will focus on feed-forward, multi-layer networks using backpropagation learning. We'll begin with a simple introduction of neural networks and their components; discuss the learning algorithm and then some problems that can arise during backpropagation learning. We'll look at an example of a simple network and walk through the backpropagation algorithm to understand its properties. Finally, we'll look at simple neural networks as a way to give life to characters within game environments.

NEURAL NETWORKS FROM THE BIOLOGICAL PERSPECTIVE

Neural networks are very simple implementations of local behavior observed within our own brains. The brain is composed of neurons, which are the individual processing elements. Neurons are connected by axons that end at the neuron in a synapse. The synapse is responsible for relaying a signal to the neuron. Synapses can be either inhibitory or excitory.

The human brain contains approximately 10^{11} neurons. Each neuron connects to approximately 1000 other neurons, except in the cerebral cortex where the density of interneuron connectivity is much higher. The structure of the brain is highly cyclic (self-referential), but it can be thought of as having a layered architecture (see Figure 5.1). In a very simplified model, the input layer to the network provides our sensory inputs from the environment, the middle layer, or cerebral cortex, processes the inputs, and the output layer provides motor control back to the environment.

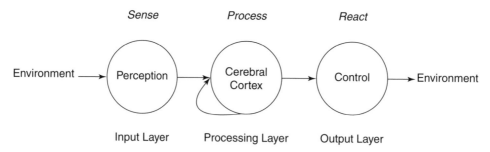

FIGURE 5.1   Layered architecture for a simple brain.

Artificial neural networks attempt to mimic the basic operation of the brain. Information is passed between the neurons, and based upon the structure and synapse weights, a network behavior (or output mapping) is provided.

SINGLE LAYER PERCEPTRONS

A single layer perceptron, or SLP, is a connectionist model that consists of a single processing unit. Each connection from an input to the cell includes a coefficient that represents a weighting factor. Each connection is specified by a weight w_i that specifies the influence of cell u_i on the cell. Positive weights indicate reinforcement and negative weights indicate inhibition. These weights, along with the inputs to the cell, determine the behavior of the network. See Figure 5.2 for a simple diagram of an SLP.

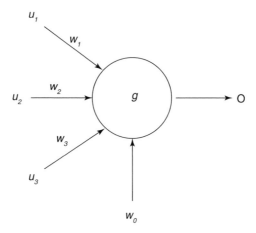

FIGURE 5.2 Single layer perceptron.

From Figure 5.2 we see that the cell includes three inputs (u_1, u_2, and u_3). A bias input (w_0) is provided, which will be discussed later. Each input connection also includes a weight (w_1, w_2, and w_3). Finally, a single output is provided, O. The cell that represents our function is defined as γ, and is shown in Equation 5.1.

$$\gamma = w_0 + \sum_{i=1}^{3} u_i w_i \tag{5.1}$$

The equation shown in Equation 5.1 is simply a function that sums the products of the weights and inputs, finally adding in the bias. The output is then provided to an activation function, which can be defined as shown in Equation 5.2.

$$\gamma = -1, if(\gamma \le 0)$$
$$\gamma = 1, if(\gamma > 0) \tag{5.2}$$

Or, simply, whenever the output is greater than zero, the output is thresholded at 1. If the output is less than or equal to zero, the output is thresholded at −1.

Modeling Boolean Expressions with SLP

While the SLP is a very simple model, it can be very powerful. For example, the basic digital logic gates can easily be constructed as shown in Figure 5.3.

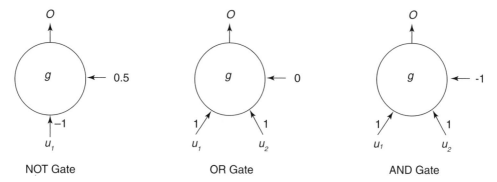

FIGURE 5.3   Logic gates built from single layer perceptrons.

Recall that an AND gate emits a '1' value if both inputs are '1', otherwise a '0' is emitted. Therefore, if both inputs are set (u vector of $[1, 1]$) and using the activation function from Equation 5.2 as *threshold*, we get:

$\gamma = \text{bias} + u_1 w_1 + u_2 w_2$, or
$1 = \text{threshold}(-1 + (1 * 1) + (1 * 1))$

Now let's try a u vector of $[0, 1]$:

$\gamma = \text{bias} + u_1 w_1 + u_2 w_2$, or
$-1 = \text{threshold}(-1 + (0 * 1) + (1 * 1))$

As both examples show, the simple perceptron model correctly implements the logical AND function (as well as the OR and NOT functions). A digital logic function that the SLP cannot model is the XOR function. The inability of the SLP to solve the XOR function is known as the *separability problem*. This particular problem was exploited by Marvin Minsky and Seymour Papert to all but destroy connectionist research in the 1960s (and support their own research in traditional symbolic AI approaches) [Minsky and Papert 1969].

The separability problem was easily resolved by adding one or more layers between the inputs and outputs of the neural network (see an example in Figure 5.4). This led to the model known as multiple-layer perceptrons (or MLP).

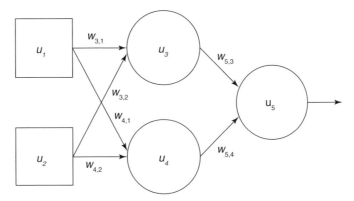

FIGURE 5.4   Multiple-layer perceptron (multi-layer network).

MULTIPLE-LAYER NETWORKS

Multiple-layer networks permit more complex, non-linear relationships of input data to output results. From Figure 5.4, we can see that the multiple-layer network is made up of an input layer, an intermediate or hidden layer, and an output layer. The input layer simply represents the inputs to the network, and is not composed of cells (neurons) in the traditional sense. The naming of cells, chosen for this example, gives each cell a u_n identifier. The two input cells are named $[u_1, u_2]$, two hidden cells $[u_3, u_4]$, and one output cell $[u_5]$. Identifying connections within the network is standardized as $w_{3,1}$, and represents the weighted connection between u_3 and u_1.

While input cells (u_1 and u_2) simply provide an input value to the network, hidden and output cells represent a function (recall Equation 5.1). The result of the sum of products is fed through a squashing function (typically a sigmoid), which results in the output of the cell. The sigmoid function is shown in Figure 5.5.

Let's now look at the complete picture of a neural network cell. In Figure 5.6, we see the output cell from the network shown in Figure 5.4. The output cell u_5 is fed by the two hidden cells, u_3 and u_4, through weights $w_{5,3}$ and $w_{5,4}$ respectively.

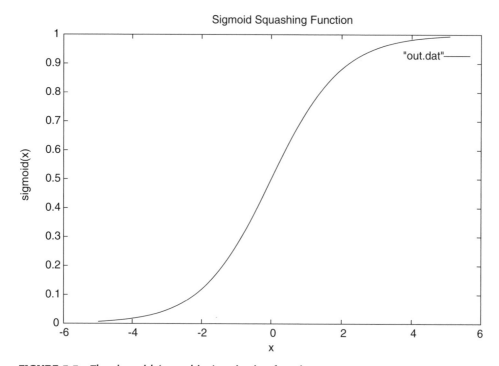

FIGURE 5.5 The sigmoid (squashing) activation function.

One important note here is that the sigmoid function should be applied to the hidden nodes in the sample network in Figure 5.6, but they are omitted in this case to illustrate the output layer processing only. The equation in Figure 5.6 illustrates the sum of products of the inputs from the hidden layer with the connection weights. The $f(x)$ function represents the sigmoid applied to the result.

In a network with a hidden layer and an output layer, the hidden layer is computed first and then the results of the hidden layer are used to compute the output layer.

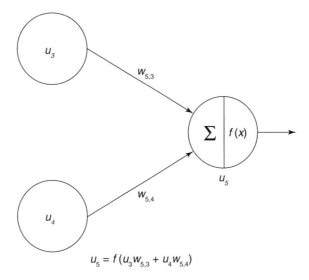

$$u_5 = f(u_3 w_{5,3} + u_4 w_{5,4})$$

FIGURE 5.6 Hidden and output layers of a sample neural network.

BACKPROPAGATION LEARNING

Backward error propagation, or simply backpropagation, is the most popular learning algorithm for connectionist learning. As the name implies, an error in the output node is corrected by back propagating this error by adjusting weights through the hidden layer and back to the input layer. While relatively simple, convergence can take some time depending upon the allowable error in the output.

Backpropagation Algorithm

The algorithm begins with the assignment of randomly generated weights for the multi-layer, feed-forward network. The following process is then repeated until the mean-squared error (MSE) of the output is sufficiently small:

1. Take a training example E with its associated correct response C.
2. Compute the forward propagation of E through the network (compute the weighted sums of the network, S_i, and the activations, u_i, for every cell).

3. Starting at the outputs, make a backward pass through the output and intermediate cells, computing the error values (Equations 5.3 and 5.4):

$$\delta_o = (C_i - u_5)u_5(1 - u_5) \qquad \text{For the output cell} \qquad (5.3)$$

$$\delta_i = (\sum_{m:m>i} w_{m,j}\delta_o)u_i(1 - u_i) \quad \text{For all hidden cells} \qquad (5.4)$$

(Note that m denotes all cells connected to the hidden node, w is the given weight vector and u is the activation).

4. Finally, the weights within the network are updated as follows (Equations 5.5 and 5.6):

$$w^*_{i,j} = w_{i,j} + \rho\delta_o u_i \qquad \text{For weights connecting hidden to output} \qquad (5.5)$$

$$w^*_{i,j} = w_{i,j} + \rho\delta_i u_i \qquad \text{For weights connecting hidden to output} \qquad (5.6)$$

where ρ represents the learning rate (or step size). This small value limits the change that may occur during each step.

The parameter ρ can be tuned to determine how quickly the backpropagation algorithm converges toward a solution. It's best to start with a small value (0.1) to test and then slowly increment.

The forward pass through the network computes the cell activations and an output. The backward pass computes the gradient (with respect to the given example). The weights are then updated so that the error is minimized for the given example. The learning rate minimizes the amount of change that may take place for the weights. While it may take longer for a smaller learning rate to converge, we minimize overshooting our target. If the learning rate is set too high, the network may never converge.

We'll see the actual code that's required to implement the functions above, listed with the numerical steps for the backpropagation algorithm as shown above.

Backpropagation Example

Let's now look at an example of backpropagation at work. Consider the network shown in Figure 5.7.

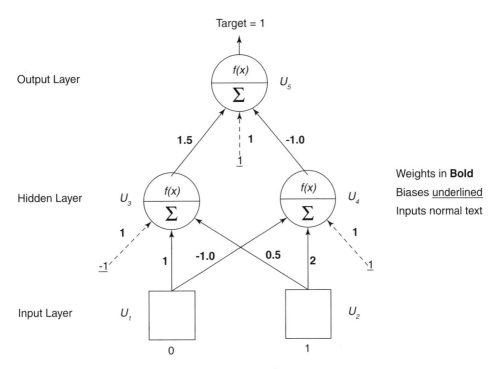

FIGURE 5.7 Numerical backpropagation example.

The Feed-forward Pass

First, we feed forward the inputs through the network. Let's look at the values for the hidden layer:

$$u_3 = f(w_{3,1}u_1 + w_{3,2}u_2 + w_b {}^*bias)$$
$$u_3 = f(1{}^*0 + 0.5{}^*1 + 1{}^*1) = f(1.5)$$
$$u_3 = 0.81757$$

$$u_4 = f(w_{4,1}u_1 + w_{4,2}u_2 + w_b {}^*bias)$$
$$u_4 = f(-1{}^*0 + 2{}^*1 + 1{}^*1) = f(3)$$
$$u_4 = 0.952574$$

Recall that $f(x)$ is our activation function, the sigmoid function (Equation 5.7):

$$f(x) = \frac{1}{1 + e^{-x}} \qquad (5.7)$$

Our inputs have now been propagated to the hidden layer; the final step is to feed the hidden layer values forward to the output layer to calculate the output of the network.

$u_5 = f(w_{5,3}u_3 + w_{5,4}u4 + w_b{}^*bias)$
$u_5 = f(1.5{}^*0.81757 + -1.0{}^*0.952574 + 1{}^*1) = f(1.2195)$
$u_5 = 0.78139$

Our target for the neural network was 1.0; the actual value computed by the network was 0.78139. This isn't too bad, but by applying the backpropagation algorithm to the network, we can reduce the error.

The mean squared error is typically used to quantify the error of the network. For a single node, this is defined as Equation 5.8:

$$err = 0.5 {}^* (o_{desired} - o_{actual})^2 \qquad (5.8)$$

Therefore, our error is:

$$err = 0.5 {}^* (1.0 - 0.78139)^2 = 0.023895$$

The Error Backward Propagation Pass

Now let's apply backpropagation, starting with determining the error of the output node and the hidden nodes. Using Equation 5.1, we calculate the output node error:

$\delta_o = (1.0 - 0.78139) {}^* 0.78139 {}^* (1.0 - 0.78139)$
$\delta_o = 0.0373$

Now we calculate the error for both hidden nodes. We use the derivative of our sigmoidal equation (Equation 5.5), which is shown as Equation 5.9.

$$val = x {}^* (1.0 - x) \qquad (5.9)$$

Using Equation 5.2, we now calculate the errors for the hidden nodes:

$\delta_{u4} = (\delta_o * w_{5,4}) * u_4 * (1.0 - u_4)$
$\delta_{u4} = (0.0373 * -1.0) * 0.952574 * (1.0 - 0.952574)$
$\delta_{u4} = -0.0016851$

$\delta_{u3} = (\delta_o * w_{5,3}) * u_3 * (1.0 - u_3)$
$\delta_{u3} = (0.0373 * 1.5) * 0.81757 * (1.0 - 0.81757)$
$\delta_{u3} = 0.0083449$

Adjusting the Connection Weights

Now that we have the error values for the output and hidden layers, we can use Equations 5.3 and 5.4 to adjust the weights. We'll use a learning rate (ρ) of 0.5. First, we'll update the weights that connect our output layer to the hidden layer.

$w^*_{i,j} = w_{i,j} + \rho \delta_o u_i$

$w_{5,4} = w_{5,4} + (\rho * 0.0373 * u_4)$
$w_{5,4} = -1 + (0.5 * 0.0373 * 0.952574)$
$w_{5,4} = -0.9822$

$w_{5,3} = w5,3 + (\rho * 0.0373 * u_3)$
$w_{5,3} = 1.5 + (0.5 * 0.0373 * 0.81757)$
$w_{5,3} = 1.51525$

Now, let's update the output cell bias:

$w_{5,b} = w_{5,b} + (\rho * 0.0373 * bias_5)$
$w_{5,b} = 1 + (0.5 * 0.0373 * 1)$
$w_{5,b} = 1.01865$

In the case of $w_{5,4}$, the weight was decreased where for $w_{5,3}$ the weight was increased. Our bias was updated for greater excitation. Now we'll show the adjustment of the hidden weights (for the input to hidden cells).

$w^*_{i,j} = w_{i,j} + \rho \delta_i u_i$

$w_{4,2} = w_{4,2} + (\rho * -0.0016851 * u_2)$

$w_{4,2} = 2 + (0.5 * -0.0016851 * 1)$
$w_{4,2} = 1.99916$

$w_{4,1} = w_{4,1} + (\rho * -0.0016851 * u_1)$
$w_{4,1} = -1 + (0.5 * -0.0016851 * 0)$
$w_{4,1} = -1.0$

$w_{3,2} = w_{3,2} + (\rho * 0.0083449 * u_2)$
$w_{3,2} = 0.5 + (0.5 * 0.0083449 * 1)$
$w_{3,2} = 0.50417$

$w_{3,1} = w_{3,1} + (\rho * 0.0083449 * u_1)$
$w_{3,1} = 1.0 + (0.5 * 0.0083449 * 0)$
$w_{3,1} = 1.0$

The final step is to update the cell biases:

$w_{4,b} = w_{4,b} + (\rho * -0.0016851 * bias_4)$
$w_{4,b} = 1.0 + (0.5 * -0.0016851 * 1)$
$w_{4,b} = 0.99915$

$w_{3,b} = w_{3,b} + (\rho * 0.0083449 * bias_3)$
$w_{3,b} = 1.0 + (0.5 * 0.0083449 * 1)$
$w_{3,b} = 1.00417$

That completes the updates of our weights for the current training example. To verify that the algorithm is genuinely reducing the error in the output, we'll run the feed-forward algorithm one more time.

$u_3 = f(w_{3,1}u_1 + w_{3,2}u_2 + w_b{}^*bias)$
$u_3 = f(1{}^*0 + 0.50417{}^*1 + 1.00417{}^*1) = f(1.50834)$
$u_3 = 0.8188$

$u_4 = f(w_{4,1}u_1 + w_{4,2}u_2 + w_b{}^*bias)$
$u_4 = f(-1{}^*0 + 1.99916{}^*1 + 0.99915{}^*1) = f(2.99831)$
$u_4 = 0.952497$

$u_5 = f(w_{5,3}u_3 + w_{5,4}u_4 + w_b{}^*bias)$

$u_5 = f(1.51525*0.8188 + -0.9822*0.952497 + 1.01865*1) = f(1.32379)$
$u_5 = 0.7898$
$err = 0.5 * (1.0 - 0.7898)^2 = 0.022$

Recall that the initial error of this network was 0.023895. Our current error is 0.022, which means that this single iteration of the backpropagation algorithm reduced the mean squared error by 0.001895.

EVOLVING GAME AI BEHAVIORS

The application that we'll use for backpropagation is the creation of neuro-controllers for game AI characters. A neurocontroller is the name commonly given to neural networks that are used in control applications. In this application, we'll use the neural network to select an action from an available set based upon the current environment perceived by the character. The usage of "character" and "agent" in the following discussion are synonymous.

The rationale for using neural networks as neurocontrollers is that we can't practically give a game AI character a set of behaviors that cover all possible combinations of perceived environments. Therefore, we train the neural network with a limited number of examples (desired behaviors for a given environment), and then let it generalize all of the other situations to provide proper responses. The ability to generalize and provide proper responses to unknown situations is the key strength of the neurocontroller design.

Another advantage to the neurocontroller approach is that the neurocontroller is not a rigid function map from environment to action. Slight changes in the environment may elicit different responses from the neurocontroller, which should provide a more believable behavior from the character. Standard decision trees or finite automata lead to predictable behaviors, which are not very gratifying in game-play.

As shown in Figure 5.8, the environment is the source of information for a character. Information is received from the environment and provided to the agent. This process of "seeing" the environment is called "perception." The neurocontroller provides the capability for "action-selection." Finally, the character manipulates the environment through "action." This alters the environment, so the character cycles back to perception to continue the sense-react cycle.

Neurocontroller Architecture

In the prior example, a neural network with a single output was discussed in detail. For the game AI agent, we'll look at another architecture called a "winner-take-all" network. Winner-take-all architectures are useful where inputs must be segmented into one of several classes (see Figure 5.9, page 97).

In the "winner-take-all" network, the output cell with the highest weighted sum is the "winner" of the group and is allowed to fire. In our application, each cell represents a distinct behavior that is available to the character within the game. Example behaviors include fire-weapon, run-away, wander, etc. The firing of a cell within the winner-take-all group causes the agent to perform the particular behavior. When the agent is again allowed to perceive the environment, the process is repeated.

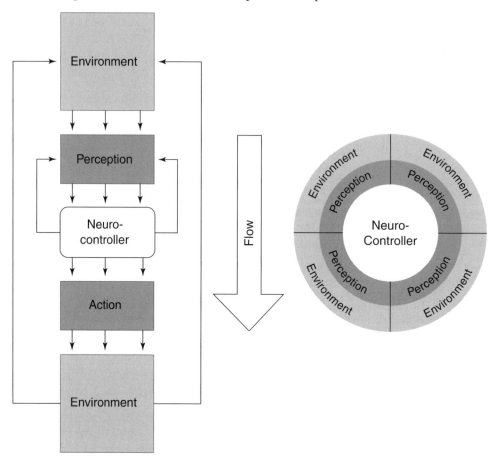

FIGURE 5.8 Example of a neurocontroller in an environment.

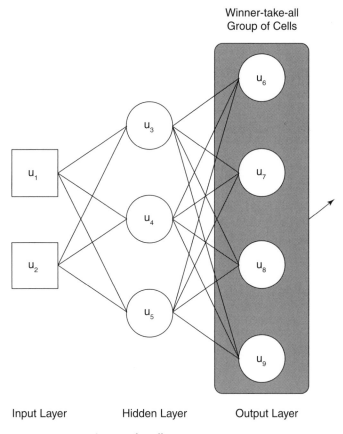

FIGURE 5.9 Winner-take-all group.

Figure 5.10 (page 98) illustrates the network that was used to test the architecture and method for action-selection. The four inputs include the *health* of the character (0-poor to 2-healthy), *has-knife* (1 if the character has a knife, 0 otherwise), *has-gun* (1 if in possession, 0 otherwise), and *enemy-present* (number of enemies in field-of-view).

The outputs select the particular behavior that the character will take. Action *attack* causes the character to attack the peers in the field-of-view, *run* causes the character to flee its current position, *wander* represents random or non-random movement of the character within the environment, and *hide* causes the character to seek shelter. These behaviors are very high-level, and it's anticipated that the behavior subsystem will take the selected action and follow-through.

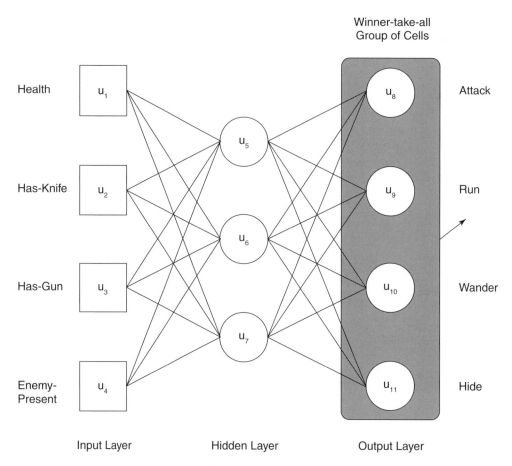

FIGURE 5.10   Game AI neurocontroller architecture for verification.

The architecture selected here (three hidden cells) was determined largely by trial-and-error. Three hidden cells could be trained for all presented examples with 100% accuracy. Decreasing the cells to two or one resulted in a network that did not successfully classify all examples.

Training the Neurocontroller

The neurocontroller within the game environment is a static element of the character's AI. The following discusses online learning of the neurocontroller within the environment.

Training the neurocontroller consists of presenting training examples from a small set of desired behaviors, and then performing the backpropagation on the network given the desired result and the actual result. For example, if the character is in possession of a gun and is healthy and in the presence of a single enemy, the desired behavior may be to attack. However, if the character is healthy, in possession of a knife, but in the presence of two enemies, the correct behavior would be to hide.

Test Data Set

The test data set consists of a small number of desired perception-action scenarios. Since we want the neurocontroller to behave in a more life-like fashion, we will not train the neurocontroller for every case. Therefore, the network will generalize the inputs and provide an action that should be similar to other scenarios for which it was trained. The examples used to train the network are presented in Table 5.1.

TABLE 5.1 Training Examples Used for the Neurocontroller.

Health	Has-Knife	Has-Gun	Enemies	Behavior
2	0	0	0	Wander
2	0	0	1	Wander
2	0	1	1	Attack
2	0	1	2	Attack
2	1	0	2	Hide
2	1	0	1	Attack
1	0	0	0	Wander
1	0	0	1	Hide
1	0	1	1	Attack
1	0	1	2	Hide
1	1	0	2	Hide
1	1	0	1	Hide
0	0	0	0	Wander
0	0	0	1	Hide
0	0	1	1	Hide
0	0	1	2	Run
0	1	0	2	Run
0	1	0	1	Hide

The data set in Table 5.1 was presented randomly to the network in backpropagation training. The mean-squared-error reduction is shown in Figure 5.11.

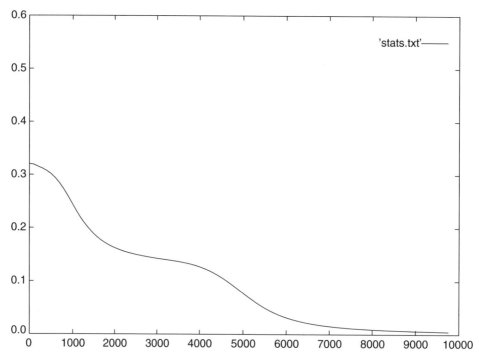

FIGURE 5.11 Sample run of the backpropagation algorithm on the neurocontroller.

In most cases, all examples shown in Table 5.1 are successfully trained. In some runs, up to two examples resulted in improper actions. Increasing the number of hidden cells resulted in perfect training. However, this would increase the computing resources needed to run the neurocontroller. Therefore, three hidden cells were chosen with multiple training cycles to ensure proper training. The neurocontroller was trained offline for as many runs as were necessary for perfect training on the given set.

To test the neurocontroller, new examples were presented to the network to identify how it would react to scenarios for which it had no specific knowledge. These tests give an understanding of how well the neurocontroller can generalize and respond with desirable actions for unseen examples.

If we present the neurocontroller with a scenario, in which it has full health, access to both weapons, and a single enemy present, or (2:1:1:1), the neurocontroller responds with an *attack* action. This is a reasonable response given the situation. Now consider a scenario where the character has full health, access to a knife, and three enemies present (2:1:0:3). The neurocontroller in this scenario responds with the *hide* action. This is another reasonable scenario. See Table 5.2 for other examples.

TABLE 5.2   Test Examples Illustrating Successful Neurocontroller Generalization.

Health	Has-Knife	Has-Gun	Enemies	Behavior
Good (2)	Yes	Yes	1	Attack
OK (1)	Yes	Yes	2	Hide
Poor (0)	No	No	0	Wander
Poor (0)	Yes	Yes	1	Hide
Good (2)	No	Yes	3	Hide
Good (2)	Yes	No	3	Hide
Poor (0)	Yes	No	3	Run

From Table 5.2, we can see that the neurocontroller successfully generalizes from the existing training set to provide reasonable actions for given environments. While it wasn't trained for these examples directly, it's able to perform a desirable behavior in response to them.

ON THE CD

The source code for the backpropagation algorithm can be found on the CD-ROM at ./software/ch5/backprop/.

SOURCE DISCUSSION

Let's now look at the source code, which implements both the backpropagation algorithm for a configurable network topology as well as training and testing for the neurocontroller example.

The global variables are shown in Listing 5.1.

Listing 5.1 Backpropagation Neural Network Globals.

```
#define INPUT_NEURONS           4
#define HIDDEN_NEURONS          3
#define OUTPUT_NEURONS          4

/* Input to Hidden Weights (with Biases) */
double wih[INPUT_NEURONS+1][HIDDEN_NEURONS];

/* Hidden to Output Weights (with Biases) */
double who[HIDDEN_NEURONS+1][OUTPUT_NEURONS];

/* Activations */
double inputs[INPUT_NEURONS];
double hidden[HIDDEN_NEURONS];
double target[OUTPUT_NEURONS];
double actual[OUTPUT_NEURONS];

/* Unit Errors */
double erro[OUTPUT_NEURONS];
double errh[HIDDEN_NEURONS];
```

The weights are defined as input to hidden layer (wih) and hidden to output layer (who). The weight for the connection between u_5 and u_1 (from Figure 5.10) is an input to hidden layer weight represented by wih[0][0] (since u_1 is the first input cell and u_5 is the first hidden cell, based from zero). This weight is referred to as $w_{5,1}$. The weight $w_{11,7}$ (connection from u_{11} in the output layer to u_7 in the hidden layer) is who[2][3]. Bias weights occupy the last row in each of the tables, as are identified by the "+1" size for the wih and who arrays.

The activations are provided by four arrays. The inputs array defines the value of the input cells, the hidden array provides the output of the hidden cells, the target array represents what is desired of the network for the given inputs, and the actual array represents what the network actually provided.

The errors of the network are provided in two arrays. The erro array represents the error for each output cell. The errh array is the hidden cell errors.

In order to find random weights for initialization of the network, a number of macros are defined, shown in Listing 5.2.

Listing 5.2 Macros and Symbolic Constants for Backpropagation.

```
#define LEARN_RATE 0.2    /* Rho */
```

```
#define RAND_WEIGHT       ( ((float)rand() / (float)RAND_MAX) -
0.5)

#define getSRand() ((float)rand() / (float)RAND_MAX)
#define getRand(x)        (int) ((float)x*rand()/(RAND_MAX+1.0))

#define sqr(x)            ((x) * (x))
```

Weights are randomly selected in the range [-0.5 – 0.5]. The learning rate (rho) is defined as 0.2. The weight range and learning rate can both be adjusted depending upon the problem and accuracy required.

Three support functions exist to assign random weights to the network and for algorithm support. These are shown in Listing 5.3.

Listing 5.3 Support Functions for Backpropagation.

```
void assignRandomWeights( void )
{
  int hid, inp, out;

  for (inp = 0 ; inp < INPUT_NEURONS+1 ; inp++) {
    for (hid = 0 ; hid < HIDDEN_NEURONS ; hid++) {
      wih[inp][hid] = RAND_WEIGHT;
    }
  }

  for (hid = 0 ; hid < HIDDEN_NEURONS+1 ; hid++) {
    for (out = 0 ; out < OUTPUT_NEURONS ; out++) {
      who[hid][out] = RAND_WEIGHT;
    }
  }

}


double sigmoid( double val )
{
  return (1.0 / (1.0 + exp(-val)));
}


double sigmoidDerivative( double val )
{
```

```
    return ( val * (1.0 - val) );
}
```

Function `assignRandomWeights` randomly assigns a weight to each of the connections within the network (including all biases). The `sigmoid` function implements the squashing function used in the feed-forward phase (Equation 5.5). The `sigmodDerivative` function implements the derivative of the `sigmoid` function and is used during error backpropagation.

The next function implements the feed-forward phase of the algorithm (see Listing 5.4).

Listing 5.4   Feed-forward Algorithm.

```
void feedForward( )
{
  int inp, hid, out;
  double sum;

  /* Calculate input to hidden layer */
  for (hid = 0 ; hid < HIDDEN_NEURONS ; hid++) {

    sum = 0.0;
    for (inp = 0 ; inp < INPUT_NEURONS ; inp++) {
      sum += inputs[inp] * wih[inp][hid];
    }

    /* Add in Bias */
    sum += wih[INPUT_NEURONS][hid];

    hidden[hid] = sigmoid( sum );

  }

  /* Calculate the hidden to output layer */
  for (out = 0 ; out < OUTPUT_NEURONS ; out++) {

    sum = 0.0;
    for (hid = 0 ; hid < HIDDEN_NEURONS ; hid++) {
      sum += hidden[hid] * who[hid][out];
    }

    /* Add in Bias */
```

```
      sum += who[HIDDEN_NEURONS][out];

      actual[out] = sigmoid( sum );

    }

  }
```

As is illustrated in Listing 5.4, the feed-forward algorithm starts by calculating the activations of the hidden layers with the inputs from the input layer. The bias is added to the cell prior to the sigmoid function. The output layer is then calculated in the same manner. Note that the network may have one or more output cells. Therefore, the output cells are looped to perform all needed output activations.

The actual backpropagation algorithm is shown in Listing 5.5.

Listing 5.5 Backpropagation Algorithm.

```
void backPropagate( void )
{
  int inp, hid, out;

  /* Calculate the output layer error (step 3 for output cell) */
  for (out = 0 ; out < OUTPUT_NEURONS ; out++) {
    erro [out] = (target[out] - actual[out]) *
                  sigmoidDerivative( actual[out] );
  }

  /* Calculate the hidden layer error (step 3 for hidden cell) */
  for (hid = 0 ; hid < HIDDEN_NEURONS ; hid++) {

    errh[hid] = 0.0;
    for (out = 0 ; out < OUTPUT_NEURONS ; out++) {
      errh[hid] += erro[out] * who[hid][out];
    }

    errh[hid] *= sigmoidDerivative( hidden[hid] );

  }

  /* Update the weights for the output layer (step 4) */
  for (out = 0 ; out < OUTPUT_NEURONS ; out++) {
```

```
for (hid = 0 ; hid < HIDDEN_NEURONS ; hid++) {
  who[hid][out] += (LEARN_RATE * erro[out] * hidden[hid]);
}

/* Update the Bias */
who[HIDDEN_NEURONS][out] += (LEARN_RATE * erro[out]);

}

/* Update the weights for the hidden layer (step 4) */
for (hid = 0 ; hid < HIDDEN_NEURONS ; hid++) {

  for (inp = 0 ; inp < INPUT_NEURONS ; inp++) {
    wih[inp][hid] += (LEARN_RATE * errh[hid] * inputs[inp]);
  }

  /* Update the Bias */
  wih[INPUT_NEURONS][hid] += (LEARN_RATE * errh[hid]);

}

}
```

This function follows the algorithm outlined in the "Backpropagation Example" section. The error for the output cell (or cells) is calculated first using the actual output and the desired output. Next, the errors for the hidden cells are calculated. Finally, the weights for all connections are updated according to whether they're in the input-hidden layer or the hidden-output layer. An important note is that in the algorithm, we don't calculate a weight for the bias, but instead simply apply the error to the bias itself. During the feed-forward algorithm, we simply add the bias in without applying any weight to it.

That's the algorithm for computing the output of a multi-layer, feed-forward neural network and adjusting the network using the backpropagation algorithm. Let's now look at the example code that drives it for the neuro-controller example.

In Listing 5.6, a structure is defined to represent the examples for our training set. The structure defines the inputs (health, knife, gun, enemy), and an array for the desired output (out array). Listing 5.6 also contains the initialization of the training set.

Listing 5.6   Representing the Neurocontroller Training Set.

```
typedef struct {
  double health;
  double knife;
  double gun;
  double enemy;
  double out[OUTPUT_NEURONS];
} ELEMENT;

#define MAX_SAMPLES 18

/*  H    K    G    E    A    R    W    H  */
ELEMENT samples[MAX_SAMPLES] = {
  { 2.0, 0.0, 0.0, 0.0, {0.0, 0.0, 1.0, 0.0} },
  { 2.0, 0.0, 0.0, 1.0, {0.0, 0.0, 1.0, 0.0} },
  { 2.0, 0.0, 1.0, 1.0, {1.0, 0.0, 0.0, 0.0} },
  { 2.0, 0.0, 1.0, 2.0, {1.0, 0.0, 0.0, 0.0} },
  { 2.0, 1.0, 0.0, 2.0, {0.0, 0.0, 0.0, 1.0} },
  { 2.0, 1.0, 0.0, 1.0, {1.0, 0.0, 0.0, 0.0} },

  { 1.0, 0.0, 0.0, 0.0, {0.0, 0.0, 1.0, 0.0} },
  { 1.0, 0.0, 0.0, 1.0, {0.0, 0.0, 0.0, 1.0} },
  { 1.0, 0.0, 1.0, 1.0, {1.0, 0.0, 0.0, 0.0} },
  { 1.0, 0.0, 1.0, 2.0, {0.0, 0.0, 0.0, 1.0} },
  { 1.0, 1.0, 0.0, 2.0, {0.0, 0.0, 0.0, 1.0} },
  { 1.0, 1.0, 0.0, 1.0, {0.0, 0.0, 0.0, 1.0} },

  { 0.0, 0.0, 0.0, 0.0, {0.0, 0.0, 1.0, 0.0} },
  { 0.0, 0.0, 0.0, 1.0, {0.0, 0.0, 0.0, 1.0} },
  { 0.0, 0.0, 1.0, 1.0, {0.0, 0.0, 0.0, 1.0} },
  { 0.0, 0.0, 1.0, 2.0, {0.0, 1.0, 0.0, 0.0} },
  { 0.0, 1.0, 0.0, 2.0, {0.0, 1.0, 0.0, 0.0} },
  { 0.0, 1.0, 0.0, 1.0, {0.0, 0.0, 0.0, 1.0} }
};
```

Recall that the health input represents three values (2 for healthy, 1 for moderately healthy, and 0 for not healthy). Knife and gun inputs are booleans (1 if item is held, 0 if not) and enemy is the number of enemies that are seen. Actions are booleans as well; a non-zero value represents the desired action to take.

Since we're implementing a winner-take-all network, we'll code a simple function to determine the output cell with the highest weighted sum. This function searches the vector for the highest output, and returns a string representing the action to take (see Listing 5.7). The return value can then be used as an offset into strings to emit the text response behavior.

Listing 5.7 Winner-take-all Determiner Function.

```c
char *strings[4]={"Attack", "Run", "Wander", "Hide"};

int action( double *vector )
{
  int index, sel;
  double max;

  sel = 0;
  max = vector[sel];

  for (index = 1 ; index < OUTPUT_NEURONS ; index++) {
    if (vector[index] > max) {
      max = vector[index]; sel = index;
    }
  }

  return( sel );
}
```

Finally, Listing 5.8 provides the main function for performing the training and testing of the neurocontroller.

Listing 5.8 Sample main Function for Neurocontroller Training and Testing.

```c
int main()
{
  double err;
  int i, sample=0, iterations=0;
  int sum = 0;

  out = fopen("stats.txt", "w");

  /* Seed the random number generator */
  srand( time(NULL) );
```

```c
assignRandomWeights();

/* Train the network */
while (1) {

  if (++sample == MAX_SAMPLES) sample = 0;

  inputs[0] = samples[sample].health;
  inputs[1] = samples[sample].knife;
  inputs[2] = samples[sample].gun;
  inputs[3] = samples[sample].enemy;

  target[0] = samples[sample].out[0];
  target[1] = samples[sample].out[1];
  target[2] = samples[sample].out[2];
  target[3] = samples[sample].out[3];

  feedForward();

  err = 0.0;
  for (i = 0 ; i < OUTPUT_NEURONS ; i++) {
    err += sqr( (samples[sample].out[i] - actual[i]) );
  }
  err = 0.5 * err;

  fprintf(out, "%g\n", err);
  printf("mse = %g\n", err);

  if (iterations++ > 100000) break;

  backPropagate();

}

/* Test the network */
for (i = 0 ; i < MAX_SAMPLES ; i++) {

  inputs[0] = samples[i].health;
  inputs[1] = samples[i].knife;
  inputs[2] = samples[i].gun;
  inputs[3] = samples[i].enemy;

  target[0] = samples[i].out[0];
  target[1] = samples[i].out[1];
```

```c
    target[2] = samples[i].out[2];
    target[3] = samples[i].out[3];

    feedForward();

    if (action(actual) != action(target)) {

      printf("%2.1g:%2.1g:%2.1g:%2.1g %s (%s)\n",
          inputs[0], inputs[1], inputs[2], inputs[3],
          strings[action(actual)], strings[action(target)]);

    } else {
      sum++;
    }

  }

  printf("Network is %g%% correct\n",
          ((float)sum / (float)MAX_SAMPLES) * 100.0);

  /* Run some tests */

  /*  Health          Knife           Gun             Enemy
   */
  inputs[0] = 2.0; inputs[1] = 1.0; inputs[2] = 1.0; inputs[3] =
    1.0;
  feedForward();
  printf("2111 Action %s\n", strings[action(actual)]);

  inputs[0] = 1.0; inputs[1] = 1.0; inputs[2] = 1.0; inputs[3] =
    2.0;
  feedForward();
  printf("1112 Action %s\n", strings[action(actual)]);

  inputs[0] = 0.0; inputs[1] = 0.0; inputs[2] = 0.0; inputs[3] =
    0.0;
  feedForward();
  printf("0000 Action %s\n", strings[action(actual)]);

  inputs[0] = 0.0; inputs[1] = 1.0; inputs[2] = 1.0; inputs[3] =
    1.0;
  feedForward();
  printf("0111 Action %s\n", strings[action(actual)]);
```

```
      inputs[0] = 2.0; inputs[1] = 0.0; inputs[2] = 1.0; inputs[3] =
        3.0;
      feedForward();
      printf("2013 Action %s\n", strings[action(actual)]);

      inputs[0] = 2.0; inputs[1] = 1.0; inputs[2] = 0.0; inputs[3] =
        3.0;
      feedForward();
      printf("2103 Action %s\n", strings[action(actual)]);

      inputs[0] = 0.0; inputs[1] = 1.0; inputs[2] = 0.0; inputs[3] =
        3.0;
      feedForward();
      printf("0103 Action %s\n", strings[action(actual)]);


  fclose(out);

  return 0;
}
```

After seeding the random number generator with srand, the connection weights of the network are randomly generated. A while loop is then performed to train the network. Each of the samples is taken in order, rather than random selection of the examples. The feed-forward algorithm is performed, followed by a check of the mean-squared-error. Finally, the backpropagation algorithm runs to adjust the weights in the network. After a number of iterations are performed, the loop exits and the network is tested with the training set to verify its accuracy. After the network is tested with the training set, a set of examples are checked that were not part of the original training set.

If the neural network were to be used within a game environment, the weights would be emitted to a file for later inclusion within source. The network could also be optimized at this stage to minimize the computing resources needed for its use within game environments.

NEUROCONTROLLER LEARNING

When the neurocontroller is embedded within a game environment, its training is complete and no further learning is possible. To include the ability for the character to learn, portions of backpropagation could be included with the game to adjust weights based upon game play.

A very simple mechanism could adjust the weights of the neurocontroller based upon the last action made by the character. If the action led to negative consequences, such as the death of the character, the weights for this action given the current environment could be inhibited to make it less likely to occur in the future.

Further, all game AI characters could learn these same lessons, in a form of Lamarckian evolution (whereby children inherit the traits of their parents, which would include lessons learned). After numerous games played, the game AI characters would become slowly better at avoiding negative situations.

NEUROCONTROLLER MEMORY

The feature of memory could also be created within the neural network by creating tapped-delay lines for each of the inputs (extending the input vector from one to two dimensions). Therefore, the prior input from the environment doesn't disappear, but becomes part of another input to the network. This could be extended for a number of elements giving the character quite a bit of history, as well as many new intelligent abilities.

This method could also include feedback, so that the last actions could be fed back into the network providing the neurcontroller with action history. Additional internal feedback could include the health of the character as well as the simulated affective state (the character's emotional state). These mechanisms further the generation of rich and believable action selection.

OTHER APPLICATIONS

The backpropagation algorithm can be used to train neural networks for a variety of applications. A short list of applications includes:

- General Pattern Recognition
- Fault Diagnosis

- Monitoring Patients in Medical Settings
- Character Recognition
- Data Filtering
- Odor/Aroma Analysis
- Fraud Detection

SUMMARY

In this chapter, an introduction to neural networks was provided with a discussion of the backpropagation algorithm. To illustrate the algorithm, the training of game AI neurocontrollers was presented and found to properly generalize to provide proper responses to unseen situations. While the approach presented here may not be possible in all game architectures due to computational requirements, it does provide a believable character architecture including non-linear relationships between perceived environment and action selection.

REFERENCES

[Minsky and Papert 1969] Minsky, Marvin and Seymour Papert. (1969). *Perceptrons: An Introduction to Computational Geometry*. Cambridge, Mass.: MIT Press.

RESOURCES

Gallant, Stephen L., *Neural Network Learning and Expert Systems*. Cambridge, Mass.: MIT Press, 1994.

Waggoner, Ben and Brian Speer. "Jean-Baptiste Lamarck (1744–1829)," available online at *http://www.ucmp.berkeley.edu/history/lamarck.html* (accessed January 17, 2003)

6 Introduction to Genetic Algorithms

In this chapter, we'll look at simulated evolution as a way to solve computational problems. The genetic algorithm, developed by John Holland [Holland 1962], is a search algorithm that operates over a population of encoded candidate solutions to solve a given problem. To illustrate the use of the algorithm, we'll use evolutionary computation to evolve sequences of instructions that represent a simple algorithm. This is otherwise known as genetic programming as defined by John Koza [Koza 1992].

BIOLOGICAL INSPIRATION

The genetic algorithm is an optimization technique that simulates the phenomenon of natural evolution (as first observed by Charles Darwin). In natural evolution, species search for increasingly beneficial adaptations for survival within their complex environments. The search takes place in the species' chromosomes where changes, and their effects, are graded by the survival and reproduction of the species. This is the basis for survival of the fittest—survival and the passing on of these characteristics to future generations. Survival in nature is the ultimate utility function.

THE GENETIC ALGORITHM

The genetic algorithm, instead of trying to optimize a single solution, works with a population of candidate solutions that are encoded as chromosomes. Within the chromosome are separate genes that represent the independent variables for the problem at hand (see Figure 6.1).

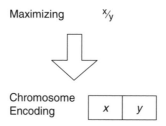

FIGURE 6.1 Encoding candidate solutions into chromosomes.

From the simple example in Figure 6.1, we take the parameters from our problem and create a chromosome that represents the two unique independent parameters. The parameters could represent bit strings, floating-point variables, or simple binary-encoded integers.

Through selection of fit chromosomes from the population and use of genetic operators such as recombination and mutation, better fit chromosomes will result in the population. This represents a summary for Holland's schema theorem and is the basis by which it works.

The genetic algorithm consists of three fundamental steps (with a large number of variations possible within each step). These steps are shown in Figure 6.2.

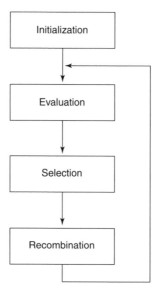

FIGURE 6.2 Genetic algorithm high-level flow.

The genetic algorithm is performed in three distinct steps, excluding the initial creation of the population. During the *evaluation* process, the fitness of the population is calculated. Next, a subset of the population is *selected* based upon a predefined selection criterion. Finally, the selected subpopulation is *recombined* and the result is a new population. The algorithm begins again with the new population and the process continues until some constraint is reached and the algorithm ends.

Initialization

Creating the initial population provides the starting point for the algorithm. Typically, this is done by randomly creating chromosomes, but can also be done by seeding the population with known fit chromosomes (see Figure 6.3).

One important constraint is that the initial population must be diverse. This can be ensured by performing a secondary step to check that each chromosome is somewhat different. Without adequate diversity, the algorithm may not produce good solutions.

NOTE

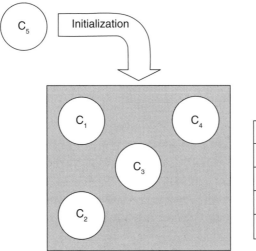

Population of Chromosomes (t_0)   Fitness Table

FIGURE 6.3   Initialization of the genetic pool.

Evaluation

The evaluation step simply provides a way to rate how each chromosome (candidate solution) solves the problem at hand. This step involves decoding the chromosome into the variable space of the problem and then checking the result of the problem using these parameters. The fitness is then computed from this result (see Figure 6.4).

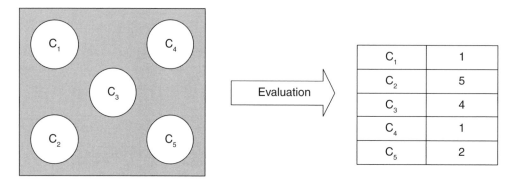

Population of Chromosomes (t_0)   Fitness Table

FIGURE 6.4   Evaluation of the population.

Selection

Selection is quite possibly the most important and most misunderstood step of the genetic algorithm. In the selection step, chromosomes are selected for propagation to future populations based upon their fitness (how well they solve the problem at hand). This is a double-edged sword since if selection involves only the highest-fit chromosomes; the solution-space becomes very limited due to a lack of diversity. If selection is performed randomly, there is no guarantee that future generations will increase in fitness. The result of the selection process is a set of chromosomes that will take part in recombination (mating, if you will). See Figure 6.5 for a depiction of the selection process.

Large varieties of selection algorithms exist. Figure 6.5 shows a selection algorithm known as "Roulette-wheel" selection. Roulette-wheel selection performs selection from the population based upon the fitness of

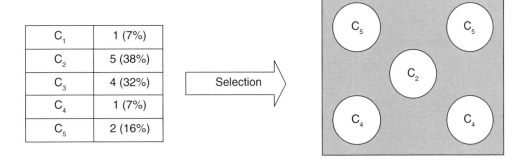

C$_1$	1 (7%)
C$_2$	5 (38%)
C$_3$	4 (32%)
C$_4$	1 (7%)
C$_5$	2 (16%)

Selection →

Fitness Table

Population of Chromosomes (t$_0$)

FIGURE 6.5   Selecting chromosomes based upon their fitness.

the chromosome. The higher-fit the chromosome, the more likely it will be chosen (and re-chosen) for propagation to the next generation. Put another way, the probability of selection is proportional to the fitness of the chromosome. From Figure 6.5, chromosome 2 has been chosen twice for propagation, chromosome 3 twice, and chromosome 5 only once. Chromosomes 1 and 4 were not selected at all, and disappear from the subsequent population.

Recombination

In recombination, pairs of chromosomes are recombined, possibly modified, and then placed back into the population as the next generation. The original sets of chromosomes are commonly referred to as the "parents" with the resulting chromosomes being the "children." One or more genetic operators are applied with some probability. Some of the possible operators include mutation and crossover, which are analogous to natural genetics. Samplings of genetic operators are covered in the next section. The process of recombination is illustrated in Figure 6.6.

The result of recombination is a new population of chromosomes. The process continues again at evaluation until the problem represented by the chromosomes is solved, or some other exit criterion is met (such as convergence, or a maximum number of generations).

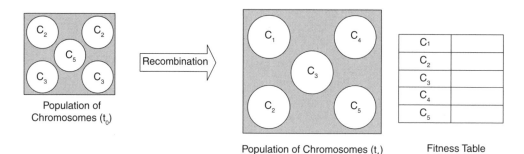

FIGURE 6.6   Recombining chromosomes for a new population.

GENETIC OPERATORS

While the variety of genetic operators is quite large, only a handful are useful in general problems. The operators discussed below, crossover and mutation, are direct descendents of natural mechanisms.

Crossover

The crossover operator takes two chromosomes, separates them at a random site (in both chromosomes) and then swaps the tails of the two, resulting in two new chromosomes. Cutting the chromosome at one location, called single-point crossover is not the only possibility. Multi-point crossover can also be used (see Figure 6.7).

The crossover does not create new material within the population, but simply intermixes the existing population to create new chromosomes. This allows the genetic algorithm to search the solution space for new candidate solutions to solve the problem at hand. The crossover operator is generally accepted as the most important operator. While it is important, the next operator provides for the introduction of new material within the population.

Mutation

The mutation operator introduces a random change into a gene in the chromosome (sometimes more than one, depending upon the rate of application). The mutation operator provides the ability to introduce new material into the population. Since chromosomes simply intermix with existing chromosomes, mutation provides the opportunity to "shake-up" the population to expand the solution space (see Figure 6.8).

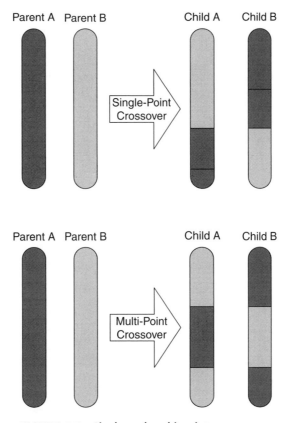

FIGURE 6.7   Single and multi-point crossover.

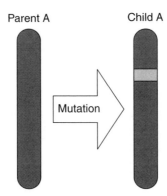

FIGURE 6.8   Mutating a
single chromosome.

GA THROUGH EXAMPLE

Thus far, much of this discussion has been conceptual. Let's now walk through an iteration of the algorithm to see how it actually works. In this example, we're trying to find a pair of parameters that maximize Equation 6.1.

$$f(x, y) = \frac{1}{1 + x^2 + y^2} \tag{6.1}$$

This equation is shown graphically in Figure 6.9 (3-dimensional plot) and Figure 6.10 (contour plot).

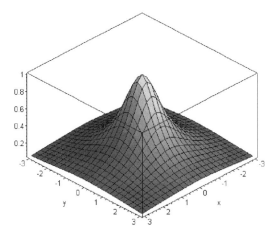

FIGURE 6.9   Graphical plot of Equation 6.1.

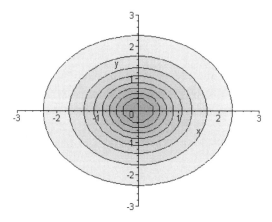

FIGURE 6.10   Contour plot of Equation 6.1 showing z-dimension via shading.

Our chromosome for this example is built from two genes, or two parameters, x and y. The first step is to create a pool of chromosomes from which we'll apply the genetic algorithm to find a solution. Figure 6.11 shows our initial population as selected randomly.

	x	y	fitness
C_0	-1	2	?
C_1	-2	3	?
C_2	1.5	0	?
C_3	0.5	-1	?

FIGURE 6.11   Initial population (t_0).

Now that our initial population is available, we begin the evaluation process. To evaluate the chromosomes in our population, we determine their individual fitness. The fitness in this case is simply Equation 6.1. The larger the value resulting from the equation, the higher is the fitness of the chromosome. Figure 6.12 shows the fitness values of the evaluated chromosomes.

	x	y	fitness
C_0	-1	2	0.167
C_1	-2	3	0.007
C_2	1.5	0	0.31
C_3	0.5	-1	0.44

FIGURE 6.12   Fitness of initial population.

From Figure 6.12, we can see that chromosome C_1 is very small, and therefore it is very unlikely to be selected. We select two pairs of parents for recombination. Each parent will contribute via crossover to children in the next generation. Based upon fitness, we select C_3 and C_2 as the first set of parents and C_3 and C_0 as the second set of parents. Since only two genes exist within the chromosome, we swap at the gene level resulting in each chromosome swapping its x and y elements. Figure 6.13 shows the new population (with the gene sources shown in parenthesis) as well as the new evaluated fitness of each new chromosome.

Let's now observe the fitness values shown in Figure 6.12 compared to the fitness values in the new population of Figure 6.13. It's clear that the fitness

	x	y	fitness
C_0 $(x_{c3}\, y_{c2})$	0.5	0	0.8
C_1 $(x_{c2}\, y_{c3})$	1.5	-1	0.24
C_2 $(x_{c3}\, y_{c0})$	0.5	2	0.19
C_3 $(x_{c0}\, y_{c3})$	-1	-1	0.33

FIGURE 6.13   Next generation with fitness evaluated (population at t_1).

values have increased (the largest fitness in t_0 was 0.44 while the largest in t_1 is 0.8). This means that the best solution within the population is better than the prior best solution from the old population. The average fitness in the first population was 0.231 while the average fitness in the new population is 0.39. This flow shows an obvious improvement in the population and the key elements of the genetic algorithm.

The mutation operator was not used in this example. For this type of problem, mutation could be implemented as slight random changes to the gene values (such as adding or subtracting a small value such as 0.1).

From this example, it should be clear that the crossover operator will not evolve into a perfect solution. The crossover operator uses the existing genetic material within the population to search the solution space. Only a limited number of combinations are possible, therefore, mutation would be necessary to introduce new material into the population to extend the search space.

NOTE

SAMPLE PROBLEM

Now that we have a basic understanding of the genetic algorithm, let's use it to solve what will be an unconventional optimization problem. Rather than focus on the traditional numerical optimization problems, let's try to optimize a more symbolic problem of sequences of instructions (under the genre of evolutionary programming).

Overview

Consider a simple instruction set for a zero-address architecture (a stack architecture). Our virtual computer has no registers, only a stack for which instructions can manipulate the values on the stack. Our virtual computer recognizes only a handful of instructions; these are shown in Table 6.1.

TABLE 6.1 Simple Instruction Set.

Instruction	Description
DUP	Duplicate the top of the stack (stack: A => A A)
SWAP	Swap the top two elements of the stack (stack: A B => B A)
MUL	Multiply the top two elements of the stack (stack: 2 3 => 6)
ADD	Add the top two elements of the stack (stack: 2 3 => 5)
OVER	Duplicate the second item on the stack (stack: A B => B A B)
NOP	No-operation (filler)

These instructions are very simple, and can be used to solve a variety of functions. For example, if we wanted to compute the square of the top element of the stack, the following instruction sequence could be used (assuming the top of the stack contains our input value):

DUP

MUL

This sequence duplicates the top of the stack and then multiples the two elements together ($X * X$, or X^2).

Solution Encoding

Recall that we encode the solution of the problem, not the problem itself (since the problem is used as the fitness measure for our chromosomes). This problem is quite easy, since our chromosome simply represents a string of instructions in a contiguous block. We assign numerical values to each of the instructions (DUP = 0, through NOP = 5). Our encoding is then a contiguous string of bytes representing the stream of instructions.

Fitness Evaluation

Evaluating the fitness of a given chromosome is a simple process of executing the string of instructions that are contained within the chromosome. We prepare a simple stack of some depth, load the initial values onto the stack, and then execute each instruction sequentially until the program reaches the end, or the END instruction is reached.

The fitness value is then calculated as the difference between the resulting value on the stack to what was expected per our objective function (predefined for the test).

Recombination

For this problem, we'll use both crossover and mutation. The crossover operator simply breaks an instruction stream at a single point, and swaps the tails of each parent. Mutation is a random reassignment of the gene with a new instruction (since the chromosome represents the program, each gene is a single instruction).

ON THE CD   The source code for the genetic algorithm can be found on the CD-ROM at ./software/ch6/genalg/.

SOURCE DISCUSSION

The source code for the genetic algorithm, as well as the virtual computer that evaluates the chromosomes, is very simple. Let's first look at the virtual computer implementation (otherwise known as a virtual machine).

Virtual Machine Implementation

The virtual machine (or VM) is a very simple architecture that supports a single integer stack and six instructions that use operands on the stack. Listing 6.1 shows the VM symbolics (from common.h) as well as the virtual machine (stm.c).

Listing 6.1   Virtual Machine Implementation.

```
#define DUP            0x00
#define SWAP           0x01
#define MUL            0x02
#define ADD            0x03
#define OVER           0x04
#define NOP            0x05
```

```
#define MAX_INSTRUCTION          (NOP+1)

#define NONE                     0
#define STACK_VIOLATION          1
#define MATH_VIOLATION           2


#define STACK_DEPTH        25

int stack[STACK_DEPTH];
int stackPointer;

#define ASSERT_STACK_ELEMENTS(x) \
     if (stackPointer < x) { error = STACK_VIOLATION ; break; }

#define ASSERT_STACK_NOT_FULL \
     if (stackPointer == STACK_DEPTH) { error = STACK_VIOLATION ;
       break; }

#define SPUSH(x) (stack[stackPointer++] = x)
#define SPOP     (stack[--stackPointer])
#define SPEEK    (stack[stackPointer-1])


/*
 *  interpretSTM
 *
 *    program    – sequence of simple instructions
 *    progLength – length of program
 *    args       - arguments on the virtual stack
 *    argsLength – number of arguments on the virtual stack
 *
 */

int interpretSTM(const int *program, int progLength,
                 const int *args, int argsLength)
{
  int pc = 0;
  int i, error = NONE;
  int a, b;

  stackPointer = 0;

  /* Load the arguments onto the stack */
```

```
for (i = argsLength-1 ; i >= 0 ; i--) {
  SPUSH(args[i]);
}

/* Execute the program */
while ((error == NONE) && (pc < progLength)) {

  switch(program[pc++]) {

    case DUP:
      ASSERT_STACK_ELEMENTS(1);
      ASSERT_STACK_NOT_FULL;
      SPUSH(SPEEK);
      break;

    case SWAP:
      ASSERT_STACK_ELEMENTS(2);
      a = stack[stackPointer-1];
      stack[stackPointer-1] = stack[stackPointer-2];
      stack[stackPointer-2] = a;
      break;

    case MUL:
      ASSERT_STACK_ELEMENTS(2);
      a = SPOP; b = SPOP;
      SPUSH(a * b);
      break;

    case ADD:
      ASSERT_STACK_ELEMENTS(2);
      a = SPOP; b = SPOP;
      SPUSH(a + b);
      break;

    case OVER:
      ASSERT_STACK_ELEMENTS(2);
      SPUSH(stack[stackPointer-2]);
      break;

  } /* Switch opcode */

} /* Loop */
```

```
      return(error);
  }
```

The symbolics section of Listing 6.1 shows the creation of the instructions and their values that will be used by the algorithm. A number of other constants are defined to understand how the program exited (whether successfully NONE, or by an error). We create a simple integer stack with a defined depth and a number of macros that simplify the development of the VM. The assert_ macros are used to identify violations within the program (such as blowing out the stack or trying to use an element that's not there). The macros SPEEK, SPUSH, and SPOP simplify stack-based operations.

Function interpretSTM (or interpret Stack Machine) is the virtual machine. This function accepts a program (program) and the length of the passed program (progLength) as well as a set of arguments (args), and the number passed (argsLength). The first operation of the VM is to store the passed arguments onto the stack. We walk through the list backwards, so whatever element the user specified as element zero is at the top of the stack.

Finally, we walk through the program that was passed in, executing each of the instructions. When we reach the end of the user program, we return with the error status. If an error was encountered along the way, the error variable is set and we return automatically.

Genetic Algorithm Implementation

The genetic algorithm that will be implemented here follows the basic flow discussed earlier in this chapter (see Figure 6.2). We'll discuss the implementation from the top down, starting with the main program, initialization, evaluation, selection, and recombination.

C main Function

The main function, shown in Listing 6.2, illustrates the basic flow of the algorithm.

Listing 6.2   C Main Routine for the Genetic Algorithm.

```
int main()
{
  int generation = 0, i;
```

```
FILE *fp;
extern float minFitness, maxFitness, avgFitness;
extern int curCrossovers, curMutations;
extern int   curPop;

void printProgram( int, int );

/* Seed the random number generator */
srand(time(NULL));

curPop = 0;

fp = fopen("stats.txt", "w");

if (fp == NULL) exit(-1);

/* Initialize the initial population and check each element's
 * fitness.
 */
initPopulation();
performFitnessCheck( fp );

/* Loop for the maximum number of allowable generations */
while (generation < MAX_GENERATIONS) {

  curCrossovers = curMutations = 0;

  /* Select two parents and recombine to create two children */
  performSelection();

  /* Switch the populations */
  curPop = (curPop == 0) ? 1 : 0;

  /* Calculate the fitness of the new population */
  performFitnessCheck( fp );

  /* Emit statistics every 100 generations */
  if ((generation++ % 100) == 0) {
    printf("Generation %d\n", generation-1);
    printf("\tmaxFitness = %f (%g)\n", maxFitness, MAX_FIT);
    printf("\tavgFitness = %f\n", avgFitness);
    printf("\tminFitness = %f\n", minFitness);
    printf("\tCrossovers = %d\n", curCrossovers);
    printf("\tMutation   = %d\n", curMutations);
```

```
      printf("\tpercentage = %f\n", avgFitness / maxFitness);
    }


    /* Check the diversity of the population after _ of the
     * generations has completed. If the population has
prematurely
     * converged, exit out to allow the user to restart.
     */
    if ( generation > (MAX_GENERATIONS * 0.25) ) {
      if ((avgFitness / maxFitness) > 0.98) {
        printf("converged\n");
        break;
      }
    }


    if (maxFitness == MAX_FIT) {
      printf("found solution\n");
      break;
    }


  }

  /* Emit final statistics */
  printf("Generation %d\n", generation-1);
  printf("\tmaxFitness = %f (%g)\n", maxFitness, MAX_FIT);
  printf("\tavgFitness = %f\n", avgFitness);
  printf("\tminFitness = %f\n", minFitness);
  printf("\tCrossovers = %d\n", curCrossovers);
  printf("\tMutation   = %d\n", curMutations);
  printf("\tpercentage = %f\n", avgFitness / maxFitness);

  /* Emit the highest fit chromosome from the population */
  for (i = 0 ; i < MAX_CHROMS ; i++) {

    if (populations[curPop][i].fitness == maxFitness) {
      int index;
      printf("Program %3d : ", i);

      for (index = 0 ; index < populations[curPop][i].progSize ;
           index++) {
        printf("%02d ", populations[curPop][i].program[index]);
      }
      printf("\n");
      printf("Fitness %f\n", populations[curPop][i].fitness);
```

```
        printf("ProgSize %d\n\n", populations[curPop][i].progSize);

        printProgram(i, curPop);

        break;
      }

    }

  return 0;
}
```

A summarized flow of the main function is as follows. We begin by seeding the random number generator with the srand call. We also open a file to store the fitness information (for which we'll see a plot in the next section). The population is then initialized with random chromosomes (initPopulation), and the fitness check is performed on the population (performFitnessCheck). This fitness check is done now because the fitness of each chromosome is necessary for selection (performSelection). This is because we're using probabilistic selection based upon the fitness value. Recombination is not shown specifically in this listing, as it is performed with the selection process.

Once selection has been performed, we switch the variable called curPop. This variable defines the current population. The population of chromosomes is defined as a 2-dimensional array that defines two populations (symbolically, old and new). See Listing 6.3 for this declaration.

Listing 6.3 Declaration of Populations.

```
typedef struct population {
  float fitness;
  int   progSize;
  int   program[MAX_PROGRAM];
} POPULATION_TYPE;

POPULATION_TYPE populations[2][MAX_CHROMS];

int curPop;
```

A population is made up of a number of chromosomes (as defined by MAX_CHROMS), where each chromosome is a program, program size (progSize), and `fitness`. The actual `populations` declaration shows two populations, as discussed before representing the old and new. The `curPop` variable defines which population is currently under view; the alternate is the target for any changes. When recombination occurs, we select parents from the current population (as defined by `curPop`) and introduce the children into the alternate population (as defined by `!curPop`).

Returning to the main function, the main loop (while loop of generations) simply performs selection, checks the fitness, and continues (swapping populations each iteration). The remainder of the loop emits debugging information and checks for a couple of exit conditions. If the average fitness is 98% of the maximum fitness, the population has converged and we exit. If the maximum fitness is the actual maximum allowable by the objective function, we also exit since we've found a solution to the problem at hand. Once a solution has been found, we emit more information to the user and display the highest fit program from the pool.

Initialization

Initializing the population is a simple process. We simply walk through the available chromosomes of the population, and assign each of the genes with a random instruction. We also initialize the fitness of each chromosome to zero and set the program size to the maximum (see Listing 6.4).

Listing 6.4   Initializing the Population.

```
void initMember( pop, index )
{
  int progIndex;

  populations[pop][index].fitness = 0.0;
  populations[pop][index].progSize = MAX_PROGRAM-1;

  /* Randomly create a new program */
  progIndex = 0;
  while (progIndex < MAX_PROGRAM) {
    populations[pop][index].program[progIndex++] =
                        getRand(MAX_INSTRUCTION);
  }

}
```

```
void initPopulation( void )
{
  int index;

  /* Initialize each member of the population */
  for (index = 0 ; index < MAX_CHROMS ; index++) {
    initMember(curPop, index);
  }
}
```

The initPopulation function is called from our main function, which in turn calls the initMember function to initialize each chromosome within the population.

Evaluating the Fitness

Fitness evaluation is performed through the performFitnessCheck function (shown in Listing 6.5).

Listing 6.5   Evaluating the Fitness of the Population.

```
float maxFitness;
float avgFitness;
float minFitness;

extern int stackPointer;
extern int stack[];

static int x = 0;
float totFitness;

int performFitnessCheck( FILE *outP )
{
  int chrom, result, i;
  int args[10], answer;

  maxFitness = 0.0;
  avgFitness = 0.0;
  minFitness = 1000.0;

  for ( chrom = 0 ; chrom < MAX_CHROMS ; chrom++ ) {
```

```
populations[curPop][chrom].fitness = 0.0;

for ( i = 0 ; i < COUNT ; i++ ) {

  args[0] = (rand() & 0x1f) + 1;
  args[1] = (rand() & 0x1f) + 1;
  args[2] = (rand() & 0x1f) + 1;

  /* Sample Problem: x^3 + y^2 + z */
  answer = (args[0] * args[0] * args[0]) +
           (args[1] * args[1]) + args[2];

  /* Call the virtual stack machine to check the program */
  result = interpretSTM(populations[curPop][chrom].program,
                        populations[curPop][chrom].progSize,
                        args, 3);

  /* If no error occurred, add this to the fitness value */
  if (result == NONE) {
    populations[curPop][chrom].fitness += TIER1;
  }

  /* If only one element is on the stack, add this to the
     fitness
   * value.
   */
  if (stackPointer == 1) {
    populations[curPop][chrom].fitness += TIER2;
  }

  /* If the stack contains the correct answer, add this to the
   * fitness value.
   */
  if (stack[0] == answer) {
    populations[curPop][chrom].fitness += TIER3;
  }

}

/* If this chromosome exceeds our last highest fitness, update
 * the statistics for this new record.
 */
if (populations[curPop][chrom].fitness > maxFitness) {
  maxFitness = populations[curPop][chrom].fitness;
```

```
      } else if (populations[curPop][chrom].fitness < minFitness) {
        minFitness = populations[curPop][chrom].fitness;
      }

      /* Update the total fitness value (sum of all fitnesses) */
      totFitness += populations[curPop][chrom].fitness;

    }

    /* Calculate our average fitness */
    avgFitness = totFitness / (float)MAX_CHROMS;

    if (outP) {
      /* Emit statistics if we have an output file pointer */
      fprintf(outP, "%d %6.4f %6.4f %6.4f\n",
                x++, minFitness, avgFitness, maxFitness);
    }

    return 0;
  }
```

Function `performFitnessCheck` walks through every chromosome in the current population and evaluates its fitness. The fitness is then stored with the chromosome in the `populations` structure.

The algorithm begins by clearing out the fitness measures in preparation for evaluating the current population. A loop is then defined to walk through each chromosome. Once the current fitness is cleared, another loop walks through the tests for the chromosome. To avoid a chromosome providing the correct answer, but working in only one case, we test the chromosome a number of times (in this case 10 times). The `args` array contains the arguments for the problem. This array is loaded onto the stack upon a call to the `evaluation` function. In each case, the `args` array is loaded with a random set of parameters. This is to ensure that it actually solves the problem at hand.

Once the arguments for the problem have been defined, we calculate the value that should result and load it into the `answer` variable. We then call the function `interpretSTM` (interpret stack machine) to evaluate the fitness (see Listing 6.1). From the result of the evaluation function, we calculate the fitness for the chromosome. The fitness is based upon a three-tiered measure. If the program exited successfully (no math error or program error), then we give it a TIER1 value. If only one value was left on the stack, we add in TIER2.

Finally, if the top of the stack is the correct value (expected value of answer) we add in TIER3. The tier values are defined such that TIER3 is greater than (more important than) TIER2, and so on for TIER1. This measure gives the genetic algorithm information to work with during the selection process. The genetic algorithm works best with gradual improvement of the calculated to expected response of the chromosome, this is not quite the case with this problem but it still works.

Once we finish checking the fitness for the current chromosome, we check to see if it is either the highest or lowest fit chromosome. This indication is stored within the maxFitness and minFitness variables accordingly. We then calculate the totFitness and once the loop to check all of the chromosomes is complete, we calculate the average fitness of the population (stored in avgFitness).

Finally, we store the current generation's information to our output file. This can later be used to plot the fitnesses of the populations to monitor their progress.

Selection and Recombination

During selection and recombination, we select parents from the current population to recombine as the children in the next. This is performed very succinctly in Listing 6.6.

Listing 6.6   Performing Selection.

```c
int performSelection( void )
{
  int par1, par2;
  int child1, child2;
  int chrom;

  /* Walk through the chromosomes, two at a time */
  for (chrom = 0 ; chrom < MAX_CHROMS ; chrom+=2) {

    /* Select two parents, randomly */
    par1 = selectParent();
    par2 = selectParent();

    /* The children are loaded at the current index points */
    child1 = chrom;
    child2 = chrom+1;
```

```
  /* Recombine the parents to the children */
  performReproduction( par1, par2, child1, child2 );

}
return 0;
}
```

This function operates from the indices into the population tables. The variables par1 and par2 are indexes into the current population, while child1 and child2 are indexes into the new population. The algorithm simply selects child indexes starting at zero and incrementing by two each count. The parent indexes are selected using the selectParent function. Once we have four index values, the performReproduction function is called to perform the actual recombination. The selectParent call is shown in Listing 6.7.

Listing 6.7   Selecting a Parent.

```
int selectParent( void )
{
  static int chrom = 0;
  int ret = -1;
  float retFitness = 0.0;

  /* Roulette-wheel selection process */
  do {

    /* Select the target fitness value */
    retFitness = (populations[curPop][chrom].fitness /
                   maxFitness);

    if (chrom == MAX_CHROMS) chrom = 0;

    /* If we've walked through the population and have reached our
     * target fitness value, select this member.
     */
    if (populations[curPop][chrom].fitness > minFitness) {
      if (getSRand() < retFitness) {
        ret = chrom++;
        retFitness = populations[curPop][chrom].fitness;
        break;
      }
    }
  }
```

```
      chrom++;

   } while (1);

   return ret;
}
```

Parent selection operates on the principal that a chromosome's chances of being selected are proportional to that chromosome's fitness compared to the overall population. We calculate this probability (stored within retFitness) at the start of the do loop. We then check to ensure that the current chromosome is greater than the minimum fitness of the population. In other words, we don't select from the least fit of the population (elitist in some manner). We then calculate a random number (from 0 to 1) and compare this to our fitness value. If the random number is less than our fitness value, we select the parent and allow the function to return. Otherwise, we continue to the top of the loop and calculate the fitness ratio for the next chromosome.

Once we've selected both parents, we perform recombination. This process is shown in Listing 6.8.

Listing 6.8   Recombining Parent Chromosomes to Create Two New Children.

```
int performReproduction( int parentA, int parentB,
                         int childA,  int childB )
{
  int crossPoint, i;
  int nextPop = (curPop == 0) ? 1 : 0;

  int mutate( int );

  /* If we meet the crossover probability, perform crossover of the
   * two parents by selecting the crossover point.
   */
  if (getSRand() > XPROB) {
    crossPoint =
        getRand(MAX(populations[curPop][parentA].progSize-2,
                    populations[curPop][parentB].progSize-2))+1;
    curCrossovers++;
  } else {
```

```
    crossPoint = MAX_PROGRAM;
}

/* Perform the actual crossover, in addition to random mutation
 */
for (i = 0 ; i < crossPoint ; i++) {
  populations[nextPop][childA].program[i] =
      mutate(populations[curPop][parentA].program[i]);
  populations[nextPop][childB].program[i] =
      mutate(populations[curPop][parentB].program[i]);
}

for ( ; i < MAX_PROGRAM ; i++) {
  populations[nextPop][childA].program[i] =
      mutate(populations[curPop][parentB].program[i]);
  populations[nextPop][childB].program[i] =
      mutate(populations[curPop][parentA].program[i]);
}

/* Update the program sizes for the children (based upon the
 * parents).
 */
populations[nextPop][childA].progSize =
  populations[curPop][parentA].progSize;
populations[nextPop][childB].progSize =
  populations[curPop][parentB].progSize;

return 0;
}
```

We first check to see if we are to perform the crossover operator (random number greater than XPROB). If so, we calculate the crossover point (cross-Point) based upon the maximum length of the chromosome. This is based upon the larger of the two parents. The chromosomes may be different sizes (though in this simulation, they are always the maximum). The crossover point is ensured never to be the first or last gene of the chromosome (since then no crossover is actually occurring). If no crossover is to be performed, the crossover point is defined as the size of the program.

The next step is to perform the crossover (or tail swapping) of the two chromosomes. We copy parent A to child A and parent B to child B, up until the crossover point. At this point (the next for loop), we copy parent A to child B and parent B to child A. Note that if the crossover point was the size of the program, the first for loop would have copied the entire chromosome and the second for loop would have nothing to copy (the desired result in this case).

Finally, the children in the new population inherit the program sizes of their parents. In this case, the program size is constant, but this can easily be changed during the init process.

Note that we create a variable called nextPop, which is based upon curPop. Variable nextPop defines the population that the children will be created in; curPop defines where the parents are read. This provides a ping-pong population buffer from old population to new.

The final function is mutate, shown in Listing 6.9. This function simply redefines a gene in the current chromosome to a new instruction, based upon the mutation probability.

Listing 6.9   Mutation Operator.

```
int mutate(int gene)
{
  float temp = getSRand();

  /* If we've met the mutation probability, randomly mutate this
   * gene to a new instruction.
   */
  if (temp > MPROB) {
      gene = getRand(MAX_INSTRUCTION);
      curMutations++;
  }

  return gene;
}
```

SAMPLE RUNS

Let's now look at some sample runs of the application. While the application emits quite a bit of debugging data, including the fitness trends to file stats.txt, we'll look simply at the results.

The first test was to create an instruction sequence that solved Equation 6.2:

$$x^8 \tag{6.2}$$

The resulting program evolved with the application was:

DUP MUL DUP MUL DUP MUL

In summary, the sequence first calculates the square of x, then squares that value and squares it once more, each time using the DUP instruction.

The next test involved three variables, shown in Equation 6.3:

$$(x * 2) + (y * 2) + z \tag{6.3}$$

The instruction sequence evolved for this equation was:

ADD DUP ADD SWAP ADD

The evolved program is an optimization of the equation where x and y are first summed before multiplying them by 2 (through a DUP ADD sequence). The final ADD instruction adds in the z component. Note that in this case a SWAP instruction was generated. This instruction has no value, but it still resulted in a working program.

Another interesting evolution was found for Equation 6.4:

$$(x * y) + (y * y) + z \tag{6.4}$$

The resulting program evolved with the application was:

OVER ADD MUL ADD

This program first duplicates the second item on the stack (y) and places it on the top of the stack. Next, it adds x and y together, and multiplies it by y. Finally, z is added in with the final ADD instruction. This is yet another optimization (simplification) of the original equation.

Finally, let's look at a more complicated example in Equation 6.5:

$$x^3 + y^2 + z \tag{6.5}$$

This equation was solved by the following evolved instruction sequence:

DUP DUP MUL MUL SWAP DUP MUL SWAP ADD SWAP SWAP
ADD

The first four instructions (DUP DUP MUL MUL) calculate the x^3 term. Next, we swap the top two elements of the stack so that the y element is now on top. The DUP MUL sequence calculates the y^2 term. Finally, the remaining five instructions add the three terms together. Note that the SWAP instructions are superfluous, but did not destroy the sequence and were therefore not evolved away.

Figure 6.14 shows the progress of the algorithm in evolving the instruction sequence for Equation 6.5. It's interesting to note the gradual improvement of the average fitness in this example. After 10,000 generations, the plot shows gradual improvement until around 20,000 generations. At this point, there is a step improvement in the maximum and average fitness of the population. The maximum fitness of the population then hovers near the highest fitness (2510) until around 30,000 generations when the problem is finally solved.

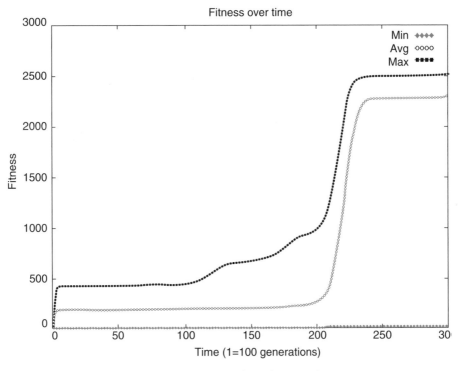

FIGURE 6.14 Plot of fitness over time in evolving for Equation 6.5.

What's interesting about this plot is the gradual improvement of the fitness. This proves that the genetic algorithm is useful in solving symbolic problems such as these. While chromosomes are selected that don't solve the problem completely, mutating and crossing-over with other chromosomes in the population lead to increased fitness until the problem is ultimately solved.

TWEAKING THE PARAMETERS AND PROCESSES

While there are a variety of methods that can be altered for the genetic algorithm (such as the method for selection or recombination), the rates at which operators are applied can also be manipulated. It turns out that there is no optimal set of methods and parameters that can be used to universally solve all problems. Each problem must be tweaked to solve it faster, or in a more optimal way (and in some cases, just to solve it at all). In this section, we'll discuss a number of ways that the genetic algorithm can be tailored for a particular application.

Selection Method

We've discussed the *probabilistic* selection method, the higher the fit of the chromosome, the higher the probability that it will be selected. The problem with probabilistic selection is that a fit chromosome might not be propagated to the following generation. To ensure that the most fit chromosomes are retained, a strategy called *elitist* selection ensures that the best chromosomes are selected for recombination in the next. This is done by automatically propagating the top 10% of the chromosomes to the next generation.

One final interesting selection mechanism is called *tournament* selection. In tournament selection, two or more chromosomes are selected from the population. Those chromosomes then compete for the right to move into the next generation. The winner of the competition is based upon the highest fitness. This process is performed twice, resulting in two parents that are used for recombination.

Population Size

The size of the population is a very important element of the genetic algorithm. If the population is too small, too little genetic material may be present to find a solution to the problem at hand. The population size is also linked to the rates at which the crossover and mutation operators should be applied.

Genetic Operators

We've discussed the crossover and mutation operators, but many others exist which can be useful for experimentation for a given problem. Another operator known as *inversion* has been shown to be useful in certain classes of problems. This operator simply reverses some subset of the genes within the chromosome (useful in an asexual context).

Other Mechanisms

Population seeding is an interesting technique to give the genetic algorithm a good start in optimizing a problem. Rather than initializing the population with random chromosomes, the developer inserts chromosomes that represent known good solutions to the problem. This can lead to premature convergence (loss of diversity within the genetic pool) so extra care must be taken with this technique.

Breeding schemes are another interesting avenue for experimentation, some of which have roots in practices of animal husbandry and horticulture. R. Hollstein investigated a variety of selection methods, as shown in Table 6.2 [Hollstein 1971].

TABLE 6.2   Selection Methods Investigated by R. Hollstein (table created by author).

Method	Description
Progeny Testing	Fitness of offspring controls subsequent breeding of parents
Individual Selection	Fitness of individual controls future use as a parent
Family Selection	Fitness of family controls use of all family members as parents
Within-family Selection	Fitness of individuals within a family controls selection of parents for breeding within family
Combined Selection	Two or more of the prior methods combined

A final option is the self-adaption of the genetic operators and/or rates by which they are applied. Thomas Back [Back 1992] reported interesting results in evolving the rates of mutation and crossover along with the chromosome. Using this, not only does the GA find the solution to the problem at hand, but also the correct rates by with the genetic operators should be applied.

Probabilities

The probabilities for which the genetic operators are applied to the population are very important. For example, if the mutation operator is set too high, the result is the destruction of any useful genetic material within the population and a shift to simple random search. If the rates are set too low, the search for a solution to the given problem may take much longer than is necessary.

Unless self-adaption is used (per Thomas Back), the correct rates are typically found through experimentation. A good starting point is to set the rate so that 70% of the selected parents have the crossover operator applied to them and one mutation is permitted in every other selection.

Depending upon the encoding method selected for the problem, some genetic operators can simply be destructive. A good understanding of the encoding and the effects of operators is therefore necessary to know when and how often to use them.

PROBLEMS WITH THE GENETIC ALGORITHM

The genetic algorithm is not without its problems. This section will discuss some of the issues that should be understood when applying the genetic algorithm.

Premature Convergence

The problem of premature convergence is one of a lack of diversity within the population. When a majority of the chromosomes in the population is similar, the selection process has less material to work with and the rate of fitness increase slows. Premature convergence can be detected by comparing the average fitness of the population with the maximum fitness. If they are fairly close to one another, then premature convergence has occurred.

The most common reason for premature convergence is a population that is too small for the problem. Increasing the size of the population easily solves this problem. Another common reason is the selection algorithm used. If an elitist algorithm is used, only the highest-fit chromosomes may be selected, leading to a population that is likely descendent from a small percentage of the initial population. One solution here is called *restart*. This simply means that if the population has prematurely converged without finding a decent solution, simply start over. The desire is that by restarting, new material will be introduced into the population that may not have a small number of dominating chromosomes.

Epistasis

Epistasis is defined as the interdependence among the variables (genes) encoded in the chromosome. If no gene is related to another in the chromosome, epistasis is small or non-existent. If genes are dependent on one another, epistasis is high and can create difficulties for the recombination algorithms.

A common solution to the problem is to keep genes (variables) that are related close to one another in the chromosome. Grouping the dependent genes means they are much less likely to be disrupted during operators such as crossover.

The "No-Free-Lunch" Theorem

The "No-Free-Lunch" theorem is based upon the idea that there is no optimal optimization method. Any encoding, selection-method, and set of parameter probabilities will not blindly work for all classes of problems. The key is to use knowledge of the problem at hand to choose the best approach [Shaffer 1993].

OTHER APPLICATIONS

The genetic algorithm can be used in a variety of optimization problems. Since the usefulness of the genetic algorithm depends most highly on the representation of the solution, any number of numerical and symbolic problems may be optimized. For example, in addition to simple function optimization, symbolic problems such as the Towers of Hanoi problem can be very easily solved.

Genetic algorithms have been applied to many other practical applications, such as:

- Computer-Aided Design
- Scheduling Problems
- Economics and Game Theory
- many others

The author has applied the genetic algorithm, as part of star tracker research, to the problem of absolute attitude determination using a star tracker. In this application, star quadrilaterals were matched from an onboard star catalog to a set of stars in the star-tracker's field of view to determine where the spacecraft was pointing.

SUMMARY

In this chapter, we've had our first look at the genetic algorithm. We discussed the general operation of the algorithm and a saw sample run through the algorithm to demonstrate initialization, fitness evaluation, selection, and recombination. We then discussed source code that implements an evolver for instruction sequences and looked at some of the sample equations that were solved with it. Since the GA knows nothing about the equations themselves, only if it's correct in solving them, the GA provides alternate solutions to the problem (within the defined instruction set) that demonstrated an optimization of the actual algorithm. Finally, we discussed the parameters that can be tweaked for the genetic algorithm and some of the problems that the algorithm presents.

REFERENCES

[Back 1992] Back, T. (1992). *The Interaction of Mutation Rate, Selection, and Self-Adaption within a Genetic Algorithm*. Germany: University of Dortmund.

[Holland 1962] Holland, J. (1962). "Concerning efficient adaptive systems." *Self-Organizing Systems*, (pp. 215-230). Washington, D.C.: Spartan Books.

[Hollstein 1971] Hollstein, R. (1971). "Artificial Genetic Adaption in Computer Control Systems." Ph.D diss., University of Michigan.

[Koza 1992] Koza, J. (1992). *Genetic Programming: On the Programming of Computers by Means of Natural Selection*. Cambridge, Mass.: MIT Press.

[Shaffer 1993] Shaffer, R. (1993). "Practical Guide to Genetic Algorithms," available online at *http://chemdiv-www.nrl.navy.mil/6110/6112/sensors/chemometrics/practga.html* (accessed January 17, 2003)

RESOURCES

Holland, J. 1975. *Adaption in Natural and Artificial Systems*. Ann Arbor: The University of Michigan Press.

Koza, J. "Genetic Programming, Inc. Home Page," available online at *http://www.genetic-programming.com*

7 ■ Artificial Life

A rtificial life, or Alife is a term coined by Chris Langton [Langton] to describe a wide variety of computational mechanisms used to model natural systems. Artificial life has been used to model agents trading resources in artificial economies, ecologies of insects, the behavior of animals, and entities negotiating with one another to study models in game theory. In this chapter, we'll investigate artificial life and then implement a simulation that demonstrates agents within a food chain competing in an artificial environment.

INTRODUCTION

While artificial life is a large discipline with a variety of concerns, we'll focus here on what is called *synthetic ethology*. This is defined most succinctly by Bruce MacLennan:

> Synthetic ethology is an approach to the study of animal behavior in which simple, synthetic organisms are allowed to behave and evolve in a synthetic world. Because both the organisms and their worlds are synthetic, they can be constructed for specific purposes, particularly for testing specific hypotheses. [MacLennan]

Artificial life can then be described as the theory and practice for biological system modeling and simulation. One hope of researchers working with artificial life is that by modeling biological systems, we can come to a better understanding of why and how they work. Through the models, researchers can manipulate their environments to play "what if" games to understand how systems and environments respond to change.

SIMULATING FOOD CHAINS

A food chain describes the hierarchy of living organisms within an ecosystem. For instance, consider a very simple abstracted food chain made up of three entities. At the bottom of the food chain is the plant. It derives its energy from the environment (rain, soil, and the sun). The next level is herbivores— a herbivore consumes plant life to survive. Finally, at the top are carnivores. Carnivores, within this simulation, consume herbivores in order to survive. Ignoring the effect of dead herbivores and carnivores on the environment, the food chain can be illustrated as shown in Figure 7.1.

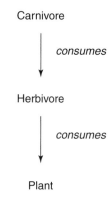

FIGURE 7.1   Simple food chain.

By viewing Figure 7.1 as a dependency graph, it should be very clear that a delicate balance exists between the entities. What happens if the abundance of plant life diminishes through a drought or other natural or artificial event? The lack of plant life affects the sustainability of herbivores within the environment, which results in a decrease in their population. This effect cascades up through the food chain, ultimately affecting the carnivore population at the top. This balance can be modeled and studied within the domain of artificial life and synthetic ethology.

FOOD CHAIN MODEL

To model a simple food chain, a number of aspects of the simulation must be defined. These include the environment (physical space in which the agents interact), the agents themselves (and their perception and actuation within the environment), and a set of laws that describe how and when interaction takes place. These elements will be described in the following sections.

Overview

Based upon our discussion of the simple food chain, our simulation will consist of an environment and three types of entities. A plant is a stationary food source that exists within the environment and exists as a food source for herbivores. Herbivores are migratory agents that sense their environment and can eat plants. The predators of herbivores are carnivores that are the other migratory agent within the environment. Carnivores can eat only herbivores, while herbivores can eat only plants. If either agent lives for a certain amount of time within the environment without eating, the agent dies of starvation. When an agent consumes enough food, it is permitted to reproduce which creates a new agent (of the particular type) in the environment. Through reproduction, evolution occurs through the mutation of the agent's brain (simple neural network).

It's important to note that the agents initially have no idea how to survive within the environment. They don't know that eating will allow them to live longer. Nor do they know that they must avoid their predators. All of these details must be experienced and learned by the agents through a simple form of evolution.

The following sections will discuss the elements of the simulation in detail.

Environment

Agents live within a grid world whose edges are connected in a toroid fashion. When an agent moves beyond the edge of a particular dimension, it reappears on the other side (see Figure 7.2).

Plants occupy unique cells within the environment, but it's possible for a single cell to be occupied by one or more agents (herbivore and/or carnivore).

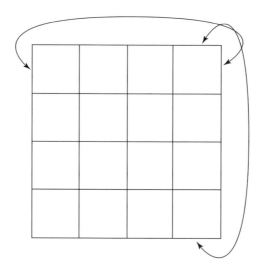

FIGURE 7.2 Toroid grid world for the food chain simulation.

Anatomy of an Agent

An agent is a generic entity within the simulation. It is defined as being a particular type (herbivore or carnivore), but the way it perceives the environment and how it acts upon it are the same (see Figure 7.3). The agent can be thought of as a simple system with a set of inputs (its perception of the world), how it reacts given its perception (its brain), and actuation into the environment (taking its particular action).

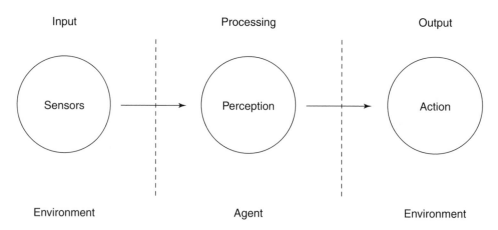

FIGURE 7.3 Agent systems model.

The agent, as depicted by Figure 7.3, is made up of three distinct parts. These are sensors, perception (determining which action to take based upon the sensors), and actuation (taking the action). Note that the agent model is reactionary; it simply reacts to the environment. Agents have no capacity to plan, and other than their ability to reproduce, they have no ability to learn. Even with this simple mode, learning occurs through what is known as Lamarckian inheritance. Through reproduction, the characteristics of the parent are passed down to its progeny.

Jean-Baptiste Lamarck (1744–1829) proposed an alternate mechanism for evolution than that offered by Charles Darwin. Instead of the process of natural selection driving the gradual improvement of the species, Lamarck believed that heredity, or the inheritance of acquired traits, drove the process.

Sensors

Agents within the environment have the ability to sense what is around them. An agent cannot view the entire environment—only a set of local cells can be sensed (see Figure 7.4).

	Front	Front	Front	Front	Front	
	Left	Proximity	Proximity	Proximity	Right	
	Left	Proximity	Agent	Proximity	Right	

FIGURE 7.4   Agent's area of perception (facing north).

The local environment that the agent can perceive is split up into four separate areas. The area local to the agent is called *Proximity* and is the area in which the agent can act (such as eating an object). The area in front of the agent (5 cells) makes up the *Front*. Finally, the two cells at the left and right edges are *Left* and *Right*, respectively.

The agent is provided with a numerical count of the objects in view in each of the distinct areas. Therefore, for the four separate areas, three quantities are provided for each to identify the types of objects present (plants, herbivores, and carnivores). This provides twelve inputs to the agent.

Actuators

The agent can perform a limited set of actions within the environment. It can move a single step (in a given direction), turn left or right, or eat an object in its local proximity. The action performed by the agent is provided through its brain, as a function of the inputs provided at the sensory stage.

Agent Brain

The brain of the agent could be one of a variety of different computational constructs. Existing artificial life simulations have used finite automata (state machines), classifier systems, or neural networks. In keeping with the biological motivation of this simulation, we'll use a simple, fully-interconnected, winner-takes-all neural network (as was used in Chapter 5) as the behavioral element of the agent. Figure 7.5 shows a complete network for the agent.

Recall that sensor inputs represent the count of the objects in view in a particular area. After each of the inputs has been captured from the environment, we propagate these inputs through the network to the outputs. This is done using Equation 7.1.

$$o_j = b_j + \sum_{i=0}^{n} u_i w_{i,j} \tag{7.1}$$

In other words, for each output cell (o_j) in the network, we sum the products of the input cells (u_i) by the weights of the connections from the inputs cells to the output cells (w_{ij}). The bias for the output cell is also added. The result is a set of values in the output cells. The action element of the agent then uses these values.

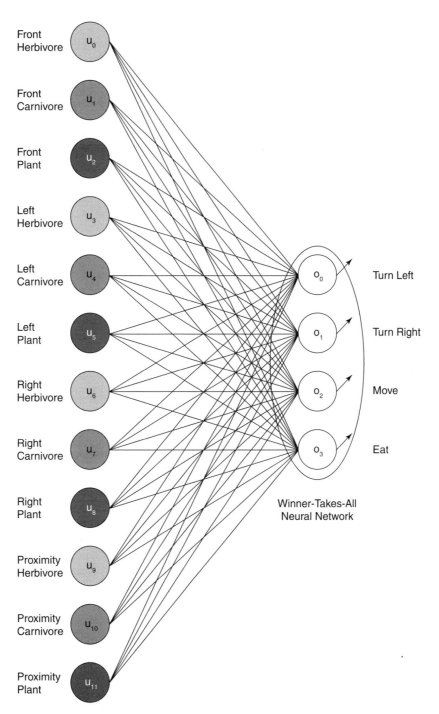

FIGURE 7.5 Winner-takes-all: neural network as the agent brain.

The initial weights of the agent's neural network are randomly selected, but through reproduction, the weights should become tuned for survival within the environment.

Agent Action Selection

Recall that the agent can perform one of four actions, as defined by the output cells of the neural network. The process of action selection is simply finding the output cell with the largest value and performing this action. This is the "winner-takes-all" aspect of the network. Once the action has taken place, the environment is modified (if warranted by the agent's action) and the process continues.

Energy and Metabolism

Agents survive in the environment given adequate energy. When an agent's internal energy falls to zero, the agent dies. Agents create energy by eating other objects in the environment. An agent can only eat an object that is defined as legal per the food chain. Carnivores can eat only herbivores, and herbivores can eat only plants. Agents also have a metabolism, a rate at which they consume energy to stay alive. Carnivores consume a single energy unit each time step, while herbivores consume two energy units. This means that herbivores must consume twice as much food as carnivores to stay alive. While carnivores do not need to consume as much food, they do have to find it. Herbivores have an advantage in that their food does not move within the environment; however, they must still locate it.

Reproduction

When an agent consumes enough food to reach 90% of its maximum energy, it is permitted to asexually reproduce. Reproduction permits those agents who are able to successfully navigate their environments and stay alive to create offspring (natural selection). By creating offspring, the agents evolve through random mutation of the weights of their neural networks. No learning takes place within the environment, but the capability of an agent to reproduce means that its neural network is passed down to its child. This mimics Lamarckian evolution in which the characteristics of the agent are passed down to the child (the child inherits the neural network of the parent).

When a parent reproduces, it is not without consequences. The parent and the child share the available energy of the parent (cutting the parent's energy in half). This keeps an agent from continually reproducing and provides an implicit timer to avoid continual reproduction of the agent.

Death

Agents can die in one of two ways. Either the agent is unable to find sufficient food to sustain itself and starves to death, or an agent further up the food chain eats it. In either case, the agent in question is removed from the simulation.

COMPETITION

During the simulation, a subtle game of competition occurs. Carnivores slowly evolve neural networks that are good at locating and eating herbivores. At the same time, herbivores slowly evolve neural networks that find plants in the environment while simultaneously avoiding carnivores. While these strategies are visible by watching the simulation, analyzing the resulting neural networks can also provide insight into the strategies. We'll peer into some of these in the results section to better understand the agents' motives.

SAMPLE ITERATION

Let's now look at a sample action-selection iteration of an evolved agent. In this example, we'll look at an herbivore that has evolved during the simulation. While not perfect, this particular agent survived in the environment for over 300 time steps. It was able to do this by avoiding predators (carnivores) as well as finding and eating plants. Figure 7.6 shows the neural network for this agent.

Solid lines in the neural network are excitory connections, while dashed lines are inhibitory. Within the output cells are the biases that are applied to each output cell as it is activated. From Figure 7.6, we can see that an excitory connection exists for the *eat* action when a plant is in proximity (a plant can only be eaten when it is in proximity of the agent). Also of interest is the inhibitory connection for the *move* action when a carnivore is in front. This is another beneficial action for the survival of the herbivore.

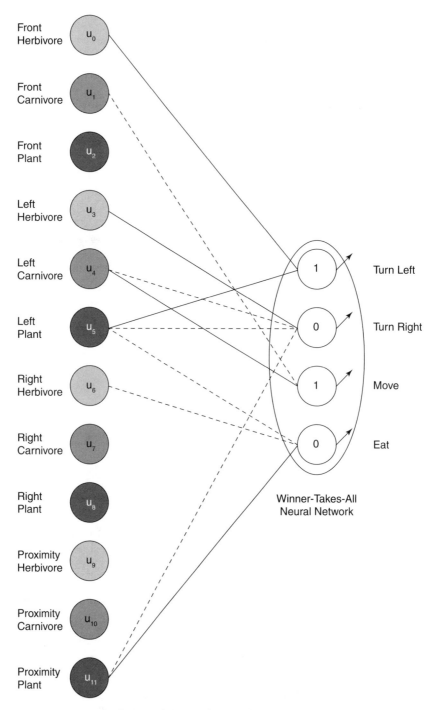

FIGURE 7.6 Neural network for evolved herbivore.

An agent's actions are not formed by a single connection. Instead, the action with the largest value is permitted to fire based upon the combination of the sensor inputs. Let's look at a couple of iterations of the herbivore described by the neural network in Figure 7.6.

Recall from Equation 7.1 that we multiply the weights vector (for the particular action) by the inputs vector and then add the bias.

In our first epoch, our herbivore is presented with the scene as shown in Figure 7.7. The different zones are shaded to illustrate them (recall Figure 7.4). In this scene, the 'X' denotes the location of the herbivore (its reference point to the scene). A plant is located within *proximity* and a carnivore is located in *front*.

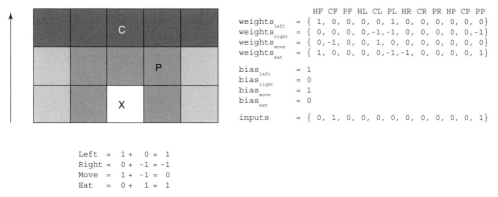

$$
\begin{array}{lll}
& \text{HF CF PF HL CL PL HR CR PR HP CP PP} \\
\text{weights}_{\text{left}} & = \{ 1, 0, 0, 0, 0, 1, 0, 0, 0, 0, 0, 0\} \\
\text{weights}_{\text{right}} & = \{ 0, 0, 0, 0,-1,-1, 0, 0, 0, 0, 0,-1\} \\
\text{weights}_{\text{move}} & = \{ 0,-1, 0, 0, 1, 0, 0, 0, 0, 0, 0, 0\} \\
\text{weights}_{\text{eat}} & = \{ 1, 0, 0, 0, 0,-1,-1, 0, 0, 0, 0, 1\} \\
\\
\text{bias}_{\text{left}} & = 1 \\
\text{bias}_{\text{right}} & = 0 \\
\text{bias}_{\text{move}} & = 1 \\
\text{bias}_{\text{eat}} & = 0 \\
\\
\text{inputs} & = \{ 0, 1, 0, 0, 0, 0, 0, 0, 0, 0, 0, 1\}
\end{array}
$$

```
Left  = 1 +  0 =  1
Right = 0 + -1 = -1
Move  = 1 + -1 =  0
Eat   = 0 +  1 =  1
```

FIGURE 7.7 Herbivore at time t_0.

The first step is assessing the scene. We count the number of objects of each type in each of the four zones. As shown in Figure 7.7, the weights and inputs are labeled with type/zone (HF is herbivore-*front*, CF is carnivore-*front*, PP is plant-*proximity*, etc.). In this example, our input's vector has non-zero values in only two of the vector elements. As shown in the scene, these are a carnivore in the *front* zone and a plant in *proximity*.

To evaluate the function to take, we multiply the input vector by the weights vector for the defined action and then add in the respective bias. This is shown below in Figure 7.7. Per our action-selection algorithm, we take the action with the largest resulting value. In the case of a tie, as is shown in Figure 7.7, we take the largest value that appeared last. In this case, the *eat* action is performed (a desirable action given the current scene).

Once the plant is consumed, it disappears from the scene. The herbivore is then left with the scene as shown in Figure 7.8.

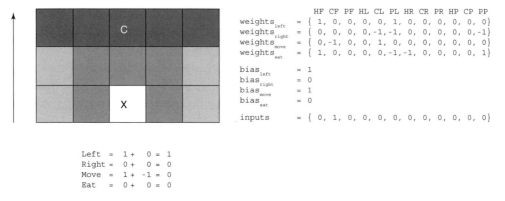

$$
\begin{aligned}
&\phantom{weights_{left} = \{~} \text{HF CF PF HL CL PL HR CR PR HP CP PP}\\
&weights_{left} = \{~~1,~~0,~~0,~~0,~~0,~~1,~~0,~~0,~~0,~~0,~~0,~~0\}\\
&weights_{right} = \{~~0,~~0,~~0,~~0,-1,-1,~~0,~~0,~~0,~~0,~~0,-1\}\\
&weights_{move} = \{~~0,-1,~~0,~~0,~~1,~~0,~~0,~~0,~~0,~~0,~~0,~~0\}\\
&weights_{eat} = \{~~1,~~0,~~0,~~0,~~0,-1,-1,~~0,~~0,~~0,~~0,~~1\}
\end{aligned}
$$

$$
\begin{aligned}
bias_{left} &= 1\\
bias_{right} &= 0\\
bias_{move} &= 1\\
bias_{eat} &= 0
\end{aligned}
$$

$$
inputs = \{~0,~1,~0,~0,~0,~0,~0,~0,~0,~0,~0,~0\}
$$

```
Left  =  1 +  0 = 1
Right =  0 +  0 = 0
Move  =  1 + -1 = 0
Eat   =  0 +  0 = 0
```

FIGURE 7.8 Herbivore at time T_1.

The scene is assessed once again, and as shown, the plant no longer exists, but the carnivore remains. This is illustrated by the inputs (changes are shown in bold from the prior iteration). We again compute the output cells of the neural network by multiplying the input vector times the respective weights vector. In this case, the largest value is associated with the *left* action. Given the current scene, this is a reasonable action to take.

Finally, in Figure 7.9, we see the final iteration of the herbivore. Note that the agent's view has changed because it changed direction in the last iteration. With the change in the scene, the inputs have now changed as well. Instead of a carnivore in the *front* zone, it has moved to the *right* zone due to our new view of the scene.

Computing the output cells once again results in the move action being the largest, but more importantly, last in this case. The herbivore's behavior allowed it to find food and eat it, and then avoid a carnivore within its field of view. From this short demonstration of the herbivore's neural network, it is not surprising that it was able to navigate and survive in the environment for a long period of time.

The source for the Alife simulation can be found on the accompanying CD-ROM at ./software/ch7.

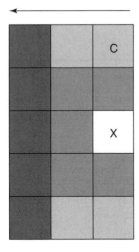

```
                                HF CF PF HL CL PL HR CR PR HP CP PP
          weights      = {  1,  0,  0,  0,  0,  1,  0,  0,  0,  0,  0,  0}
                 left
          weights      = {  0,  0,  0,  0, -1, -1,  0,  0,  0,  0,  0, -1}
                 right
          weights      = {  0, -1,  0,  0,  1,  0,  0,  0,  0,  0,  0,  0}
                 move
          weights      = {  1,  0,  0,  0,  0, -1, -1,  0,  0,  0,  0,  1}
                 eat

          bias         = 1
              left
          bias         = 0
              right
          bias         = 1
              move
          bias         = 0
              eat

          inputs       = {  0,  0,  0,  0,  0,  0,  0,  1,  0,  0,  0,  0}



          Left   =   1 +   0 =  1
          Right  =   0 +   0 =  0
          Move   =   1 +   0 =  1
          Eat    =   0 +   0 =  0
```

FIGURE 7.9   Herbivore at time T_2.

SOURCE DISCUSSION

The source code for the Alife simulation is very straightforward. Let's first walk through the structures for the simulation that describe not only the environment but also the agents and other objects within the environment.

Listing 7.1 shows the agent type. Most elements of this structure are self-explanatory, type defines the agent as herbivore or carnivore, energy is the available energy to the agent, age is the age in time steps, and generation is a value that describes this agent in the lineage of agents that reproduced.

The location of the agent (as defined by the locType type) specifies the x/y coordinate of the agent within the landscape. The inputs vector defines the values of the inputs to the neural network during the perception stage. The actions vector is the output layer of the neural network that defines the action to be taken. Finally, weight_oi (weight value from output to input) and biaso represent the weights and biases for the output layer of the network. We'll see later how the weights are structured within this single vector.

Listing 7.1   Agent Types and Symbolics.

```
typedef struct {
  short type;
```

```
  short energy;
  short parent;
  short age;
  short generation;
  locType location;
  unsigned short direction;
  short inputs[MAX_INPUTS];
  short weight_oi[MAX_INPUTS * MAX_OUTPUTS];
  short biaso[MAX_OUTPUTS];
  short actions[MAX_OUTPUTS];
} agentType;

#define TYPE_HERBIVORE  0
#define TYPE_CARNIVORE  1
#define TYPE_DEAD      -1

typedef struct {
  short x;
  short y;
} locType;
```

The input vector defines the inputs as object and zone (such as herbivore and front). To give an agent the ability to differentiate each of these elements separately, each is given its own input into the neural network. The outputs are also well-defined with each output cell in the output vector representing a single action. Listing 7.2 provides the symbolic constant definitions for the input and output cells.

Listing 7.2   Sensor Input and Action Output Cell Definitions.

```
#define HERB_FRONT       0
#define CARN_FRONT       1
#define PLANT_FRONT      2
#define HERB_LEFT        3
#define CARN_LEFT        4
#define PLANT_LEFT       5
#define HERB_RIGHT       6
#define CARN_RIGHT       7
#define PLANT_RIGHT      8
#define HERB_PROXIMITY   9
#define CARN_PROXIMITY  10
#define PLANT_PROXIMITY 11
```

```
#define MAX_INPUTS       12


#define ACTION_TURN_LEFT      0
#define ACTION_TURN_RIGHT     1
#define ACTION_MOVE           2
#define ACTION_EAT            3


#define MAX_OUTPUTS      4
```

The agent environment is provided by a three dimensional cube. Three planes exist for the agents, with each plane being occupied by a single type of object (plant, herbivore, or carnivore). The agent's world is still viewed as a two dimensional grid, but three dimensions exist to more efficiently account for the objects present. Listing 7.3 provides the types and symbolics used to represent the landscape.

Listing 7.3   Agent Environment Types and Symbolics

```
#define HERB_PLANE       0
#define CARN_PLANE       1
#define PLANT_PLANE      2

#define MAX_GRID   30

/* Agent environment in 3 dimensions (to have independent planes
 * for plant, herbivore and carnivore objects.
 */
int landscape[3][MAX_GRID][MAX_GRID];

#define MAX_AGENTS 36
#define MAX_PLANTS 30

agentType agents[MAX_AGENTS];
int agentCount = 0;

plantType plants[MAX_PLANTS];
int plantCount = 0;
```

The size of the grid, number of agents that exist, and the amount of plant life are all parameters that can be manipulated for different experiments. The header file (common.h) includes a section for parameters that can be adjusted.

Finally, a set of macros is provided in the header file for commonly used functions associated with random number generation (see Listing 7.4).

Listing 7.4   Simulation Macro Functions.

```
#define getSRand()      ((float)rand() / (float)RAND_MAX)
#define getRand(x)      (int) ((float)x*rand()/(RAND_MAX+1.0))

#define getWeight()     (getRand(9)-1)
```

The getSRand function returns a random number between 0 and 1, while getRand returns a number from 0 to x-1. Finally, the getWeight function returns a weight used for the agent neural networks. This includes biases used with the output cells.

We'll now walk through the source of the simulation. We begin with the main function, which has been simplified to remove the command-line processing and statistics collection. The unedited source can be found on the CD-ROM.

ON THE CD

The main function sets up the simulation and then loops for the number of time steps allotted for the simulation within the header file (via the MAX_STEPS symbolic constant). The simulate function is the primary entry point of the simulation where life is brought to the agents and the environment (see Listing 7.5).

Listing 7.5   main Function for the Alife Simulation.

```
int main( int argc, char *argv[] )
{
  int i;

  /* Seed the random number generator */
  srand( time(NULL) );

  /* Initialize the simulation */
  init();

  /* Main loop for the simulation. */
  for (i = 0 ; i < MAX_STEPS ; i++) {

    /* Simulate each agent for one time step */
    simulate();
```

```
    }

    return 0;
}
```

The init function initializes both the environment and the objects within the environment (plants, herbivores, and carnivores). Note that when agents are initialized, the type of the agent is filled in. This is done so that the initAgent can be reused for other purposes within the simulation. With the type filled in, the initAgent function knows which kind of agent is being initialized and treats it accordingly (see Listing 7.6).

Listing 7.6   Function init to Initialize the Simulation.

```
void init( void )
{

  /* Initialize the landscape */
  bzero( (void *)landscape, sizeof(landscape) );

  bzero( (void *)bestAgent, sizeof(bestAgent) );

  /* Initialize the plant plane */
  for (plantCount = 0 ; plantCount < MAX_PLANTS ; plantCount++) {
    growPlant( plantCount );
  }

  /* Randomly initialize the Agents */
  for (agentCount = 0 ; agentCount < MAX_AGENTS ; agentCount++) {

    if (agentCount < (MAX_AGENTS / 2)) {
      agents[agentCount].type = TYPE_HERBIVORE;
    } else {
      agents[agentCount].type = TYPE_CARNIVORE;
    }

    initAgent( &agents[agentCount] );

  }

}
```

The plant plane is first initialized by creating plants of a count defined by the MAX_PLANTS symbolic constant. Function growPlants provides this function (see Listing 7.7). Next, the agents are initialized. For the maximum number of agents allowed (defined by MAX_AGENTS), half of the space is reserved for each time. We initialize the herbivores first and then the carnivores. The actual initialization of the agents is provided by the initAgent function (shown in Listing 7.8).

The growPlant function simply finds an empty spot in the plant plane and places a plant in that position (see Listing 7.7). The function also ensures that no plant exists there already (so that we can control the number of unique plants available in the environment).

Listing 7.7 Function growPlant to Introduce Foliage into the Simulation.

```
void growPlant( int i )
{
  int x,y;

  while (1) {

    /* Pick a random location in the environment */
    x = getRand(MAX_GRID); y = getRand(MAX_GRID);

    /* As long as a plant isn't already there */
    if (landscape[PLANT_PLANE][y][x] == 0) {

      /* Update the environment for the new plant */
      plants[i].location.x = x;
      plants[i].location.y = y;
      landscape[PLANT_PLANE][y][x]++;
      break;

    }

  }

  return;
}
```

The agent planes are next initialized with the herbivore and carnivore species (see Listing 7.8). A reference pointer to an agent is passed (as shown in Listing 7.6) which represents the agent element to initialize. Recall that the agent type has already been defined. We first initialize the energy of the agent to half of the maximum available to the agent. This is done because when an agent reaches a large percentage of its maximum allowable energy, it is permitted to reproduce. Setting the energy to half of the maximum requires that the agent must quickly find food within the environment in order to reproduce. The age and generation are also initialized for a new agent. We keep a count of the number of agents within agentTypeCounts. This ensures that we maintain a 50/50 split between the two agent species within the simulation. Next, we find a home for the agent using the findEmptySpot function. This function, shown in Listing 7.8, finds an empty element in the given plane (defined by the agent type) and stores the coordinates of the agent within the agent structure. Finally, we initialize the weights and biases for the agent's neural network.

Listing 7.8   Function initAgent to Initialize the Agent Species.

```
void initAgent( agentType *agent )
{
  int i;

  agent->energy = (MAX_ENERGY / 2);
  agent->age = 0;
  agent->generation = 1;

  agentTypeCounts[agent->type]++;

  findEmptySpot( agent );

  for (i = 0 ; i < (MAX_INPUTS * MAX_OUTPUTS) ; i++) {
    agent->weight_oi[i] = getWeight();
  }

  for (i = 0 ; i < MAX_OUTPUTS ; i++) {
    agent->biaso[i] = getWeight();
  }

  return;
}

void findEmptySpot( agentType *agent )
{
  agent->location.x = -1;
```

```
agent->location.y = -1;

while (1) {

  /* Pick a random location for the agent */
  agent->location.x = getRand(MAX_GRID);
  agent->location.y = getRand(MAX_GRID);

  /* If an agent isn't there already, break out of the loop */
  if (landscape[agent->type]
              [agent->location.y][agent->location.x] == 0)
    break;

}

/* Pick a random direction for the agent, and update the map */
agent->direction = getRand(MAX_DIRECTION);
landscape[agent->type][agent->location.y][agent->location.x]++;

return;
}
```

Note in function findEmptySpot, that the landscape is represented by counts. This records whether an object is contained at the coordinates of the grid. As objects die, or are eaten, the landscape is decremented to identify the removal of an object.

We've now completed our discussion of the initialization of the simulation; let's now continue with the actual simulation. Recall that our main function (shown in Listing 7.5) calls the simulate function to drive the simulation. The simulate function (shown in Listing 7.9) permits each of the agents to perform a single action within the environment. The herbivores are simulated first and then the carnivores. This gives a slight advantage to the herbivores, but since herbivores must contend with starvation and a predator, it seemed like a way to level the playing field, if only slightly.

Listing 7.9 The simulate Function.

```
void simulate( void )
{
  int i, type;

  /* Simulate the herbivores first, then the carnivores */
```

```
for (type = TYPE_HERBIVORE ; type <= TYPE_CARNIVORE ; type++) {

  for (i = 0 ; i < MAX_AGENTS ; i++) {

    if (agents[i].type == type) {

      simulateAgent( &agents[i] );

    }

  }

}

}
```

The simulate function (Listing 7.9) calls the simulateAgent function to simulate a single step of the agent. This function can be split into four logical sections. These are perception, network propagation, action selection, and energy test.

The perception algorithm is likely the most complicated of the simulation. Recall from Figure 7.4 that an agent's field of view is based upon its direction and is split into four separate zones (*front, proximity, left,* and *right*). For the agent to perceive the environment, it must first identify the coordinates of the grid that make up its field of view (based upon the direction of the agent) and then split these up into the four separate zones. We can see how this is done in the switch statement of the simulateAgent function (Listing 7.11). The switch statement determines the direction in which the agent is facing. Each call to the percept function sums the objects for the particular zone. Note that each call identifying HERB_<zone> represents the first plane for the zone (herbivore, carnivore, and then plant).

The percept call is made with the agents current coordinates, the offset into the inputs array and a list of coordinate offsets and bias. Note that when the agent is facing north, the north<zone> offsets are passed, but when the agent is facing south, we again pass the north<zone> offsets but with a -1 bias. This is done similarly with the west<zone>. The coordinate offsets for the agent to each of the zones are defined for a given direction, but can be reversed to identify the coordinates in the opposite direction.

So what do we mean by this? Let's look at the coordinate offsets in Listing 7.10.

Listing 7.10   Coordinate Offsets to Sum Objects in the Field of View.

```
const offsetPairType northFront[]=
      {{-2,-2}, {-2,-1}, {-2,0}, {-2,1}, {-2,2}, {9,9}};
const offsetPairType northLeft[]={{0,-2}, {-1,-2}, {9,9}};
const offsetPairType northRight[]={{0,2}, {-1,2}, {9,9}};
const offsetPairType northProx[]=
      {{0,-1}, {-1,-1}, {-1,0}, {-1,1}, {0,1}, {9,9}};

const offsetPairType westFront[]=
      {{2,-2}, {1,-2}, {0,-2}, {-1,-2}, {-2,-2}, {9,9}};
const offsetPairType westLeft[]={{2,0}, {2,-1}, {9,9}};
const offsetPairType westRight[]={{-2,0}, {-2,-1}, {9,9}};
const offsetPairType westProx[]=
      {{1,0}, {1,-1}, {0,-1}, {-1,-1}, {-1,0}, {9,9}};
```

Two sets of coordinate offset vectors are provided, one for north and one for west. Let's take the northRight vector as an example. Let's say our agent is sitting at coordinates <7,9> within the environment (using an <y,x> coordinate system). Using the northRight vector as coordinate biases, we calculate two new coordinate pairs (since <9,9> represents the list end): <7,11> and <6,11>. These two coordinates represent the two locations for the right zone given an agent facing north. If the agent were facing south, we would negate the northRight coordinates before adding them to our current position, resulting in: <7,7> and <8,7>. These two coordinates represent the two locations for the right zone given an agent facing south.

Now that we've illustrated the coordinate offset pairs, let's continue with our discussion of the simulateAgent function (see Listing 7.11).

Listing 7.11   Function simulateAgent.

```
void simulateAgent( agentType *agent )
{
  int x, y;
  int out, in;
  int largest, winner;

  /* Use shorter names… */
  x = agent->location.x;
  y = agent->location.y;

  /* Determine inputs for the agent neural network */
```

```
switch( agent->direction ) {

  case NORTH:
    percept( x, y, &agent->inputs[HERB_FRONT], northFront, 1 );
    percept( x, y, &agent->inputs[HERB_LEFT], northLeft, 1 );
    percept( x, y, &agent->inputs[HERB_RIGHT], northRight, 1 );
    percept( x, y, &agent->inputs[HERB_PROXIMITY], northProx, 1
      );
    break;

  case SOUTH:
    percept( x, y, &agent->inputs[HERB_FRONT], northFront, -1 );
    percept( x, y, &agent->inputs[HERB_LEFT], northLeft, -1 );
    percept( x, y, &agent->inputs[HERB_RIGHT], northRight, -1 );
    percept( x, y, &agent->inputs[HERB_PROXIMITY], northProx, -1
      );
    break;

  case WEST:
    percept( x, y, &agent->inputs[HERB_FRONT], westFront, 1 );
    percept( x, y, &agent->inputs[HERB_LEFT], westLeft, 1 );
    percept( x, y, &agent->inputs[HERB_RIGHT], westRight, 1 );
    percept( x, y, &agent->inputs[HERB_PROXIMITY], westProx, 1
      );
    break;

  case EAST:
    percept( x, y, &agent->inputs[HERB_FRONT], westFront, -1 );
    percept( x, y, &agent->inputs[HERB_LEFT], westLeft, -1 );
    percept( x, y, &agent->inputs[HERB_RIGHT], westRight, -1 );
    percept( x, y, &agent->inputs[HERB_PROXIMITY], westProx, -1
      );
    break;

}

/* Forward propogate the inputs through the neural network */
for ( out = 0 ; out < MAX_OUTPUTS ; out++ ) {

  /* Initialize the output node with the bias */
  agent->actions[out] = agent->biaso[out];

  /* Multiply the inputs by the weights for this output node */
  for ( in = 0 ; in < MAX_INPUTS ; in++ ) {
```

```
          agent->actions[out] +=
            ( agent->inputs[in] *
              agent->weight_oi[(out * MAX_INPUTS)+in] );

      }

    }

    largest = -9;
    winner = -1;

    /* Select the largest node (winner-takes-all network) */
    for ( out = 0 ; out < MAX_OUTPUTS ; out++ ) {
      if (agent->actions[out] >= largest) {
        largest = agent->actions[out];
        winner = out;
      }
    }

    /* Perform Action */
    switch( winner ) {

      case ACTION_TURN_LEFT:
      case ACTION_TURN_RIGHT:
        turn( winner, agent );
        break;

      case ACTION_MOVE:
        move( agent );
        break;

      case ACTION_EAT:
        eat( agent );
        break;

    }

    /* Consume some amount of energy.
     * Herbivores, in this simulation, require more energy to
     * survive than carnivores.
     */
    if (agent->type == TYPE_HERBIVORE) {
      agent->energy -= 2;
```

```
  } else {
    agent->energy -= 1;
  }

  /* If energy falls to or below zero, the agent dies. Otherwise,
     we
   * check to see if the agent has lived longer than any other
     agent
   * of the particular type.
   */
  if (agent->energy <= 0) {
    killAgent( agent );
  } else {
    agent->age++;
    if (agent->age > agentMaxAge[agent->type]) {
      agentMaxAge[agent->type] = agent->age;
      agentMaxPtr[agent->type] = agent;
    }
  }

  return;
}
```

Having discussed perception, we now continue with the remaining three stages of the simulateAgent function. The next step is to forward propagate our inputs collected in the perception stage to the output cells of the agent's neural network. This process is performed based upon Equation 7.1. The result is a set of output cells representing a value calculated using the input cells and the weights between the inputs cell and output cells. We then select the action to take based upon the highest output cell (in a winner-takes-all network fashion). A switch statement is used to call the particular action function. As shown in Listing 7.11, available actions are ACTION_TURN_LEFT, ACTION_TURN_RIGHT, ACTION_MOVE and ACTION_EAT.

The final stage of agent simulation is an energy test. At each step, an agent loses some amount of energy (differs for carnivores and herbivores). If the agent's energy falls to zero, the agent dies of starvation and ceases to exist within the simulation. If the agent survives, then its age is incremented. Otherwise, the agent is killed using the killAgent function.

We'll now walk through the functions referenced within the simulateAgent function, in the order in which they were called (percept, turn, move, eat, and killAgent).

While the earlier discussion of percept may have given the impression that a complicated function was required, as is shown in Listing 7.12, it's quite simple. This is because much of the functionality is provided by the data structure; the code simply follows the data structure to achieve the intended function.

Listing 7.12   percept **Function.**

```
void percept( int x, int y, short *inputs,
              const offsetPairType *offsets, int neg )
{
  int plane, i;
  int xoff, yoff;

  /* Work through each of the planes in the environment */
  for (plane = HERB_PLANE ; plane <= PLANT_PLANE ; plane++) {

    /* Initialize the inputs */
    inputs[plane] = 0;
    i = 0;

    /* Continue until we've reached the end of the offsets */
    while (offsets[i].x_offset != 9) {

      /* Compute the actual x and y offsets for the current
       * position.
       */
      xoff = x + (offsets[i].x_offset * neg);
      yoff = y + (offsets[i].y_offset * neg);

      /* Clip the offsets (force the toroid as shown by Figure 7.2.
       */
      xoff = clip( xoff );
      yoff = clip( yoff );

      /* If something is in the plane, count it */
      if (landscape[plane][yoff][xoff] != 0) {
        inputs[plane]++;
      }

      i++;

    }
```

```
   }

   return;
}

int clip( int z )
{
   if (z > MAX_GRID-1) z = (z % MAX_GRID);
   else if (z < 0) z = (MAX_GRID + z);
   return z;
}
```

Recall that each call to percept provides the calculation of the number of objects in a given zone, but for all three planes. Therefore, percept uses a for-loop to walk through each of the three planes and calculates the sums based upon the particular plane of interest. For a given plane, we walk through each of the coordinate offset pairs (as defined by the offsets argument). Each coordinate offset pair defines a new set of coordinates based upon the current position. With these new coordinates, we increment the inputs element if anything exists at the location. This means that the agent is unaware of how many objects exist at the coordinate for the given plane, only that at least one object exists there.

Also shown in Listing 7.12 is the clipfunction. This function is used by percept to achieve a toroid (wrap) effect on the grid.

The turn function, shown in Listing 7.13, is very simple, as the agent simply changes direction. As is shown in Listing 7.13, given the agent's current direction and the direction to turn, a new direction results.

Listing 7.13 Function turn.

```
void turn ( int action, agentType *agent )
{
   /* Since our agent can turn only left or right, we determine
    * the new direction based upon the current direction and the
    * turn action.
    */
   switch( agent->direction ) {

      case NORTH:
         if (action == ACTION_TURN_LEFT) agent->direction = WEST;
```

```
      else agent->direction = EAST;
      break;

   case SOUTH:
      if (action == ACTION_TURN_LEFT) agent->direction = EAST;
      else agent->direction = WEST;
      break;

   case EAST:
      if (action == ACTION_TURN_LEFT) agent->direction = NORTH;
      else agent->direction = SOUTH;
      break;

   case WEST:
      if (action == ACTION_TURN_LEFT) agent->direction = SOUTH;
      else agent->direction = NORTH;
      break;

   }

   return;
}
```

The move function is just slightly more complicated. Using a set of offsets to determine the new coordinate position, and the direction to determine which pair of offsets to use, a new set of coordinates is calculated. Also shown in Listing 7.14, is maintenance of the landscape. Prior to the agent's move, the landscape for the given plane (as defined by the agent type) is decremented to represent an agent moving from the location. Once the agent has moved, the landscape is updated again to show an agent now located at the coordinates in the given plane.

Listing 7.14 Function move.

```
void move( agentType *agent )
{
   /* Determine new position offset based upon current direction */
   const offsetPairType offsets[4]={{-1,0},{1,0},{0,1},{0,-1}};

   /* Remove the agent from the landscape. */
   landscape[agent->type][agent->location.y][agent->location.x]--;
```

```
/* Update the agent's X,Y position (including clipping) */
agent->location.x =
  clip( agent->location.x + offsets[agent->direction].x_offset
    );
agent->location.y =
  clip( agent->location.y + offsets[agent->direction].y_offset
    );

/* Add the agent back onto the landscape */
landscape[agent->type][agent->location.y][agent->location.x]++;

return;
}
```

The eat function is split into two stages, locating an object to eat within the agent's proximity (if one exists) and then the record keeping required to document and remove the eaten item (see Listing 7.15).

Listing 7.15 Function eat.

```
void eat( agentType *agent )
{
  int plane, ax, ay, ox, oy, ret=0;

  /* First, determine the plane that we'll eat from based upon
   * our agent type (carnivores eat herbivores, herbivores eat
   * plants).
   */
  if (agent->type == TYPE_CARNIVORE) plane = HERB_PLANE;
  else if (agent->type == TYPE_HERBIVORE) plane = PLANT_PLANE;

  /* Use shorter location names */
  ax = agent->location.x;
  ay = agent->location.y;

  /* Choose the object to consume based upon direction (in the
   * proximity of the agent).
   */
  switch( agent->direction ) {

    case NORTH:
```

```
      ret = chooseObject( plane, ax, ay, northProx, 1, &ox, &oy );
      break;

   case SOUTH:
      ret = chooseObject( plane, ax, ay, northProx, -1, &ox, &oy );
      break;

   case WEST:
      ret = chooseObject( plane, ax, ay, westProx, 1, &ox, &oy );
      break;

   case EAST:
      ret = chooseObject( plane, ax, ay, westProx, -1, &ox, &oy );
      break;

  }

  /* Found an object -- eat it! */
  if (ret) {

    int i;

    if (plane == PLANT_PLANE) {

      /* Find the plant in the plant list (based upon position) */
      for (i = 0 ; i < MAX_PLANTS ; i++) {
        if ((plants[i].location.x == ox) &&
            (plants[i].location.y == oy))
          break;
      }

      /* If found, remove it and grow a new plant elsewhere */
      if (i < MAX_PLANTS) {
        agent->energy += MAX_FOOD_ENERGY;
        if (agent->energy > MAX_ENERGY) agent->energy =
MAX_ENERGY;
        landscape[PLANT_PLANE][oy][ox]--;
        growPlant( i );
      }

    } else if (plane == HERB_PLANE) {

      /* Find the herbivore in the list of agents (based upon
```

```
     * position).
     */
    for (i = 0 ; i < MAX_AGENTS ; i++) {
      if ( (agents[i].location.x == ox) &&
           (agents[i].location.y == oy))
        break;
    }

    /* If found, remove the agent from the simulation */
    if (i < MAX_AGENTS) {
      agent->energy += (MAX_FOOD_ENERGY*2);
      if (agent->energy > MAX_ENERGY) agent->energy =
MAX_ENERGY;
      killAgent( &agents[i] );
    }

  }

  /* If our agent has reached the energy level to reproduce,
     allow
   * it to do so (as long as the simulation permits it).
   */
  if (agent->energy > (REPRODUCE_ENERGY * MAX_ENERGY)) {
    if (noRepro == 0) {
      reproduceAgent( agent );
      agentBirths[agent->type]++;
    }
  }

}

  return;
}
```

The first step is to identify the plane of interest, which is based upon the type of agent doing the consumption. If the agent is an herbivore, we'll look into the plant plane, otherwise, as a carnivore, we'll look into the herbivore plane.

Next, using the agent's direction, we call the `chooseObject` function (shown in Listing 7.16) to return the coordinates of an object of interest in the desired plane. Note that we use the coordinate offset pairs again (as used in

Listing 7.11), but concentrate solely on the proximity zone per the agent's direction. If an object was found, the chooseObject function returns a non-zero value and fills the coordinates into the ox/oy coordinates as passed in by the eat function.

Listing 7.16 Function chooseObject.

```
int chooseObject( int plane, int ax, int ay,
                  const offsetPairType *offsets,
                  int neg, int *ox, int *oy )
{
  int xoff, yoff, i=0;

  /* Work through each of the offset pairs */
  while (offsets[i].x_offset != 9) {

    /* Determine next x,y offset */
    xoff = ax + (offsets[i].x_offset * neg);
    yoff = ay + (offsets[i].y_offset * neg);

    xoff = clip( xoff );
    yoff = clip( yoff );

    /* If an object is found at the check position, return
     * the indices.
     */
    if (landscape[plane][yoff][xoff] != 0) {
      *ox = xoff; *oy = yoff;
      return 1;
    }

    /* Check the next offset */
    i++;

  }

  return 0;
}
```

The chooseObject function is very similar to the percept function shown in Listing 7.12, except that instead of accumulating the objects found in the given plane in the given zone, it simply returns the coordinates of the first object found.

The next step is consuming the object. If an object was returned, we check the plane in which the object was found. For the plant plane, we search through the `plants` array and remove this plant from the `landscape`. We then grow a new plant, which will be placed in a new random location. For the herbivore plane, we identify the particular herbivore with the `agents` array and then kill it using the `killAgent` function (shown in Listing 7.17). The current agent's energy is also increased, per its consumption of the object.

Finally, if the agent has reached the level of energy required for reproduction, the `reproduceAgent` function is called to permit the agent to asexually give birth to a new agent of the given type. The `reproduceAgent` function is shown in Listing 7.18.

Killing an agent is primarily a record-keeping task. We first remove the agent from the landscape and record some statistical data (number of deaths per agent type and number of agents of a given `type`). Then we store the agent away if it is the oldest found for the given species.

Once record keeping is done, we decide whether we want to initialize a new random agent (of the given type) is its place. The decision point is the number of agents that exist for the given type. Since the evolutionary aspect of the simulation is the most interesting, we want to maintain a number of open agent slots so that when an agent does desire to reproduce, it can. Therefore, we allow a new random agent to fill the dead agents place when the population of this agent species fills less than 25% of the overall population. This leaves 25% of the agent slots available (for a given species) open for reproduction.

Listing 7.17   Function `killAgent`.

```
void killAgent( agentType *agent )
{
  agentDeaths[agent->type]++;

  /* Death came to this agent (or it was eaten)... */
  landscape[agent->type][agent->location.y][agent->location.x]--;
  agentTypeCounts[agent->type]--;

  if (agent->age > bestAgent[agent->type].age) {
    memcpy( (void *)&bestAgent[agent->type],
```

```
                          (void *)agent, sizeof(agentType) );   }

       /* 50% of the agent spots are reserved for asexual reproduction.
        * If we fall under this, we create a new random agent.
        */
       if (agentTypeCounts[agent->type] < (MAX_AGENTS / 4)) {

         /* Create a new agent */
         initAgent( agent );

       } else {

         agent->location.x = -1;
         agent->location.y = -1;
         agent->type = TYPE_DEAD;

       }

       return;
   }
```

The final function within the simulation is the reproduceAgent function. This is by far the most interesting function because it provides the Lamarckian learning aspect to the simulation. When an agent gives birth in the simulation, it does so by passing on its traits (its neural network) to its child. The child inherits the parent's traits with a slight probability of mutating the weights of the neural network. This permits the evolutionary aspect of the simulation, a desired increasing level of competence for survival within the environment. The reproduceAgent function is provided in Listing 7.18.

Listing 7.18   Function reproduceAgent.

```
void reproduceAgent( agentType *agent )
{
  agentType *child;
  int i;

  /* Don't allow an agent type to occupy more than half of
   * the available agent slots.
   */
  if ( agentTypeCounts[agent->type] < (MAX_AGENTS / 2)) {
```

```
/* Find an empty spot and copy the agent, mutating one of the
 * weights or biases.
 */
for (i = 0 ; i < MAX_AGENTS ; i++) {
  if (agents[i].type == TYPE_DEAD) break;
}

if (i < MAX_AGENTS) {

  child = &agents[i];

  memcpy( (void *)child, (void *)agent, sizeof(agentType) );

  findEmptySpot( child );

  if (getSRand() <= 0.2) {
    child->weight_oi[getRand(TOTAL_WEIGHTS)] = getWeight();
  }

  child->generation = child->generation + 1;
  child->age = 0;

  if (agentMaxGen[child->type] < child->generation) {
    agentMaxGen[child->type] = child->generation;
  }

  /* Reproducing halves the parent's energy */
  child->energy = agent->energy = (MAX_ENERGY / 2);

  agentTypeCounts[child->type]++;
  agentTypeReproductions[child->type]++;

  }

}

return;
}
```

The first step is to identify whether space is available for the new child. For this test, we check to see if less than 50% of the total agent slots are filled for the given species. This provides an even distribution of agents within the environment. This may not be biologically correct, but we can simulate one species dominating another in a special playback mode (to be discussed later).

If an open slot is found for the child, we copy the parent's agent structure to the child's and then find an empty spot for the child to occupy. Next, we mutate a single weight within the agent's neural network. Note that we use a TOTAL_WEIGHTS symbolic to find the weight to modify. This encompasses not only the weights but also the biases (as they are contiguous within the agent structure). We then do a little record keeping and halve the energy between the parent and child. This then requires them to navigate their environments to find food before they are permitted to reproduce again.

SAMPLE RESULTS

We'll now look at a few summaries of the simulation in action. The operation of the simulation will also be discussed including the available command-line options that are available.

The simulation can be run by simply executing the application with no options, such as:

```
./sim
```

This will run the simulation given the parameters defined in the header file common.h. The defaults within common.h include 36 agents (18 herbivores and 18 carnivores) and 35 plants within a 30x30 grid. The maximum number of simulation steps is set to 1 million. Figure 7.10 shows the maximum age reached for each of the two species.

It's interesting to note the trend of increasing age in the agents. When the carnivore species finds an interesting strategy that increases its longevity, shortly thereafter, herbivores find another strategy that gives them the ability to live a little longer. In some ways, the species compete with one another. When a species evolves an interesting strategy, the other species must evolve to counteract this new strategy.

Once a run is complete, the two best agents of the species are saved off into a file called agents.dat. These agents can then be pitted against one another in a simulation called *playback*. This mode doesn't seed the population

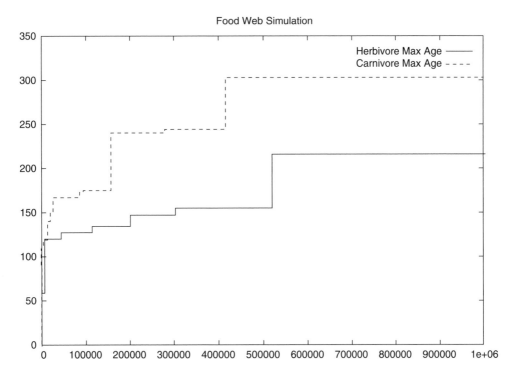

FIGURE 7.10 Age progression in a sample simulation.

with random members, but instead starts with the best members from the last run. This can be performed using the following command:

```
./sim -prn
```

The 'p' argument defines that we want to run in playback mode. The 'r' specifies that we wish to save off the run-time trend information, and 'n' defines that no reproduction is permitted. The trend data stored in *playback* mode includes agent birth and death counts (for both species).

Using agents evolved in the prior run, Figure 7.11 shows a plot of the run-time trend data that was created.

As we've defined that no reproduction may occur, this simulation shows no births occurring, only deaths. When the playback simulation has begun, the landscape is initialized with herbivores and carnivores. It's clear from the

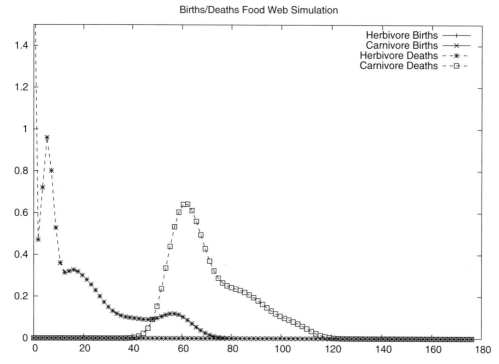

FIGURE 7.11 Run-time trend data from a playback simulation. Herbivore and carnivore births, while represented in the graph, are not visible due to the graph scaling and frequency of the herbivore and carnivore deaths.

plot that the carnivores have a field day with the abundance of herbivores that are available to consume. Once this winds down, carnivore deaths begin a steep increase as the landscape has been stripped of prey and starvation sets in. With the loss of food for the carnivores, their demise is certain.

The simulation provides a number of options. These are shown in Table 7.1.

One interesting scenario is provided by the following parameters:

```
./sim -prncg
```

This provides a circular food web in which carnivores hunt and eat herbivores, but conversely, once carnivores die, they become food available to herbivores.

TABLE 7.1   Command-line Options for the Simulation.

Option	Description
-h	Command-line help
-p	Playback mode (read agents.dat)
-r	Save run-time trend data (runtime.dat)
-g	Don't regrow plants
-c	Convert carnivores to plants when they die
-n	No reproduction is permitted
-s	Manual step (carriage-return required)

INTERESTING STRATEGIES

While this simulation is simple and agents are provided with a minimal number of input sensors and available actions, very interesting behaviors can result.

One interesting herbivore strategy entailed herding. An herbivore would follow another herbivore if it were in front. The analogy could be strength in numbers—as long as you're not the herbivore in front. Carnivores found numerous interesting strategies one of which was finding plants and then waiting for herbivores to wander by. This strategy was successful but short-lived as herbivores finally evolved the ability to avoid carnivores, even if plants were in the vicinity.

ADJUSTING THE PARAMETERS

The size of the environment, number of agents, and number of plants in the simulation is all related. For a balanced simulation, the number of plants must be at least equal to the number of herbivores (half the number of agents in the simulation). Any less and herbivores quickly die, followed quickly by the carnivores. The number of agents must not be so large that the species are crowded within the simulation. If the number of agents and grid dimension are similar, the simulation will be balanced.

The simulation parameters are provided within the header file (`common.h`). The simulation can also be adjusted using the command-line parameters, as shown in Table 7.1.

SUMMARY

In this chapter, we investigated artificial life (Alife) by simulating a very simple food web. Alife provides a platform for the study of a variety of different phenomena within biological and social systems. The greatest strength of Alife in the field of synthetic ethology is the ability to play "what-if" games by changing the variables of the simulation and monitoring their effects. We demonstrated the concepts of synthetic ethology using a very simple predator/prey simulation, which resulted in interesting strategies by both predator and prey.

REFERENCES

[Langton]. Langton, Chris. "What Is Artificial Life," available online at *http://www.biota.org/papers/cgalife.html* (accessed January 17, 2003)

[MacLennan] MacLennan, Bruce. "Artificial Life and Synthetic Ethology," available online at *http:www.cs.utk.edu/~mclennan/alife.html* (accessed January 17, 2003)

RESOURCES

CALResCo. "The Complexity & Artificial Life Research Concept for Self-Organizing Systems," available online at *http://www.calresco.org* (accessed January 17, 2003)

Digital Life Lab at Caltech. "Aveda Software," available online at *http://dllab.caltech.edu/avida/* (accessed January 17, 2003)

International Society for Artificial Life. "Home Page," available online at
    http://www.alife.org
MacLennan, Bruce. "Bruce MacLennan's Home Page," Available online at
    http://www.cs.utk.edu/~mclennan/

8 Introduction to Rules-Based Systems

In this chapter, we'll look at one of the original symbolic AI systems, the knowledge-based system. These systems are also called expert systems (or production systems), where knowledge is encoded in rules. Knowledge (or facts) is stored in a working memory, and the rules are applied to the knowledge to create more knowledge. This process continues until some goal state is reached. We'll investigate a simple rules-based system in this chapter along with an application in the domain of fault tolerance.

INTRODUCTION

While a number of different types of rules-based systems exist, we'll focus on a combination of two particular kinds called the deduction system and the reaction system. A deduction system consists of rules representing antecedents and consequents. An antecedent is a condition (an "if" statement, if you will) while the consequent represents the resulting action (the "then" portion). By deduction, the rules insert new facts into the working memory that were "deduced" (reasoned by deduction) from the existing working memory by a given rule. A reaction system includes "actions" that are performed as part of the consequent, such as issuing a command in an embedded system to alter the environment.

ANATOMY OF A RULES-BASED SYSTEM

A rules-based system is made up of a number of distinct elements. A set of rules exists that operate over a collection of facts stored in a working memory.

Logic is provided to identify which rule to fire (based upon the antecedents) and then modify working memory (based upon the consequents). Figure 8.1 provides a graphical depiction of a simple rules-based system.

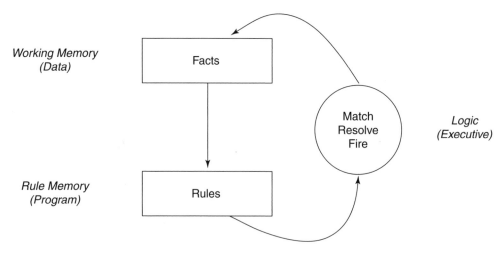

FIGURE 8.1   Rules-based system illustration.

Rules operate over the body of facts stored within the working memory. Once a rule is matched, it is permitted to fire, which may (or may not) alter the working memory. This process continues until a goal state is reached.

Working Memory

The working memory is the structure where the currently known facts are stored. This is a persistent space that can be altered only through the consequent of a rule (and from which a rule may only be fired if its antecedents are true). Consider the following example of working memory:

```
(sensor-failed sensor1)
(mode normal)
```

In this example, two facts are known. These are encoded in pairs of type and value. For example, the first fact is defined as a type `sensor-failed` and its value is `sensor1`. The knowledge being demonstrated by this fact is that `sensor1` is a failed sensor. The second fact defines that the particular `mode` is `normal`. All facts are coded in this representation (though in commercial rules-based systems, a richer representation is often provided).

Rules Memory

The rules memory contains a set of rules that operate over the working memory. Rules are constructed in two parts and include an "antecedent" and a "consequent." The antecedent defines the facts that must be true for the rule to be triggered. The consequent defines those actions that will be taken if the rule is triggered. Consider the following example:

```
(defrule sensor-check
      (sensor-failed sensor1)
=>
      (add (disable sensor1))
)
```

The `defrule` token specifies that we're defining a rule for the system, and is followed by a text name for the rule. This is followed by one or more antecedents (in this case `(sensor-failed sensor1)`). The '`=>`' symbol separates the antecedents from the consequents. One or more consequents are then provided. These actions are performed only if the rule is triggered. Finally, the rule is closed by the trailing parenthesis. The actions are defined as two elements. The first is the command that is to be issued and the second is a parameter on which the command operates. In this example, if the rule were triggered, the fact `(disable sensor1)` would be added to the working memory.

Logic

The system of reasoning behind the rules-based system is the logic that identifies the rules to trigger and permits them to fire. This process is commonly defined as a match-resolve-act cycle, and is discussed in the section "Phases of a Rules-Based System."

TYPES OF RULES-BASED SYSTEMS

Before we descend into the logic behind the rules-based system, it's important to understand that there are fundamentally two different types of systems. These are forward chaining systems and backward chaining systems.

Backward Chaining

The backward chaining system is an inference strategy that begins with a hypothesis (a goal state) and works backwards through the rules to generate a new hypothesis and ultimately the currently known set of facts. By arriving at the initial set of facts from the hypothesis, the hypothesis is proven.

Forward Chaining

The forward chaining system is an inference strategy that begins with known facts. The rules memory is then consulted to identify the rules that match the given set of facts, which may introduce new facts into the working memory. This process continues until either no new facts may be derived, or a goal state is reached. This is a deduction process, which simply uses the known facts to flow through the working memory (and rules) to generate new facts.

This chapter will focus on forward chaining in both the examples and sample implementation.

PHASES OF A RULES-BASED SYSTEM

Let's now look at the phases of a rules-based system, per the forward chaining inference strategy (as shown in Figure 8.2).

Match Phase

In the match phase, each of the rules is checked to see if the set of antecedents for the rule can be matched with facts in the working memory. If so, then the rule is added to the conflict set. Rules whose antecedents are not matched are ignored. Once all rules have been checked, the conflict set is then reviewed by the next phase, the conflict resolution phase.

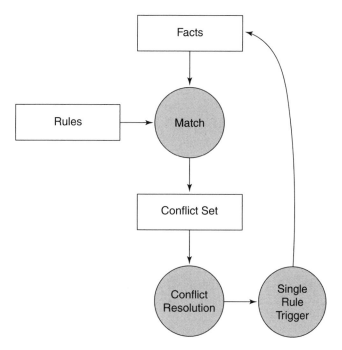

FIGURE 8.2   Rules-based system phases.

Conflict Resolution Phase

The purpose of the conflict resolution phase is to pick a rule to fire out of the conflict set. If only one rule exists in the set, then the process is simple. Given more than one rule in the set, some criteria must be defined to determine which rule to fire. This can be as elaborate as identifying the rule with the greatest number of antecedents (or consequents), or as simple as picking the first rule matched. Upon identifying the rule to be fired, it is passed on to the action phase.

Action Phase

The action phase performs the set of consequents for the particular rule to be fired. These actions could be adding facts to working memory, removing facts from working memory, or performing some other action. For example, if our rules-based system was connected to the outside world, the actions could manipulate the environment (such as moving a robotic arm or disabling a switch).

SIMPLE EXAMPLE

Let's now look at a simple example that includes a number of rules and a variety of facts in a working memory. We'll use a subset of the ZOOKEEPER rules first proposed by Patrick Henry Winston, the Ford Professor of the Artificial Intelligence and Computer Science Department at the Massachusetts Institute of Technology [Winston 1993].

Consider the following rules shown in Listing 8.1.

Listing 8.1   Sample Problem Adapted from Winston's ZOOKEEPER Example.

```
(defrule bird-test
     (has-feathers ?)
=>
     (bird ?)
)

(defrule mammal-test
     (gives-milk ?)
=>
     (mammal ?)
)

(defrule ungulate-test1
     (mammal ?)
     (chews-cud ?)
=>
     (is-ungulate ?)
)

(defrule ungulate-test2
     (mammal ?)
     (has-hoofs ?)
=>
     (is-ungulate ?)
)
```

Now consider that our working memory contains the following facts:

```
(gives-milk animal)
```

```
(has-hoofs animal)
```

We begin with the match phase where we try to match the facts in our working memory with the antecedents in our rule set. Neither fact matches the antecedents of the first rule (`bird-test`), but an antecedent is matched in the second test (`mammal-test`). We save this rule off into our conflict set and continue our search through the remaining rules. No other rules match given the current working memory, so in this case we have the simple case of a conflict set containing one rule. Since there is no conflict, the `mammal-test` rule is permitted to fire (the action phase), resulting in the working memory as shown below:

```
(gives-milk animal)
```

```
(has-hoofs animal)
```

```
(mammal animal)
```

We begin again at the match phase and walk through the rules looking for matching antecedents. In this case, our conflict set contains two rules, `mammal-test` and `ungulate-test2`. Conflict resolution is also simple given this case, because only one rule here has any affect on the working memory (`ungulate-test2`). The first rule has previously fired; therefore, nothing new can be added to our working memory and the rule can be omitted from the conflict set. Moving on to the action phase and firing the `ungulate-test2` rule results in the following working memory:

```
(gives-milk animal)
```

```
(has-hoofs animal)
```

```
(mammal animal)
```

```
(ungulate animal)
```

From this very simple example, our rules system has deduced that the animal in question is an ungulate (a hoofed animal). It reasoned this after first determining that the animal was a mammal (knowing that it gave milk) and then using this information, along with the hoof information, determined that the animal was an ungulate.

Conflict resolution in the example shown included two of the most basic mechanisms for determining which rule to fire. Other mechanisms could be provided for scenarios that are more complicated. For example, the conflict resolver could pick the rule to fire from the conflict set that had the largest number of antecedents. This provides for the most complicated case and could help the system reason to the most relevant goal state and ignore the simpler cases, which might lead the system down unnecessary paths.

SAMPLE APPLICATION

We'll now look at another example that provides a form of fault tolerance within an embedded domain. While reviewing this application, we'll also present the other consequent primitives that are available.

Fault Tolerance

In a very simple application, we'll encode rudimentary knowledge of sensor management into our rules. A redundant set of sensors exists from which one can be set as the active sensor (and thus be used by the larger system). Either of the sensors may be working (or failed), but only one may be active at any given time. If neither of the sensors is working, then neither can be active. Additionally, our mode must change to denote that a problem exists within the sensor subsystem.

In this application, it is assumed that we're operating in a blackboard architecture (see Figure 8.3). Blackboard architecture contains a number of agents that use and produce data on the blackboard. The blackboard serves as a working space where facts are communicated amongst the agents. Agents are triggered by data on the blackboard and can manipulate the data (adding, changing, or removing), which may trigger other agents to continue the work process.

The blackboard architecture is interesting because it not only provides the ability for agents to communicate with one another, but also to coordinate and synchronize their activities.

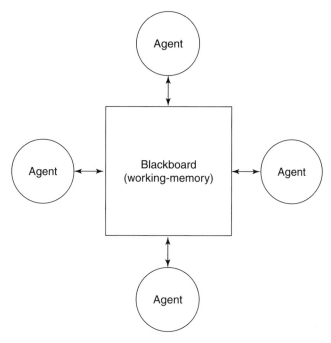

FIGURE 8.3   Graphical depiction of a blackboard architecture.

Rules Definition

The rules file for our sample fault tolerance demonstration is shown in Listing 8.2. This set of rules introduces a number of new consequents (actions) that can be performed.

Listing 8.2   Fault Tolerance Demonstration Rules File.

```
(defrule init
     (true null)                        ; antecedent
=>
     (add (sensor-active none))         ; consequents
     (add (sensor-working sensor1))
     (add (sensor-working sensor2))
     (add (mode failure))
     (enable (timer 1 10))
     (print ("default rule fired!"))
     (disable (self))
```

```
)

;
; Define active rule-set
;

(defrule sensor-failed
     (sensor-working ?)
     (sensor-failed ?)
=>
     (delete (sensor-working ?))
)

(defrule check-active
     (sensor-active ?)
     (sensor-failed ?)
=>
     (delete (sensor-active ?))
     (add (sensor-active none))
)

(defrule make-working
     (sensor-active none)
     (sensor-working ?)
=>
     (add (sensor-active ?))
     (delete (mode failure))
     (add (mode normal))
     (delete (sensor-active none))
)

(defrule failure
     (mode normal)
     (sensor-active none)
     (sensor-failed sensor1)
     (sensor-failed sensor2)
=>
     (add (mode failure))
     (delete (mode safe))
     (delete (mode normal))
)


; Use triggers to simulate timed events...
```

```
(defrule trigger1
    (timer-triggered 1)
=>
    (print ("Sensor 1 failure.\n"))
    (add (sensor-failed sensor1))
    (enable (timer 2 10))
    (delete (timer-triggered 1))
)

(defrule trigger2
    (timer-triggered 2)
=>
    (print ("Sensor 2 failure.\n"))
    (add (sensor-failed sensor2))
    (enable (timer 3 10))
    (delete (timer-triggered 2))
)

(defrule trigger3
    (timer-triggered 3)
=>
    (print ("Sensor 1 is now working.\n"))
    (delete (sensor-failed sensor1))
    (add (sensor-working sensor1))
    (enable (timer 4 10))
    (delete (timer-triggered 3))
)

(defrule trigger4
    (timer-triggered 4)
=>
    (print ("Sensor 2 is now working.\n"))
    (delete (sensor-failed sensor2))
    (add (sensor-working sensor2))
    (enable (timer 1 10))
    (delete (timer-triggered 4))
)
```

This example contains nine rules, but only four are actual operating rules. The first rule (init) in Listing 8.2 is an initialization rule. Note that the antecedent is (true null), which always resolves to true. This initialization rule permits us to seed the working memory with an initial set of facts (as defined by the add commands). The enable command allows us to enable a timer, which when fired can trigger another rule. We'll use timers in this example to perform simulated events from the environment. These would be events (facts) placed into the working memory from other agents operating within the environment (recall Figure 8.3). [Note: The timers used in this example are modeled after Microsoft's *The Age of Kings*, which uses a rules file to define the game AI.] The timer command uses two arguments, the numeric id of the timer and the number of seconds until the timer should fire (in this case, timer 1 will fire in 10 seconds). The print command is a debugging command that provides us with some visibility into the reasoning of the system. The final command in this rule, disable, is very important. It provides the ability to disable the rule from the set of available rules. This rule can then never be fired again, an obvious need for rules whose antecedents are always matched (such as the init rule).

Once the init rule has fired, the working memory will contain:

```
(sensor-active none)
(sensor-working sensor1)
(sensor-working sensor2)
(mode failure)
```

Rule make-working would be the next rule to fire (using sensor1 as the matched parameter), leaving working memory as:

```
(sensor-working sensor1)
(sensor-working sensor2)
(sensor-active sensor1)
(mode normal)
```

At this point, no further rules can fire and the system remains in this state until the timer fires (after 10 seconds). When a timer fires, the system simply adds the fact to working memory ((timer-triggered 1)). This new fact in working memory then causes the rule to fire that handles the particular timer (using the trigger event as the rule's antecedent). The event triggered by the timer simulates the failure of sensor1, modifying working memory as follows:

```
(sensor-working sensor1)
(sensor-working sensor2)
(sensor-active sensor1)
(mode normal)
(sensor-failed sensor1)
```

Rules `sensor-failed` and `check-active` then fire, leaving working memory in the following state:

```
(sensor-working sensor2)
(mode normal)
(sensor-failed sensor1)
(sensor-active none)
```

Finally, rule `make-working` fires, leaving working memory as:

```
(sensor-working sensor2)
(mode normal)
(sensor-failed sensor1)
(sensor-active sensor2)
```

At this point, the system is operational with a working sensor from the redundant pair. The rules also provide for no working sensors with an indication of this event using the `mode` fact. The derivation of the remaining rule firings is left for the reader.

This example can be performed with the rules-based system application on the CD-ROM. The fault-tolerance example shown above is contained in the file `fault.rbs`.

The source code for the rules based system can be found on the CD-ROM at ./software/ch8/rbs/.

SOURCE DISCUSSION

Let's now look at a simple implementation of a rules-based system using the rules and fact format discussed thus far.

The basic flow of the software is shown in Figure 8.4. After initializing (clearing) the working memory and the rules-set, the rules file specified by the user is parsed and the rules loaded into the rules-set. The software then goes into a loop trying to match a rule given the current working memory. When a rule is matched, the execution logic is called to perform the consequents of the particular rule. Whether or not a rule was fired, the software continues by trying to match another rule. This is the basic simplified flow of the rules-based system.

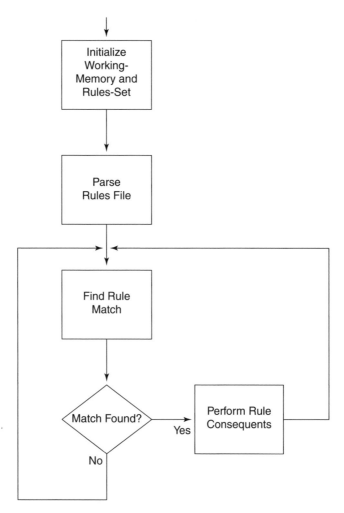

FIGURE 8.4 Basic flow of the rules-based system.

Let's first look at the data structures that are used by the source (Listing 8.3).

Listing 8.3   Rules-Based System Data Structures.

```
#define MEMORY_ELEMENT_SIZE     80
#define MAX_MEMORY_ELEMENTS     40
#define MAX_RULES               40
#define MAX_TIMERS              10

typedef struct memoryElementStruct *memPtr;

typedef struct memoryElementStruct {
  int active;
  char element[MEMORY_ELEMENT_SIZE+1];
  struct memoryElementStruct *next;
} memoryElementType;


typedef struct {
  int active;
  char ruleName[MEMORY_ELEMENT_SIZE+1];
  memoryElementType *antecedent;
  memoryElementType *consequent;
} ruleType;


typedef struct {
  int active;
  int expiration;
} timerType;
```

The memoryElementType is the structure that is used not only to represent a fact in working memory, but also a rule in the rules-set. The element field holds the fact, in the working memory context. Type ruleType represents a single rule within the rules-set. The active word defines whether this rule is active in the system. The ruleName is the name of the rule (parsed after the "defrule" token). This is used primarily for debugging, but can also aid the knowledge-developer when dealing with a large number of rules. The antecedent and consequent elements represent linked-lists of terms. Recall that memoryElementType contains a next element; this either represents the address of the next term, or 0 to represent the end of the chain. The timerType represents a single timer. It again uses an active word to identify whether the timer is in use. The expiration field specifies when the timer should fire.

Listing 8.4 shows the declaration of the working variables used by the rules-based system. These are global variables used by the various subsystems in the software.

Listing 8.4 Global Structures Declaration.

```
memoryElementType workingMemory[MAX_MEMORY_ELEMENTS];

ruleType ruleSet[MAX_RULES];

timerType timers[MAX_TIMERS];

int endRun = 0;
int debug = 0;
```

Declarations workingMemory, ruleSet, and timers were discussed with data structures (from Listing 8.3). Two new items are endRun, which allows the rule-set to end the run of the system (via the quit command), and debug, which specifies whether debugging information should be emitted.

The main function, as shown in Listing 8.5 provides the initialization of the system as well as loop (match-rule/fire). The function begins with parsing of the command-line using the getopt function. Three command-line parameters are supported, 'h' to emit the help information, 'd' to enable debugging and 'r' to specify the rules-file to use. Note that if no file is specified (the 'r' option is not found), then the help information is emitted by default and the software exits.

The working structures in the system are then cleared, and based upon the active word specified in each record, all are clear. A call is then made to parseFile (see Listing 8.6) to read and parse the rules-file into the ruleSet structure.

Listing 8.5 The Rules-Based System main Function.

```
int main( int argc, char *argv[] )
{
  int opt, ret;
  char inpfile[80]={0};

  extern void processTimers( void );
  extern int parseFile( char * );
```

```
extern void interpret( void );

while ((opt = getopt(argc, argv, "hdr:")) != -1) {

  switch( opt ) {

    case 'h':
      emitHelp();
      break;

    case 'd':
      debug = 1;
      printf("Debugging enabled\n");
      break;

    case 'r':
      strcpy(inpfile, optarg);
      break;

  }

}

if (inpfile[0] == 0) emitHelp();

bzero( (void *)workingMemory, sizeof(workingMemory) );
bzero( (void *)ruleSet, sizeof(ruleSet) );
bzero( (void *)timers, sizeof(timers) );

ret = parseFile( inpfile );

if (ret < 0) {
  printf("\nCould not open file, or parse error\n\n");
  exit(0);
}

while (1) {

  interpret();

  if (debug) {
    printWorkingMemory();
  }
```

```
        processTimers();

        if (endRun) break;

        sleep(1);

    }

    return 0;
}
```

The main loop is the final element shown in Listing 8.5. This loop performs the match/fire logic within the interpret function. If debugging is enabled, the working memory is emitted to follow along with the execution of rules and associated changes to working memory. The timers are processed through the call processTimers. If the 'quit' command was found, the loop is exited (via endRun) and the program exits. Finally, to simulate timed-processing of the rules, a simple call to sleep is used (in addition to slowing the system down so that it can be viewed in operation). In a production system, this would be removed and the function processTimers would utilize the current time to fire off the necessary rule.

The file parser (see Listing 8.6) takes the rules stored in the file and parses them to rules containing antecedents and consequents. The parser is very simple since the structure of the file is simple. The rules file is made up of one or more rules. Figure 8.5 shows the format of each rule.

The "defrule(" token starts off a new rule and is followed by a string name for the rule. One or more antecedents follow with the "=>" token separating the set of one or more consequents. The ")" symbol closes out the rule. Examples of rules following this form are shown in Listing 8.2.

Given this very regular and predictable structure, rules' parsing is performed using a predictive parser. The parser very simply searches for the start

```
(defrule <rule-name>
        (antecedent-terms)
=>
        (consequent-terms)
)
```

FIGURE 8.5   Format of rules within
the system.

token and then parses the antecedents. Once the separator token is found, the consequents are parsed. Finally, the closing symbol is checked to ensure the rule had proper form. If everything passes, the loop continues looking for a new rule. Listing 8.6 also shows calls to the function skipWhiteSpace. This function is used to skip around comments, spaces, and other text that is not part of the rule.

Listing 8.6   The File Parsing Function (parseFile).

```
int parseFile( char *filename )
{
  FILE *fp;
  char *file, *cur;
  int fail = 0;

  extern int debug;

  file = (char *)malloc(MAX_FILE_SIZE);

  if (file == NULL) return -1;

  fp = fopen(filename, "r");

  if (fp == NULL) {
    free(file);
    return -1;
  }

  fread( file, MAX_FILE_SIZE, 1, fp);

  cur = &file[0];

  while (1) {

    /* This will parse an entire rule */

    /* Find the "(defrule" start of a rule */
    cur = strstr( cur, "(defrule" );

    if (cur == NULL) {
      fail = 1;
      break;
    }
```

```
if (!strncmp(cur, "(defrule", 8)) {
  int i=0;

  cur+=9;

  while (*cur != 0x0a) {
    ruleSet[ruleIndex].ruleName[i++] = *cur++;
  }
  ruleSet[ruleIndex].ruleName[i++] = 0;

  cur = skipWhiteSpace( cur );

  /* Parse the antecedents */
  cur = parseAntecedent( cur, &ruleSet[ruleIndex] );

  if (cur == NULL) {
    fail = 1;
    break;
  }

  /* Should be sitting on the '=>' */
  if (!strncmp(cur, "=>", 2)) {

    cur = skipWhiteSpace( cur+2 );

    /* Parse the consequents */
    cur = parseConsequent( cur, &ruleSet[ruleIndex] );

    if (cur == NULL) {
      fail = 1;
      break;
    }

    /* Ensure we're closing out the current rule */
    if (*cur == ')') {
      cur = skipWhiteSpace( cur+1 );
    } else {
      fail = 1;
      break;
    }

  } else {
    fail = 1;
```

```
          break;
        }

        ruleSet[ruleIndex].active = 1;
        ruleIndex++;

    } else {

        break;

    }

  }

  if (debug) {
    printf("Found %d rules\n", ruleIndex);
  }

  free( (void *)file );

  fclose(fp);

  return 0;
}
```

Parsing the antecedents and consequents entails the use of two functions that parse each type (see Listing 8.7). Each function uses the parseElement function to parse the actual term from the file.

Listing 8.7   Antecedent and Consequent Parsing Functions.

```
char *parseAntecedent( char *block, ruleType *rule )
{
  while (1) {

    block = skipWhiteSpace( block );

    if (*block == '(') {

      block = parseElement( block, &rule->antecedent );

    } else break;
```

```
    }

    return block;
}

char *parseConsequent( char *block, ruleType *rule )
{
  while (1) {

    block = skipWhiteSpace( block );

    if (*block == '(') {

      block = parseElement(block, &rule->consequent);

    } else break;

  }

  return block;
}
```

Note the use of skipWhiteSpace before element parsing in the two functions. This allows comments after each consequent or antecedent in the file.

The parseElement function pulls a fact from the file, taking care to match
the parenthesis (since they're may be one pair, or two, depending upon the
type of consequent fact). The function uses the parenthesis as state variables
to know when a term has been completely parsed (and stored). Once the element has been parsed, it is added to the chain representing either the antecedent or consequent (see Listing 8.8).

Listing 8.8   The parseElement Function.

```
char *parseElement( char *block, memoryElementType **met )
{
  memoryElementType *element;
  int i=0;
  int balance = 1;

  element =
(memoryElementType *)malloc(sizeof(memoryElementType));
```

```
element->element[i++] = *block++;

while (1) {

  if (*block == 0) break;

  if (*block == ')') balance--;
  if (*block == '(') balance++;

  element->element[i++] = *block++;

  if (balance == 0) break;

}

element->element[i] = 0;
element->next = 0;

if (*met == 0) *met = element;
else {
  memoryElementType *chain = *met;
  while (chain->next != 0) chain = chain->next;
  chain->next = element;
}

return block;
}
```

Finally, the skipWhiteSpace function completes the file parser. This function simply skips any characters that are not active symbols within a rule (such as '(' or '='). The function returns the new position of the input file where the caller will begin parsing (see Listing 8.9).

Listing 8.9   The Whitespace Consumer Function.

```
char *skipWhiteSpace( char *block )
{
  char ch;

  while (1) {

    ch = *block;
```

```
    while ((ch != '(') && (ch != ')') && (ch != '=') &&
           (ch != 0) && (ch != ';')) {
      block++;
      ch = *block;
    }

    if (ch == ';') {

      while (*block++ != 0x0a);

    } else break;


  }

  return block;
}
```

Upon completion of the parser, the ruleSet will have been populated with the rules from the file. We continue from Listing 8.5 to the interpret function (see Listing 8.10). This function simply walks through the active rules and calls the checkRule function to see if their antecedents match. The checkRule function returns one if the rule fires, zero otherwise. If the rule fired, we break from the loop and start again from the top of the rules set.

Listing 8.10 The interpret Function.

```
void interpret( void )
{
  int rule;
  int fired = 0;

  extern int checkRule( int );
  extern int debug;

  for (rule = 0 ; rule < MAX_RULES ; rule++) {

    fired = 0;

    if (ruleSet[rule].active) {

      fired = checkRule( rule );

      /* If a rule had some effect on working memory, exit,
```

```
      * otherwise test another rule.
      */
     if (fired) break;

  }

}

if (debug) {
  if (fired) printf("Fired rule %s (%d)\n",
                       ruleSet[rule].ruleName, rule);
}

return;
}
```

The checkRule function, while notably short and simple, begins the most complex portion of the rules-based system (see Listing 8.11). Function check-Rule calls the checkPattern function to try to match the antecedents of the current rule with the fact in working memory.

Listing 8.11   The checkRule Function.

```
int checkRule( int rule )
{
  int fire = 0;
  char arg[MEMORY_ELEMENT_SIZE]={0};

  extern int fireRule( int, char * );

  fire = checkPattern(rule, arg);

  if (fire == 1) {

    fire = fireRule( rule, arg );

  }

  return fire;
}
```

The checkPattern function returns one if the antecedents match. If a match is found, the rule is permitted to fire using the fireRule function. Note that we use the fire variable again for the return value of fireRule, and recall that the return of this routine defines whether the rule in question fired. When we match a rule (via checkPattern), we allow the matched rule to speculatively fire. If the rule changes working memory, then the rule *actually* fired and this status is returned. If the rule does not change working memory, we pretend that the rule did not fire and continue our search by returning a zero value. This is one element of conflict resolution, and avoids the problem of a rule firing repeatedly, simply because it appears before other rules whose antecedents match elements in the working memory.

The purpose of the checkPattern function is to match the antecedents of the current rule to facts in working memory. While this is a conceptually simple task, what happens if our rule appears as:

```
(defrule check-fully-charged
    (fully-charged ?)
=>
    (trickle-charge ?)
)
```

Recall that in this case, the rule will match for the first term of the antecedent (fully-charged), and the second element is used in the consequents. So if our working memory appears as:

```
(fully-charged battery-1)
```

Then upon firing, the rule will be added to working memory:

```
(trickle-charge battery-1)
```

Therefore, the first step in rule matching is to check whether the antecedent has a '?' as the second term of the element. If so, then we need to store each of the first terms of these rules to use in subsequent matching of the rules.

The checkPattern function is shown in Listing 8.12.

Listing 8.12 The Rule Matching Algorithm, checkPattern.

```
int checkPattern( int rule, char *arg )
{
```

```c
int ret=0;
char term1[MEMORY_ELEMENT_SIZE+1];
char term2[MEMORY_ELEMENT_SIZE+1];
memoryElementType *antecedent = ruleSet[rule].antecedent;

while (antecedent) {

  sscanf( antecedent->element, "(%s %s)", term1, term2);
  if (term2[strlen(term2)-1] == ')') term2[strlen(term2)-1] = 0;

  if (term2[0] == '?') {
    int i;
    char wm_term1[MEMORY_ELEMENT_SIZE+1];
    char wm_term2[MEMORY_ELEMENT_SIZE+1];

    for (i = 0 ; i < MAX_MEMORY_ELEMENTS ; i++) {

      if (workingMemory[i].active) {

        sscanf( workingMemory[i].element, "(%s %s)",
                wm_term1, wm_term2 );
        if (wm_term2[strlen(wm_term2)-1] == ')')
          wm_term2[strlen(wm_term2)-1] = 0;

        if (!strncmp(term1, wm_term1, strlen(term1))) {
          addToChain(wm_term2);
        }

      }

    }

  }

  antecedent = antecedent->next;

}

/* Now that we have the replacement strings, walk through
 * the rules trying the replacement string when necessary.
 */

do {
```

```
memoryElementType *curRulePtr, *temp;

curRulePtr = ruleSet[rule].antecedent;

while (curRulePtr) {

  sscanf( curRulePtr->element, "(%s %s)", term1, term2 );
  if (term2[strlen(term2)-1] == ')') term2[strlen(term2)-1]
    = 0;

  if (!strncmp( term1, "true", strlen(term1))) {
    ret = 1;
    break;
  } else {
    if ((term2[0] == '?') && (chain)) {
      strcpy(term2, chain->element);
    }
  }

  ret = searchWorkingMemory( term1, term2 );

  if (!ret) break;

  curRulePtr = curRulePtr->next;

}

if (ret) {

  /* Cleanup the replacement string chain */
  while (chain) {
    temp = chain;
    chain = chain->next;
    free(temp);
  }

  strcpy(arg, term2);

} else {

  if (chain) {
    temp = chain;
    chain = chain->next;
    free(temp);
```

```
      }

    }

  } while (chain);

  return ret;
}
```

The first portion of `checkPattern` walks through the list of antecedents for the current rule and finds each element that has a second term of '?'. The first term of this element is then searched in the working memory and when found, the second element of the fact is stored via a call to `addToChain`. This is referred to as the replacement string (the actual value in working memory for the '?' second rule term). When this loop has completed, we have a chain of elements representing the second term of facts in memory that match rules with second terms of '?'. Using this, the second loop walks through the antecedents for the current rule, using each of the stored second terms in the chain linked-list. Once the antecedent has been fully traced with a given chain element, the working memory matched the rule and the stored second term (as defined by the current element in the chain) is copied and returned to the caller. This argument (such as 'battery-1' in our previous example) is used later when working through the consequents of the rule.

The `addToChain` function, discussed previously, simply builds a chain of terms that are used in pattern matching (see Listing 8.13). The `searchWorkingMemory` function (see Listing 8.14) attempts to mach the two terms of an antecedent with a fact in working memory. Upon matching, a one is returned to the caller (otherwise zero).

Listing 8.13 Building a Chain of Elements with `addToChain`.

```
void addToChain( char *element )
{
  memoryElementType *walker, *newElement;;

  newElement =
(memoryElementType *)malloc(sizeof(memoryElementType));

  strcpy( newElement->element, element );

  if (chain == NULL) {
```

```
      chain = newElement;
    } else {
      walker = chain;
      while (walker->next) walker = walker->next;
      walker->next = newElement;
    }

    newElement->next = NULL;
  }
```

Listing 8.14 Matching Antecedents to Facts in Working Memory with
searchWorkingMemory.

```
  int searchWorkingMemory( char *term1, char *term2 )
  {
    int ret = 0;
    int curMem = 0;
    char wm_term1[MEMORY_ELEMENT_SIZE+1];
    char wm_term2[MEMORY_ELEMENT_SIZE+1];

    while (1) {

      if (workingMemory[curMem].active) {

        /* extract the memory element */
        sscanf(workingMemory[curMem].element, "(%s %s)",
               wm_term1, wm_term2);
        if (wm_term2[strlen(wm_term2)-1] == ')') {
          wm_term2[strlen(wm_term2)-1] = 0;
        }

        if ((!strncmp(term1, wm_term1, strlen(term1))) &&
            (!strncmp(term2, wm_term2, strlen(term2)))) {

          ret = 1;
          break;

        }

      }

      curMem++;
```

```
      if (curMem == MAX_MEMORY_ELEMENTS) {
        break;
      }

    }

    return ret;
  }
```

If a rule is matched to working memory, then one is returned from check-Pattern to the checkRule function (see Listing 8.11). This indicates that the rule may fire and the fireRule is invoked with the index of the rule to fire and the argument that was stored from checkPattern. Recall that this value is the matched '?' rule term from working memory.

Firing a rule is quite a bit simpler than matching a rule in working memory. To fire a rule, we simply walk through the linked-list of consequents for the rule and perform the command encoded by each element (see Listing 8.15).

Listing 8.15 Firing a Rule with fireRule.

```
int fireRule( int rule, const char *arg )
{
  int ret;
  memoryElementType *walker = ruleSet[rule].consequent;
  char newCons[MAX_MEMORY_ELEMENTS+1];

  while (walker) {

    if (!strncmp(walker->element, "(add", 4)) {

      constructElement( newCons, walker->element, arg );

      ret = performAddCommand( newCons );

    } else if (!strncmp(walker->element, "(delete", 7)) {

      constructElement( newCons, walker->element, arg );

      ret = performDeleteCommand( newCons );

    } else if (!strncmp(walker->element, "(disable", 8)) {
```

```
        ruleSet[rule].active = 0;
        ret = 1;

    } else if (!strncmp(walker->element, "(print", 6)) {

        ret = performPrintCommand( walker->element );

    } else if (!strncmp(walker->element, "(enable", 7)) {

        ret = performEnableCommand( walker->element );

    } else if (!strncmp(walker->element, "(quit", 5)) {

        extern int endRun;

        endRun = 1;

    }

    walker = walker->next;

  }

  return ret;
}
```

The fireRule function walks through each of the consequents and de-codes the command contained in each. A chain of if-then-else statements compares the known command types and calls a special function that handles the execution of the particular command. There are two cases where the working memory is manipulated (add and delete) and therefore, the proper fact must be constructed. Recall that if the antecedent was an inexact match (such as (fast-charge ?)), then we use the passed argument (arg) to con-struct the actual fact being applied to working memory. This function is shown in Listing 8.16.

Listing 8.16 Constructing a New Fact Using constructElement.

```
void constructElement( char *new, const char *old, const char *arg )
{
```

```
/* Find the second paren */
old++;
while (*old != '(') old++;

while ((*old != 0) && (*old != '?')) *new++ = *old++;

/* This was a complete rule (i.e., no ? element) */
if (*old == 0) {

  *(--new) = 0;
  return;

} else {

  /* Copy in the arg */
  while (*arg != 0) *new++ = *arg++;
  if ( *(new-1) != ')') *new++ = ')';
  *new = 0;

}

return;
}
```

The constructElement function very simply creates a new fact based upon the pattern fact (consequent) and the passed argument. If the pattern fact contains a '?', then the passed argument replaces the '?' and is returned as the new fact. Therefore, if our argument was "battery-1" and our consequent was "(fast-charge ?)", then our new fact would be "(fast-charge battery1)".

Let's now look at the functions that implement the available commands. The first is the add command which adds a new fact to working memory (see Listing 8.17). The add command has the format:

```
(add (fast-charge ?))
```

for an inexact match, or could represent an absolute fact, such as:

```
(add (fast-charge battery-2))
```

Listing 8.17   Adding a New Fact to Working Memory.

```
int performAddCommand( char *mem )
{
  int slot;

  /* Check to ensure that this element isn't already in
   * working memory
   */
  for (slot = 0 ; slot < MAX_MEMORY_ELEMENTS ; slot++) {

    if (workingMemory[slot].active) {

      if (!strcmp( workingMemory[slot].element, mem )) {

        /* Element is already here, return */
        return 0;

      }

    }

  }

  /* Add this element to working memory */

  slot = findEmptyMemSlot();

  if (slot < MAX_MEMORY_ELEMENTS) {

    workingMemory[slot].active = 1;
    strcpy( workingMemory[slot].element, mem );

  } else {
    assert(0);
  }

  return 1;
}
```

The add command first tests to see whether the fact already exists in working memory. If so, it returns a zero to the caller (and error) and exits. Otherwise, an empty slot is found (using findEmptyMemSlot, see Listing 8.18) and the fact is copied into working memory. A one is returned to indicate that working memory was changed. Note that the return status of this function is returned all the way up to `ruleFire` to support the speculative execution of the rule.

Listing 8.18   Finding an Empty Slot in Working Memory.

```
int findEmptyMemSlot( void )
{
  int i;

  for (i = 0 ; i < MAX_MEMORY_ELEMENTS ; i++) {
    if (!workingMemory[i].active) break;
  }

  return i;
}
```

The `delete` command removes a fact from working memory (see Listing 8.19). This function simply tries to match the constructed fact with a fact in working memory. If the fact is found in working memory, it is removed (by setting it inactive and zeroing out the string element). The `delete` command has the format:

```
(delete (fast-charge ?))
```

Listing 8.19   Removing a Fact from Working Memory.

```
int performDeleteCommand( char *mem )
{
  int slot;
  int ret = 0;
  char term1[MEMORY_ELEMENT_SIZE+1];
  char term2[MEMORY_ELEMENT_SIZE+1];
  char wm_term1[MEMORY_ELEMENT_SIZE+1];
  char wm_term2[MEMORY_ELEMENT_SIZE+1];

  sscanf( mem, "(%s %s)", term1, term2 );

  for ( slot = 0 ; slot < MAX_MEMORY_ELEMENTS ; slot++ ) {

    if ( workingMemory[slot].active ) {
```

```
        sscanf( workingMemory[slot].element, "(%s %s)",
               wm_term1, wm_term2 );

     if (!strncmp(term1, wm_term1, strlen(term1)) &&
          !strncmp(term2, wm_term2, strlen(term2))) {

       workingMemory[slot].active = 0;
       bzero( workingMemory[slot].element, MEMORY_ELEMENT_SIZE );
       ret = 1;

     }

   }

 }

 return ret;
}
```

As with the `performAddCommand`, the return status of this function is returned all the way up to `ruleFire` to support the speculative execution of the rule.

The `print` command simply emits the second term of a fact to standard-out (see Listing 8.20). The second term is a double-quote delimited string. The function (`performPrintCommand`) searches for the first '"' and then emits all characters until the terminating '"' character is found. Facts for emitting strings have the format:

```
(print ("this is a test."))
```

Listing 8.20   Emitting a String.

```
int performPrintCommand( char *element )
{
  char string[MAX_MEMORY_ELEMENTS+1];
  int i=0, j=0;

  /* Find initial '"' */
  while ( element[i] != '"') i++;
  i++;

  /* Copy until we reach the end */
```

```
        while ( element[i] != '"') string[j++] = element[i++];
        string[j] = 0;

        printf("%s\n", string);

        return 1;
}
```

The `enable` command is used to start a timer (see Listing 8.21). A fact for starting a timer has the format:

```
(enable (timer N T))
```

where 'N' is the timer index and 'T' is the expiration time in seconds.

Listing 8.21   Enabling a Timer.

```
int performEnableCommand( char *element )
{
  char *string;
  int timer, expiration;

  void startTimer( int, int );

  string = strstr( element, "timer" );

  sscanf( string, "timer %d %d", &timer, &expiration );

  startTimer( timer, expiration );

  return 1;
}
```

Two final commands are `disable` and `quit`. These two commands are handled inline to the `fireRule` function (see Listing 8.15). The `disable` command is used to disable a rule from the current rule-set (it will no longer be capable of firing). The `quit` command ends the run of the rules-based system. The commands have the format:

```
(disable (self))
(quit null)
```

The final set of functions relate to timer processing. The processing of timers is handled through the processTimers function (shown in Listing 8.22). This function simply decrements the expiration time for the currently active timers until they reach their trigger value (in this case, zero). Once a timer has fired, the fireTimer function is called (see Listing 8.23).

Listing 8.22   Processing the Timer List.

```
void processTimers( void )
{
  int i;

  for (i = 0 ; i < MAX_TIMERS ; i++) {

    if (timers[i].active) {

      if (--timers[i].expiration == 0) {

        fireTimer( i );

      }

    }

  }

  return;
}
```

Recall that firing a timer involves adding a fact to working memory that represents this, which will act as a trigger for an active rule. When a timer is fired, a fact such as "(timer-triggered X)" is added to working memory (where X represents the timer index). The add function (performAddCommand) is used to add the trigger fact to working memory. The assumption here is that another rule in the rule-set will have an antecedent for "(timer-triggered X)" to process the timer event.

Listing 8.23   Firing a Timer.

```
int fireTimer( int timerIndex )
{
```

```
    int ret;
    char element[MEMORY_ELEMENT_SIZE+1];

    extern int performAddCommand( char *mem );

    sprintf( element, "(timer-triggered %d)", timerIndex );

    ret = performAddCommand( element );

    timers[timerIndex].active = 0;

    return ret;
}
```

Starting a timer is called by the `enable` command. This function is provided here (see Listing 8.24) to encapsulate all timer functionality into a single file.

Listing 8.24   Starting a Timer.

```
void startTimer( int index, int expiration )
{
  timers[index].expiration = expiration;
  timers[index].active = 1;

  return;
}
```

BUILDING A RULES BASE

Building a rules base is not a simple task, but there are a number of ways to simplify the task.

Rules should be logically ordered based upon their context. For example, rules that have similar antecedents could be placed together since they are attempting to deduce the same or similar facts from the working memory. Similarly, rules that share similar consequents could also be grouped together since they result in similar actions (represent similar deductions).

For complex rule bases, state machines can be introduced using staging elements. For example, consider the following two rules in Listing 8.25.

Listing 8.25 Example of Staging Rules.

```
(defrule stage1-check
     (stage stage1)
     (battery-temp low)
=>
     (add (check battery-temp))
     (delete (stage stage1))
     (add (stage stage2))
)

(defrule stage2-check
     (stage stage2)
     (battery-temp low)

=>

     (add (check battery-pressure))
     (delete (stage stage2))

)
```

We've introduced the "(stage stageX)" facts as markers. Instead of acting as simple information in the working memory, these facts act as guards for the rules. Neither of the rules is considered unless the staging rule matches.

Finally, nothing beats pure testing. In order to fully test, there must be some way to introduce stimulus into the system. Outside of simply introducing facts through the init rule, time-triggered rules can also be used to simulate the addition of facts asynchronously. Recall from Listing 8.2 the use of time-triggered events to simulate sensor failures.

OTHER APPLICATIONS

While rules-based systems are often used as knowledge-based expert systems, it should be clear from this application that a rules-based system could also be used for simple programming tasks. When we program, we encode our knowledge about the problem at hand into the syntax and semantics of the programming language. Rules-based systems can also be used to solve interesting problems, such as the fault-tolerance application discussed above for sensor management. One of the key differences between the two approaches is that when programming in a traditional language, we encode our knowledge serially into the application using the constructs at hand. Rules-based systems require instead a mapping of the knowledge about the application into rules that define the consequents and antecedents. In some ways, this can be easier and more readily understandable.

PROBLEMS WITH RULES-BASED SYSTEMS

The greatest drawback to rules-based systems is the amount of time spent trying to match a rule with available working memory. Recall from the source discussion that there is not only the problem of one-to-one mapping of rules to working memory, but also variations based upon inexact terms. Therefore, instead of just trying to map a rule to working memory, we may have to perform multiple iterations over each rule. If a match is not found, the match process will continue through to each rule.

A solution to this problem exists, called the Rete algorithm [Forgy 1982]. The idea behind Rete is to share intermediate information between rules to limit the number of matches that must be performed. This is performed through an acyclic directed graph representing the antecedents for the rules. For example, if two rules share one common element of their antecedent, each rule would share a node within the graph for the comment element. From this node one would represent the remaining elements of their respective antecedents. In this way, a match for a given element is performed once, leading to possibly multiple rules that might match, but only computing the initial match once.

SUMMARY

In this chapter, we've investigated one of the original reasoning architectures in artificial intelligence, the rules-based system. We focused specifically on forward chaining architectures with an implementation of a simple deduction system. Even though simple, this implementation can be used in a variety of settings, including embedding it within other systems with consequent hooks for manipulating the environment. We looked not only at a classical example from [Winston 93] (the ZOOKEEPER rule-set), but also at a simple fault tolerance example, managing sensors within an environment with reliability requirements. While rules-based systems do have their drawbacks, they provide a powerful architecture for reasoning in systems that interact with a user (such as classical diagnostics systems) down to embedded systems that must manage their environment.

REFERENCES

[Forgy 1982] Forgy, C.L. (1982). "Rete: A Fast Algorithm for the Many Pattern/Many Object Pattern Match Problem," *Artificial Intelligence* 19:17–37.

[Winston 1993] Winston, P.H. (1993). *Artificial Intelligence.* 3rd ed. Addison Wesley.

9 Introduction to Fuzzy Logic

In this chapter, we'll look at the logic system defined by Lotfi Zadeh to overcome the disparity between real-world systems and software representations. In software, the Boolean logic values of true and false represent unique elements in a two-valued system. The real world rarely operates in this fashion—many conditions can be partially true or partially false (or both). Fuzzy logic was introduced to allow software to operate in the domain of degrees of truth. Instead of binary systems that represent truth or falsity, degrees of truth operate over the infinite space between 0.0 and 1.0 inclusive.

INTRODUCTION

To fully understand what Dr. Zadeh proposed in 1963, let's look at a number of examples that provide more information about fuzzy logic and its representation.

FUZZY QUALITY OF SERVICE EXAMPLE

The power of fuzzy logic appears when we begin to analyze a system using linguistics. For example, let's say that we're building a QoS (Quality of Service) algorithm that manages the output of packets over a particular link. The purpose of the QoS algorithm is to provide a given application a consistent amount of bandwidth of the link. If the application tries to use too much of the link's bandwidth, we must reduce the rate that packets are emitted for the given application. From a control perspective, we have three elements.

The first is the packet arrival rate from the application, the second is the measured utilization of the link, and the third is the gate that controls the flow of packets between the application and the link (see Figure 9.1).

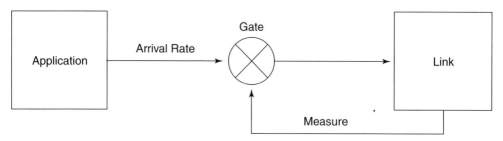

FIGURE 9.1   Quality of service scenario with rate feedback.

The purpose of the gate is to control when and how many packets are permitted to pass given the bandwidth allocated to the particular application. When we think about this problem, we consider it in terms of linguistics. For example:

> If the application utilization of the link is high, then reduce the rate of flow of packets through the gate for the application.

Conversely,

> If the application utilization of the link is low, then increase the rate of flow of packets through the gate for the application.

These rules imply that there exists a dead-zone between the high and low rates that is "about right" for the application

The question is now what is "high" and "low" for the application rate and what is "about right"? Fuzzy logic determines this using membership functions (see Figure 9.2).

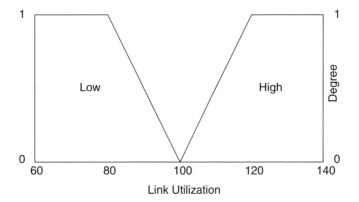

FIGURE 9.2   Membership function for packet rate.

MEMBERSHIP FUNCTIONS

A membership function defines the degree of membership (degree of truth) of a given real-world value in the membership function. From our QoS example, we have a membership function over the set of link utilization (see Figure 9.2).

From Figure 9.2, we've defined two segments, with a third centered between what exists as our target. The low range can be defined programmatically as shown in Equation 9.1:

```
m_low(x) = {
     0,                      if rate(x) >= 100
     (100-rate(x))/20        if rate(x) > 80 AND rate(x) < 100
     1,                      if rate(x) <= 80.
}                                                               (9.1)
```

The high range can then be defined as shown in Equation 9.2:

```
m_high(x) = {
     0,                      if rate(x) <= 100
     (rate(x)-100)/20        if rate(x) > 100 AND rate(x) < 120
     1,                      if rate(x) >= 120.
}                                                               (9.2)
```

FUZZY CONTROL

To illustrate the membership functions, Table 9.1 identifies sample packet rates along with their degree of membership within the two functions.

TABLE 9.1 Example Degrees of Membership.

Packet Rate	m_low(x)	m_high(x)
10	1.0	0.0
85	0.75	0.0
90	0.5	0.0
95	0.25	0.0
100	0.0	0.0
105	0.0	0.25
110	0.0	0.5
115	0.0	0.75
180	0.0	1.0

So given these two membership functions, we can determine the degree of membership for a given rate of packet flow. However, how can this be used in terms of a control strategy for adjusting the packet flow to maintain a consistent quality of service? A very simple mechanism involves the degree of membership to be used as a coefficient to the gating algorithm.

Our gating function defines how many packets may pass during a given interval (for example one second). Each second, the number of packets that are permitted to pass is adjusted to maintain consistent utilization for the application. If the utilization is too high, we decrease the number of packets. Otherwise, if the utilization is too low, we increase it accordingly. The question is, how much to increase?

A simple mechanism is to use our degree of membership as the coefficient applied to the packet delta. Consider Equation 9.3.

$$rate = rate + (m\_low(rate) * pdelta) - (m\_high(rate) * pdelta) \qquad (9.3)$$

The variable rate is the current number of packets that are permitted to pass through in the given time period (one second). Constant pdelta is a tunable parameter that defines the maximum number of packets that can be added to or subtracted from the rate. The membership functions then provide the degree of membership that is used as a coefficient in the rate-tuning algorithm.

Let's look at a few examples using a `pdelta` of 10. While our rate will represent a non-integer value, we'll round up for the tuning algorithm.

Given a `rate` of 110, how will our algorithm adjust the rate for the gating mechanism? Using our Equation 9.3, we get:

rate = 110 + (0 * 10) – (0.5 * 10) = 105

On the next iteration, if the application continues to generate at the given rate of 105, we'll get:

rate = 105 + (0 * 10) – (0.25 * 10) = 102.5

This process continues until we reach our dead-band of 100 at which point no further rate changes are performed.

If our rate had been low, such as 80, Equation 9.3 would have adjusted as follows:

rate = 80 + (1 * 10) – (0 * 10) = 90

Therefore, using the degree of membership as a coefficient for rate-change results in a very simple control mechanism.

A VISUAL FUZZY CONTROL EXAMPLE

Let's now look at another example of fuzzy control using a tracking scenario. In a simple two-dimensional world, we have an agent that serves as the predator. Another agent in the world serves as the prey. The goal is to build a set of membership functions that provide the ability for the predator to track and ultimately catch the prey. Our membership functions will use the error angle for control (representing the difference between the predator's current direction and the direction of the prey).

A plot of the predator membership function is shown in Figure 9.3. Seven distinct groups are defined that identify how much error is present and thus how much correction should be applied.

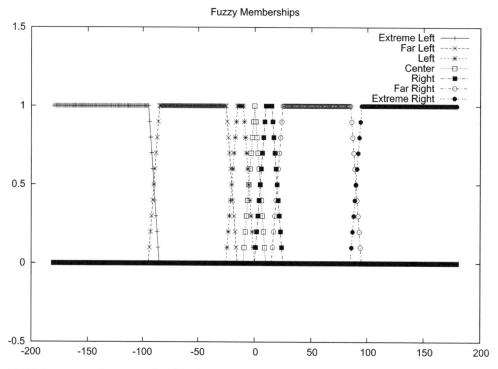

FIGURE 9.3 Predator membership functions.

The center group is the only group in which no change is made to the current direction of the predator. Left and right are [+1, -1] respectively, far left and far right are [+8, -8], and finally extreme left and extreme right represent [+15, -15]. If the predator's error angle falls into a particular membership function, the associated correction is applied to the predator's direction and the process begins again. At each time step, the predator moves one unit for each correction.

Given the membership functions in Figure 9.3, a plot of the predator in action is shown in Figure 9.4.

The predator begins at coordinates [100,100] where the prey begins at a random location (here, approximately [84,30]). The prey simply moves in

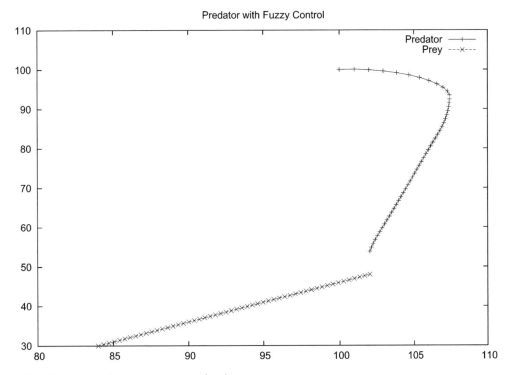

FIGURE 9.4 Predatory/prey example plot.

a 45° line from its initial location. As shown, the predator correctly alters its course to intercept the prey (come within 5 units of the prey).

THE FUZZY AXIOMS

Just like conventional Boolean logic, fuzzy logic has a set of basic operators. These follow the conventional Boolean operators, but differ in how they work. The fuzzy axioms are shown in Figure 9.5.

These operators provide the basis for logic operations for the approximate fuzzy values. Performing conditions such as:

```
if (m_warm(board_temperature) AND m_high(fan_speed)) then …
```

Truth(A OR B)	MIN(truth(A), truth(B))
Truth(A AND B)	MAX(truth(A), truth(B))
Truth(NOT A)	1.0 - truth(A)

FIGURE 9.5   The fuzzy logic axioms.

This form is not only very readable, but can also better approximate the state of the system and lead to better control.

HEDGE FUNCTIONS

An important modifier for fuzzy systems is hedges, or modifiers of fuzzy memberships. These modifiers provide an additional linguistic construct to fuzzy logic and maintain mathematical consistency. Consider the hedge functions of VERY and NOT_VERY. Hedge functions are used in conjunction with membership functions and alter their value based upon the defined linguistic purpose. The hedge functions are defined below as Equations 9.4 and 9.5.

$$VERY(m\_x) = m\_x^2 \tag{9.4}$$

$$NOT\_VERY(m\_x) = m\_x^{0.5} \tag{9.5}$$

For example, consider their use with the m_high membership function as defined by Figure 9.2. Given a packet rate of 115, m_high would result in 0.75. If we applied the VERY hedge function to the membership function (VERY(m_high(rate))), then the resulting value would be 0.5625 (in other words, it's high, but not very high). If the rate had been 119, m_high would result in 0.95. The VERY hedge function applied to this would then result in 0.903 (or, very high).

WHY USE FUZZY LOGIC?

Fuzzy logic is an important construct in the design of software as it uses approximations rather than exact values. This is important because human reasoning itself is approximate and therefore it is easier to map fuzzy logic to systems designs.

SAMPLE APPLICATION

To demonstrate the fuzzy logic functions, we'll build a very simple battery charger simulation (which will lack some physical details).

Our mythical battery charger operates within an environment where at times a charging voltage exists (for example, from a set of solar cells), and a load exists. The voltage from the solar panels provides the ability to charge the battery while the load discharges the battery into the operating circuit. Our charger provides two modes of operation, trickle charge mode and fast charge mode. In trickle charge mode, only a small amount of current is permitted to pass into the battery to provide a very small amount of charge. In fast charge mode, all available current is provided to the charger for the onboard batteries.

From a control systems perspective, what is necessary is a way to determine when to go into fast charge mode and when to switch to trickle charge mode. When a battery charges, the temperature of the battery will rise. When the battery is fully charged, the additional current arriving at the battery will be realized as heat. Therefore, when the battery gets hot, it's probably a good indication that the battery is fully charged and to switch to trickle charge mode. We can also measure the voltage of our battery to determine if it has reached its limit, and then switch it into trickle charge mode. When the battery is neither hot nor has the battery reached its voltage limit, it's safe to switch to fast charge mode. These are simplified rules, as the derivative of the battery temperature is a better indication of battery charge.

Fuzzy Battery Charge Control

As defined, the battery charger has two modes of operation: trickle and fast charge modes. Two sensors exist to monitor the battery: voltage and temperature. To control the charge of the battery we'll use the following fuzzy rules:

```
if m_voltage_high( voltage )
then mode = trickle_charge

if m_temperature_hot( temperature )
then mode = trickle_charge

if ( ( not(m_voltage_high( voltage ))) AND
     ( not(m_temperature_hot( temperature ))) )
then mode = fast_charge
```

Note that these rules are sub-optimal, since the last rule could cover all cases. We'll use three rules to cover more of the available fuzzy operators.

Identifying the fuzzy rules is one of the first steps. This is readily known from system operators or through analysis of the problem. Defining how the linguistics map to the real world is the next problem. This is the process of creating the membership functions.

Fuzzy Charge Membership Functions

Creating the membership functions takes the fuzzy linguistic names and maps them to the real world values in the particular domain. In this example, we'll specify two variables: voltage and temperature. The voltage and temperature membership graphs (showing the actual membership functions) are shown in Figures 9.6 and 9.7 respectively.

The voltage membership graph defines three membership functions within the voltage domain: low, medium, and high. Similarly, the temperature domain also defines three: cold, warm, and hot. These artificial values are for demonstration purposes only and do not represent any type of battery technology.

One can easily see patterns in the membership functions. For this reason, a number of helper functions are provided in source to facilitate creating these membership shapes (including the spike pattern, not shown in these graphs).

NOTE

ON THE CD

The source code for the fuzzy logic battery charge simulator can be found on the CD-ROM at ./software/ch9/fuzzy/.

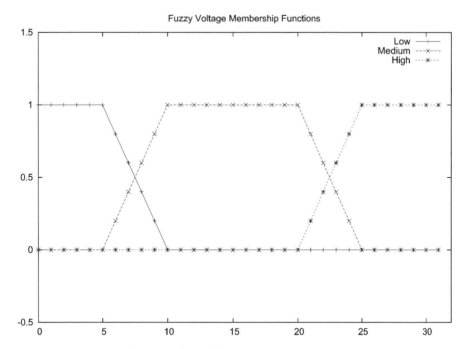

FIGURE 9.6 Fuzzy voltage membership graph.

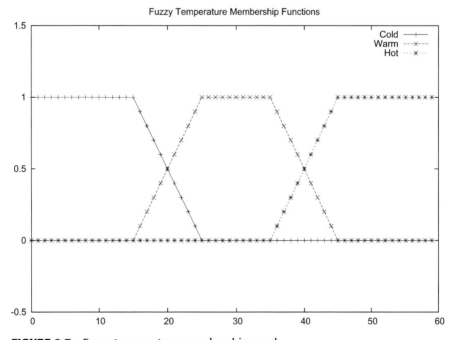

FIGURE 9.7 Fuzzy temperature membership graph.

SOURCE DISCUSSION

The source code presented in this section provides a number of patterns for fuzzy logic software development, with a sample application built around them to demonstrate the capabilities. We'll discuss the generic fuzzy logic functions first and then discuss the simulation.

Fuzzy Logic APIs

The fuzzy logic API provides two elements to fuzzy logic software developers. The first are the fuzzy operators and the second are the membership helper functions.

The fuzzy operators provide fuzzy versions of the AND, OR, and NOT functions, commonly found in conventional logic. Listing 9.1 shows these functions.

Listing 9.1   Fuzzy Logic Operators.

```
#define MAX(a,b)    ((a>b) ? a : b)
#define MIN(a,b)    ((a<b) ? a : b)


fuzzyType fuzzyAnd( fuzzyType a, fuzzyType b )
{
  return MAX(a,b);
}


fuzzyType fuzzyOr( fuzzyType a, fuzzyType b )
{
  return MIN(a,b);
}


fuzzyType fuzzyNot( fuzzyType a )
{
  return( 1.0 - a );
}
```

These functions follow the initially-discussed fuzzy axioms in Figure 9.5.

The next set of APIs provides the ability to create the membership functions very easily. These functions permit the developer to define the outline of the function with a set of values defining the functions profile. These functions are shown in Listing 9.2.

Listing 9.2   Helper Functions for Creating Membership Functions.

```
fuzzyType spikeProfile( float value, float lo, float high )
{
  float peak;

  value += (-lo);

  if      ((lo < 0) && (high < 0)) {
    high = -(high - lo);
  } else if ((lo < 0) && (high > 0)) {
    high += -lo;
  } else if ((lo > 0) && (high > 0)) {
    high -= lo;
  }

  peak = (high / 2.0);
  lo = 0.0;

  if      (value < peak) {
    return( value / peak );
  } else if (value > peak) {
    return( (high-value) / peak );
  }

  return 1.0;
}


fuzzyType plateauProfile( float value, float lo, float lo_plat,
                          float hi_plat, float hi )
{
  float upslope;
  float downslope;

  value += (-lo);

  if (lo < 0.0) {
```

```
      lo_plat += -lo;  hi_plat += -lo;
      hi      += -lo;  lo      = 0;
    } else {
      lo_plat -= lo;  hi_plat -= lo;
      hi      -= lo;  lo      = 0;
    }

    upslope = (1.0 / (lo_plat - lo));
    downslope = (1.0 / (hi - hi_plat));

    if      (value < lo) return 0.0;
    else if (value > hi) return 0.0;
    else if ((value >= lo_plat) && (value <= hi_plat)) return 1.0;
    else if (value < lo_plat) return ((value-lo) * upslope);
    else if (value > hi_plat) return ((hi-value) * downslope);

    return 0.0;
}
```

The first function, spikeProfile, defines the typical triangle-shaped membership function (for example, the center membership function in Figure 9.3). The developer provides the lo and hi values which define base endpoints for the triangle. The peak point is defined as hi/2.

The second function, plateauProfile, defines the trapezoidal-shaped membership function (as illustrated by the Warm membership function in Figure 9.7). The membership functions that extend to the boundaries (such as the Cold and Hot functions in Figure 9.7) are also created using the plateauProfile function.

The purpose of these functions is to identify the degree of membership for a given value and profile vector.

Battery Charge Simulation Membership Functions

Let's now look at the code specific to the battery simulation. The first set of functions that we'll look at are the membership functions. These functions use the previously defined helper functions to build the shapes as shown in the membership graphs.

The first set of functions are the voltage membership functions (see Listing 9.3).

Listing 9.3   Voltage Membership Functions.

```
fuzzyType m_voltage_low( float voltage )
{
  const float lo = 5.0;
  const float lo_plat = 5.0;
  const float hi_plat = 5.0;
  const float hi = 10.0;

  if (voltage < lo) return 1.0;
  if (voltage > hi) return 0.0;

  return plateauProfile( voltage, lo, lo_plat, hi_plat, hi );
}


fuzzyType m_voltage_medium( float voltage )
{
  const float lo = 5.0;
  const float lo_plat = 10.0;
  const float hi_plat = 20.0;
  const float hi = 25.0;

  if (voltage < lo) return 0.0;
  if (voltage > hi) return 0.0;

  return plateauProfile( voltage, lo, lo_plat, hi_plat, hi );
}


fuzzyType m_voltage_high( float voltage )
{
  const float lo = 25.0;
  const float lo_plat = 30.0;
  const float hi_plat = 30.0;
  const float hi = 30.0;

  if (voltage < lo) return 0.0;
  if (voltage > hi) return 1.0;

  return plateauProfile( voltage, lo, lo_plat, hi_plat, hi );
}
```

Each of the membership functions in Listing 9.3 utilizes the plateauProfile function to build the required shape. Each function accepts a voltage
value. A value is then returned which is the degree of membership to the particular membership function. Each function initially checks to see if the
passed value is outside of the limits of the membership function. If so, the respective return value is generated. Otherwise, the value is passed to the
plateauProfile function with the profile defined by the [lo, lo_plat,
hi_plat, hi] vector, and the resulting return value is returned to the caller.

The membership functions in Listing 9.3 are show graphically in Figure
9.6.

Listing 9.4 provides the temperature membership functions for the sample charging application.

Listing 9.4   Temperature Membership Functions.

```
fuzzyType m_temp_cold( float temp )
{
  const float lo = 15.0;
  const float lo_plat = 15.0;
  const float hi_plat = 15.0;
  const float hi = 25.0;

  if (temp < lo) return 1.0;
  if (temp > hi) return 0.0;

  return plateauProfile( temp, lo, lo_plat, hi_plat, hi );
}


fuzzyType m_voltage_low( float voltage )
{
  const float lo = 5.0;
  const float lo_plat = 5.0;
  const float hi_plat = 5.0;
  const float hi = 10.0;

  if (voltage < lo) return 1.0;
  if (voltage > hi) return 0.0;

  return plateauProfile( voltage, lo, lo_plat, hi_plat, hi );
}
```

```
fuzzyType m_voltage_medium( float voltage )
{
  const float lo = 5.0;
  const float lo_plat = 10.0;
  const float hi_plat = 20.0;
  const float hi = 25.0;

  if (voltage < lo) return 0.0;
  if (voltage > hi) return 0.0;

  return plateauProfile( voltage, lo, lo_plat, hi_plat, hi );
}
```

The temperature functions provided in Listing 9.4 are illustrated graphically in Figure 9.7.

Battery Charge Simulation Control Function

Controlling the mode of the battery is now a simple function of implementing the previously defined fuzzy rules. The chargeControl function in Listing 9.5 provides the controller function.

Listing 9.5   The Battery Charge Control Function.

```
void chargeControl( )
{
  static unsigned int i = 0;

  extern float voltage, temperature;

  if ( (i++ % 10) == 0 ) {

    if (normalize( m_voltage_high( voltage ) ) ) {
      chargeMode = TRICKLE_CHARGE;
    } else if (normalize( m_temp_hot( temperature ) ) ) {
      chargeMode = TRICKLE_CHARGE;
    } else if (normalize(
                  fuzzyAnd(
                    fuzzyNot( m_voltage_high( voltage ) ),
                    fuzzyNot( m_temp_hot( temperature ) ) ) ) ) {
```

```
        chargeMode = FAST_CHARGE;
    }

  }

}
```

This function changes the charge mode based upon the values of voltage and temperature using the fuzzy rules and membership functions.

Simulation Main Loop

Finally, the simulation main loop exercises the simulator and charge control function to properly charge the battery given the environmental parameters of voltage and temperature. The main loop is shown in Listing 9.6.

Listing 9.6   The Main Loop.

```
int main()
{
  int i;

  extern int simulate(void);
  extern void chargeControl( float * );

  extern float voltage;
  extern float temperature;
  extern int chargeMode;

  for (i = 0 ; i < 3000 ; i++) {

    simulate();

    chargeControl();

    printf("%d, %f, %f, %d\n", i,
            voltage,
            temperature,
            chargeMode
    );

  }
```

```
        return 0;
    }
```

As shown, the simulator simply loops through, calling the simulator and then allowing the charge controller function to identify in which mode the charger should be. The simulator is not shown here in the text, but is provided on the CD-ROM.

The simulation is visualized in Figure 9.8. This plot shows the voltage, temperature, and charge mode (as emitted by the main function). The presence of input charger voltage is a half sine wave (to simulate 50% sunlight on a set of solar panels). As shown, the battery charge maintains proper charge of the battery given the loading on the battery and presence of input current for battery charging.

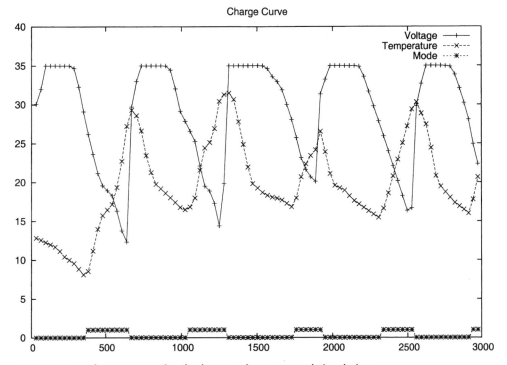

FIGURE 9.8 Charge curves for the battery charge control simulation.

While the simulation does not represent a true physical battery simulation, it models some of the basic concepts of loading and charging given the voltage and temperature constraints.

ADVANTAGES TO FUZZY LOGIC

There are a number of advantages to utilizing fuzzy logic in systems design. The fuzzy logic operators are simple like traditional Boolean logic operators. Therefore, they can be used by system operators to extend their knowledge of operation into the domain of membership functions and fuzzy logic rules, which linguistically are modeled by our own language.

For traditional systems developers, the complexity of the resulting system using fuzzy logic can be much simplified. Complex applications with a multitude of inputs and outputs can be modeled, and implemented, very simply using fuzzy logic.

Another interesting advantage is that fuzzy logic can reduce the processing requirements of a system and therefore decrease the expense of the resulting embedded control hardware. In many cases, complex mathematical modeling can be replaced with membership functions and a set of fuzzy rules to control a system. Minimizing these mathematical constraints can reduce code size and therefore allow the system to run more quickly, or on less advanced hardware.

OTHER APPLICATIONS

Fuzzy logic has been used in a variety of widely varying applications. Its most visible use is in control systems where fuzzy systems have had commercial success. Fuzzy logic has also been applied to self-focusing cameras, cement mixing systems, vehicle controls including anti-lock breaking systems, and even rules-based systems.

Probably the most successful applications are the ones that remain unknown. The name fuzzy logic itself doesn't promote a sense of reliability, though technically we know it is a sound method. As with many other AI methods, there exists a slow migration into the practical realm where someday fuzzy logic will not be associated with AI but instead seen as a visible standard technical solution.

SUMMARY

In this chapter, we've introduced fuzzy logic and fuzzy control. The fundamental fuzzy operators were defined using three very different applications (packet flow, target-tracking, and charge control). Hedge functions were also introduced as a linguistic modifier to existing fuzzy membership functions. A sample application of battery charge control was then detailed to identify how the membership functions and control elements were created using fuzzy semantics. Sample code was used to illustrate this concept, including a set of generic fuzzy logic APIs. Finally, some of the advantages of fuzzy logic were discussed including simplification and cost reduction of the hardware embodiment.

RESOURCES

Aptronix, Inc. (1996). "Why Use Fuzzy Logic," available online at *http://www.aptronix.com/fide/whyfuzzy.htm* (accessed January 17, 2003

Brule, James F. (1985). Fuzzy Systems—A Tutorial," available online eat *http://www.austinlinks.com/Fuzzy/tutorial.html* (accessed January 17, 2003)

Jantzen, Jan. (1998). "Tutorial on Fuzzy Logic." Technical Report no 98-E 868, University of Denmark, Department of Automation.

Zadeh, L.A. (1965). "Fuzzy sets." *Information and Control* 8:338–53.

10 | The Bigram Model

In this chapter, we'll look at the Markov model (named after the Russian mathematician, Andrei Markov), and a specific variation called the bigram model. These models can be very useful in describing processes that encompass a number of states and the probabilities associated with paths through these states. A number of very interesting applications exist for these models. We'll investigate the use of the bigram model for the automatic generation of interesting text.

INTRODUCTION TO MARKOV MODELS

A Markov Chain is simply a process that consists of a number of states with probabilities attached to the transitions between the states. For example, consider Figure 10.1.

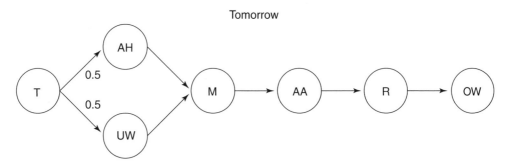

FIGURE 10.1 Example Markov Chain.

Figure 10.1 illustrates the pronunciation of the word "tomorrow." Two possible pronunciations are available within the diagram. The probability of the "**tah**morrow" pronunciation is 0.5, while the probability of the alternate "**tuw**morrow" pronunciation is also 0.5.

This is a very simple case, involving a decision at a single point within the chain. Each state involves the production of a phoneme. At the end of the chain, a completed pronunciation is available. We'll look more at the purpose for this in the applications section.

Next, let's look at a different application. Consider an email program that monitors the behavior of the user. When an email arrives, it observes what the user does with the email, and uses this information to learn how to automatically deal with subsequent emails. See the chain in Figure 10.2

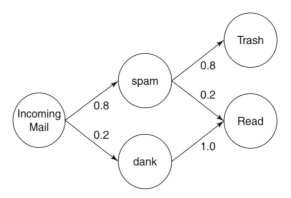

FIGURE 10.2 Learning user interaction with an email program.

Our email agent has observed that 8 out of 10 emails are spam, 2 out of 10 are from user "dank." The email agent further observes that 80% of the time, we delete the spam email without reading it. The other 20%, we read the email. From these probabilities, the email agent can deduce that we're more likely to delete the email than to read it. Using these probabilities provides an opportunity for the email agent to simplify our task of managing email.

In the examples shown here, a limited number of states and connections were defined. The Markov Chain can support a very large state space with very large numbers of connections to model very complex processes.

An interesting property of both examples is that the current state is always a function of the previous state, given a connection probability. This is called the "Markov Property." Additionally, since in our examples, a state can be reached by more than one previous state (for example, the "Read" state from Figure 10.2), these models are known as Hidden Markov Models (HMMs) or Hidden Markov Chains.

HMM APPROXIMATIONS

Note that in the prior examples, the current state of the chain was a function solely of the prior state of the chain with a defined probability. This is known as a bigram (a sequence of two words). If the current state were not a function of the prior state, the selection of state would simply be a random process. If the state were dependent upon the prior two states, it would be called a trigram. While increasing the dependence on the prior states (or context) can increase the usability of the chain (as we'll see in the applications section), the memory requirements on such models can be inhibitive [Henke 1999]. For example, consider Table 10.1 that shows the number of elements necessary for a vocabulary of 100 words.

TABLE 10.1 Context Size and the Number of Unique Elements.

n	Type	Number of Elements
2	bigram	10,000
3	trigram	1,000,000
4	4-gram	100,000,000

A corpus of 100 unique words is quite small, therefore creating anything other than bigrams over a corpus can be quite expensive.

INTERESTING APPLICATIONS

Let's now look at a few applications of Markov Chains for HMMs. The first example, speech recognition, is a practical method used to determine the words spoken in natural language processing. The following two examples are more thought provoking than useful, but provide a greater understanding of the possibilities with Markov Chains.

Speech Recognition

Recall from Figure 10.1 that the pronunciation of a word can take on one or more variations based upon the dialect or origin of the speaker. Building speech recognition systems then becomes very difficult, because the system must deal with a variety of pronunciations of a given word.

Hidden Markov Chains provide the opportunity to simplify speech recognition systems through probabilistic parsing of the phonemes of speech. For example, let's say that a speech system is designed to understand a handful of words, two of which are "tomorrow" and "today." When the system first hears the "tah" phoneme, the spoken word can be either "tomorrow" or "today." The next phoneme parsed from the speech is "m"; the probability that the word being spoken is "today" is now 0. Given our HMM, the "m" phoneme is a legal state, so we transition and then process the next phoneme. Given the probabilities at the transitions, the speech recognizer can use these to take the most likely path through the chain to identify the most likely phoneme that followed.

This example can be extended from phonemes to words. Given a set of words that can be understood by a speech recognizer, a Markov Chain can be created that identifies the probabilities of a given word following another. This would allow the recognizer to better identify which words were spoken, based upon their context (see Figure 10.3).

It's clear from these examples that HMMs can greatly simplify tasks such as speech recognition and speech understanding. In this example, the phoneme inputs caused the transition of states within the model to define words. Further, word inputs caused a transition for contextual understanding of a sentence. Next, we'll look at the use of HMMs to generate symbols based upon predefined or learned transition probabilities.

Modeling Text

In the previous examples, the Markov Chain was used to probabilistically identify the next state given the current state and an external stimulus. Let's now look at some examples where no external stimuli is provided—transi-

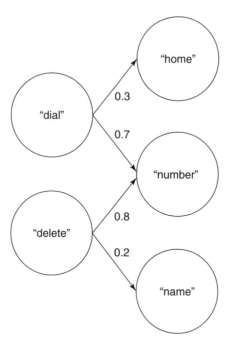

FIGURE 10.3 Higher level speech recognizer
Markov Chain.

tions between the states of the Markov Chain are based solely on the defined
probabilities as a random process.

In Figure 10.4, an example Markov Chain is shown for two sample sentences. The Markov Chain is a product of these two sentences, using the
bigram model.

The only non-unique word within this corpus is the word "is." With even
probability, the word "is" can lead either to the word "a" or "the." Note that
this now leads to four possible sentences that can be generated with the
Markov Chain (shown at the bottom of Figure 10.4).

Modeling Music

In a similar fashion to words, consider training the HMM from a vocabulary
of musical notes from a given composer [Zhang 2001]. The HMM could then
be used to compose a symphony via the probabilistic generation of notes with

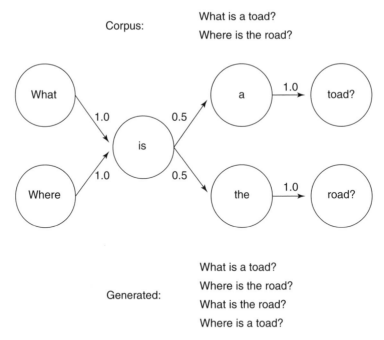

FIGURE 10.4 Sample bigram from a corpus of seven unique words.

a style of the given composer. Consider also the training of an HMM from a vocabulary of two or more composers. With a large enough n-gram, symphonies could be arranged from the combinations of great composers.

SAMPLE APPLICATION

Some suggest, using higher approximations of the HMM, that it might be possible to mimic the works of great writers such as Shakespeare [Zhang 2001]. By training the HMM with a corpus of the author's text, the HMM could then be used to emit sequences of words that are statistically similar to those from the training corpus.

For the sample application, we'll discuss the implementation of a bigram HMM that can be trained with arbitrary text. The HMM will then be used to generate random sequences of characters.

ON THE CD The source code for the bigram HMM can be found on the CD-ROM at ./software/ch10/bigram/.

SOURCE DISCUSSION

The source for parsing text into bigram chains and then building sentences from them is surprisingly simple. The bigram is implemented as a simple two-dimensional array. Each dimension is represented by the unique words that were parsed from the text. The first dimension is the first word of a bigram and the second dimension is the word that follows. The contents of the two-dimensional array at this intersection are the number of times that the second word follows the first.

Listing 10.1 contains the symbolic constants and global variables that are used within the program.

Listing 10.1   Symbolic Constants and Global Variables.

```
#define MAX_WORD_LEN      40
#define MAX_WORDS         1000

#define FIRST_WORD 0
#define MIDDLE_WORD       1
#define LAST_WORD         2

#define START_SYMBOL      0
#define END_SYMBOL 1

static int curWord = 2;

char wordVector[MAX_WORDS][MAX_WORD_LEN];

int  bigramArray[MAX_WORDS][MAX_WORDS];
int  sumVector[MAX_WORDS];
```

The largest word possible is 40 characters (MAX_WORD_LEN) and the maximum number of unique words is 1000 (MAX_WORDS). The curWord variable identifies the current word index in the wordVector and bigramArray. Symbols START_SYMBOL and END_SYMBOL represent the indices for the start and end states of our Markov Chain. Finally, the symbols FIRST_WORD, MIDDLE_WORD, and LAST_WORD are used to identify the context of a particular word (and whether it will affect the start or end of the Markov Chain).

The main program for the bigram demonstration is very simple and shown in Listing 10.2. The two major steps performed are parsing the input file that contains the corpus (parseFile), and then emitting a sentence based upon the training file (buildSentence).

Listing 10.2 Main Program.

```
int main( int argc, char *argv[] )
{
  char filename[40];
  int  debug = 0;

  /* Parse the options from the command line */
  parseOptions( argv, argc, &debug, filename );

  /* Seed the random number generator */
  srand(time(NULL));

  bzero(bigramArray, sizeof(bigramArray));

  strcpy(wordVector[0], "<START>");
  strcpy(wordVector[1], "<END>");

  /* Parse the Corpus */
  parseFile( filename );

  if (debug) emitMatrix();

  /* Randomly generate a sentence */
  buildSentence();

  return 0;
}
```

The remaining elements of the main program are parsing command-line options to alter the behavior of the program, and initializing the necessary structures. An important element to note here is the initialization of wordVector. Recall that wordVector is a list of the unique words that were found in the training set. Two symbols are loaded into wordVector to identify the start of a chain and the end. The start of the chain is always defined as element zero of wordVector, and the end of the chain as element one. All subsequent offsets represent unique words found within the corpus.

The program accepts two options, a "-f" to specify a filename for the corpus and a "-v" to enable verbose (or debug) mode. In the debug mode, the bigram array is emitted to show exactly what was parsed from the file (see Listing 10.3).

Listing 10.3   parseOptions **Function.**

```
void parseOptions( char *argv[], int argc, int *dbg, char *fname )
{
  int opt, error = 1;

  *dbg = 0;

  if (argc > 1) {

    while ((opt = getopt(argc, argv, "vf:")) != -1) {

      switch(opt) {

        case 'v':
          /* Verbose Mode */
          *dbg = 1;
          break;

        case 'f':
          /* Filename option */
          strcpy(fname, optarg);
          error = 0;
          break;

        default:
          /* Any other option is an error */
          error = 1;

      }

    }

  }
```

```
    if (error) {
      printf("\nUsage is : \n\n");
      printf("\t%s -f <filename> -v\n\n", argv[0]);
      printf("\t\t -f corpus filename\n\t\t -v verbose mode\n\n");
      exit(0);
    }

    return;
  }
```

The parseOptions function uses the standard getopt function to simplify the parsing of command-line options.

The parseFile function is used to extract the word relationships from the user-defined corpus (see Listing 10.4).

Listing 10.4   parseFile Function.

```
void parseFile( char *filename )
{
  FILE *fp;
  int  inp, index = 0;
  char word[MAX_WORD_LEN+1];
  int  first = 1;

  fp = fopen(filename, "r");

  while (!feof(fp)) {

    inp = fgetc(fp);

    if (inp == EOF) {

      if (index > 0) {
        /* For the last word, update the matrix accordingly */
        word[index++] = 0;
        loadWord(word, LAST_WORD);
        index = 0;
      }

    } else if (((char)inp == 0x0d) || ((char)inp == 0x0a) ||
                ((char)inp == ' ')) {

      if (index > 0) {
```

```
        word[index++] = 0;
        if (first) {
          /* First word in a sequence */
          loadWord(word, FIRST_WORD);
          index = 0;
          first = 0;
        } else {
          /* Middle word of a sequence */
          loadWord(word, MIDDLE_WORD);
          index = 0;
        }
      }

    } else if (((char)inp == '.') || ((char)inp == '?')) {

      /* Handle punctuation by ending the current sequence */
      word[index++] = 0;
      loadWord(word, MIDDLE_WORD);
      loadWord(word, LAST_WORD);
      index = 0;
      first = 1;

    } else {

      /* Skip white space */
      if (((char)inp != 0x0a) && ((char)inp != ',')) {
        word[index++] = (char)inp;
      }

    }

  }

  fclose(fp);
}
```

The parseFile function accepts a filename that contains the training data. The goal of the parseFile function is to extract the individual words from the file and then load them into the wordVector and bigramArray structures in a meaningful way (using the loadWord function). By meaningful we mean the loading must take into account the order in which the word was found. Was it the first word in a sentence, the last, or simply a word in the middle? Depending upon the word order, we call the loadWord function with a symbol defining the order in which the word was found. The function also properly parses word context from end-of-file markers, carriage-returns and line-feeds, and a number of punctuation symbols.

The `loadWord` function, in Listing 10.5, updates the bigram structures for the word and its defined order within the stream.

Listing 10.5   `loadWord` Function.

```
void loadWord( char *word, int order )
{
  int wordIndex;
  static int lastIndex = START_SYMBOL;

  /* First, see if the word has already been recorded */
  for (wordIndex = 2 ; wordIndex < curWord ; wordIndex++) {
    if (!strcmp(wordVector[wordIndex], word)) {
      break;
    }
  }

  if (wordIndex == curWord) {

    if (curWord == MAX_WORDS) {
      printf("\nToo may words, increase MAX_WORDS\n\n");
      exit(-1);
    }

    /* Doesn't exist, add it in */
    strcpy(wordVector[curWord++], word);
  }

  /* At this point, we have a wordIndex that points to the current
       word
   * vector.
   */

  if (order == FIRST_WORD) {

    /* Load word as the start of a sequence */
    bigramArray[START_SYMBOL][wordIndex]++;
    sumVector[START_SYMBOL]++;

  } else if (order == LAST_WORD) {
```

```
      /* Load word as the end of a sequence */
      bigramArray[wordIndex][END_SYMBOL]++;
      bigramArray[END_SYMBOL][wordIndex]++;
      sumVector[END_SYMBOL]++;

  } else {

      /* Load word as the middle of a sequence */
      bigramArray[lastIndex][wordIndex]++;
      sumVector[lastIndex]++;

  }

  lastIndex = wordIndex;

  return;
}
```

Function `loadWord` must first identify whether the current word is unique (never been seen before). A quick scan of the `wordVector` array provides for this. If the word is new, we create a new slot for it in the `wordVector` array and update the `wordVector` limit accordingly (`curWord`).

Now we have the index within the `wordVector` array for our word. Using the order argument, (which defines the order in which the word appeared within the text), we update the `bigramArray`. If the word was the first in the sentence, we update the START_SYMBOL row (the first row in the table), and increment the column offset defined by the `wordIndex`. We also update the sum or the row as defined by the `sumVector` array (used to calculate the relative probabilities for each word).

If the order of the current word is the last word, then we update the `bigramArray` using the word as the first dimension of the array and the LAST_SYMBOL as the second dimension. Finally, if the word is in the middle, we use the last word as the first index and the current word as the second index. The last word is always saved within the function within the `lastIndex` variable. See Figure 10.5 for a representation of a sample sentence.

This completes the parsing and filling in of the bigram array. The next two functions provide for emitting a sentence using the bigram array as the model.

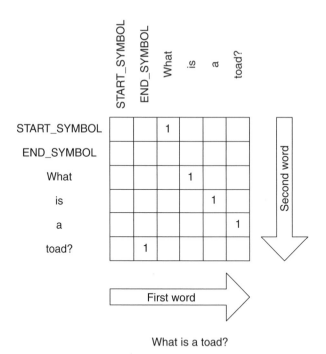

FIGURE 10.5 `bigramArray` for the sample sentence.

Function `buildSentence` walks through the `bigramArray` structure using the `sumVector` array to determine which path to take and thus which words to emit (see Listing 10.6).

Listing 10.6 Function `buildSentence`.

```
int buildSentence( void )
{
  int word = START_SYMBOL;
  int max = 0;

  printf("\n");

  /* Start with a random word */
  word = nextWord(word);

  /* Loop until we've reached the end of the random sequence */
```

```c
  while (word != END_SYMBOL) {

    /* Emit the current word */
    printf("%s ", wordVector[word]);

    /* Choose the next word */
    word = nextWord(word);

    /* Only allow a maximum number of words */
    max += getRand(12) + 1;

    /* If we've reached the end, break */
    if (max >= 100) break;

  }

  /* Emit a backspace, '.' and a blank line */
  printf("%c.\n\n", 8);

  return 0;
}
```

The `buildSentence` function creates a path through the `bigramArray` using the probabilities that are defined by the contents of the `bigramArray`. Recall that the intersection of two words within the array is the count of the number of times the second word followed the first word. A random count (`max`) is also accrued during the walk to limit the number of words that are emitted.

Function `buildSentence` uses the `nextWord` function to determine the next word in the chain (the next step through the Markov path). See Listing 10.7.

Listing 10.7   Function nextWord.

```c
int nextWord( int word )
{
  int nextWord = (word + 1);
  int max = sumVector[word];
  int lim, sum = 0;

  /* Define a limit for the roulette selection */
  lim = getRand(max)+1;

  while (nextWord != word) {
```

```
    /* Bound the limit of the array using modulus */
    nextWord = nextWord % curWord;

    /* Keep a sum of the occurrences (for the roulette wheel) */
    sum += bigramArray[word][nextWord];

    /* If we've reached our limit, return the current word */
    if (sum >= lim) {
      return nextWord;
    }

    /* For the current word (row), go to the next word column */
    nextWord++;

  }

  return nextWord;
}
```

Function nextWord uses a form of roulette wheel selection to determine the next step based upon the probabilities of the steps. A limit is defined as a random number from one to sumVector for the row (total counts for all words that follow the current). Using the random limit (lim), we walk through the row incrementing a sum variable. When the sum variable is greater than or equal to our limit, we use the current word as the next step in the path. Otherwise, we continue to sum until the limit is reached. Probabilistically, this means that words with higher counts will be selected more often for the path.

Finally, a debug function that is used when the program is in debug mode is shown in Listing 10.8 (emitMatrix). This function is used to emit the bigramArray as well as the sumVector array.

Listing 10.8   Function emitMatrix.

```
void emitMatrix( void )
{
  int x, y;

  printf("\n");
  for (x = 0 ; x < curWord ; x++) {
    printf("%20s : ", wordVector[x]);
    for ( y = 0 ; y < curWord ; y++) {
      printf("%d ", bigramArray[x][y]);
```

```
      }
      printf(" : %d\n", sumVector[x]);
    }
  }
```

SAMPLES

Let's now look at some samples of the algorithm using a variety of different text inputs.

In the first example, a set of quotes from Albert Einstein was used as the training file. This training set consists of 13 quotes with 377 unique words. See Listing 10.9 for example products from the Einstein corpus.

Listing 10.9   Emitted Text from Albert Einstein Quotes.

```
[root@plato bigram]./bigram —f einstein

Imagination is shipwrecked by language and other symbolic devices.


[root@plato bigram]./bigram —f einstein

We all ruled in the authority of imagination.
```

Each of the generated quotes from Listing 10.9 sound reasonable and is actually thought provoking.

Consider now generated text from a corpus of Albert Camus' *Absurd Man* (see Listing 10.10).

Listing 10.10   Emitted Text from Albert Camus' *Absurd Man*.

```
[root@plato bigram]./bigram —f absurdman

It is to speak only truth that is the breath of future actions.


[root@plato bigram]./bigram —f absurdman
```

```
"My field" said Goethe "is time and unfolds in a disservice to
make.
```

Finally, consider a Markov Chain that was created from two separate works (see Listing 10.11). The first work is the poem "Ode to Joy" by anonymous, and the second from book one of *The Odyssey* by Homer.

Listing 10.11   Emitted Text from a Collection of Works.

```
[root@plato bigram]./bigram –f combo

From chaos and beasts and hostile shores!  From the woods the
hunter strayed.
```

OWNERSHIP?

While the Markov Chain could be used to mimic a symphony, or the generation of text that appears similar to other literature, the question arises as to who owns the new work? The Markov Chain can emit music or text that is modeled after the original training data. Therefore, while the result is very similar to the original author's work, it is a new statistical representation of the original work.

When trigram or larger models are used to model the original work, the complexity and coherence of the resulting work will be extremely interesting.

SUMMARY

In this chapter, we investigated Markov Chains and the bigram model for text generation. Markov Chains can be used in a variety of applications, from spelling checkers to the confirmation of the authorship of an unknown work. The applications of speech recognition and text and music modeling were discussed as well as an implementation of a bigram text generator that emits interesting phrases. Finally, the issue of legal ownership was touched upon since emitted works of Markov Chains are based solely on the statistical representations of another author's work.

REFERENCES

[Henke 1999] Henke, Jonathon. (1999). "Statistical Inference: n-gram Models over Sparse Data", TDM Seminar. Available online at *http://www.sims.berkeley.edu/courses/is296a-4/ f99/Lectures/henke-ch6.ppt* (accessed January 17, 2003)

[Zheng 2001] Zheng, Byoung-Tak. (2001). "Course 4190.515: Bioinformatics (Machine Learning)," Seoul National University School of Computer Science and Engineering. Available online at *http://bi.snu.ac.kr/Courses/g-ai01/g-ai01.html* (accessed January 17, 2003)

RESOURCES

Baker, J.K. (1975). "Stochastic Modeling for Automatic Speech Understanding." In R. Reddy (ed.), *Speech Recognition* (pp. 521–42). Academic Press.

Baldi, P., and S. Brunak. (1998). *Bioinformatics: The Machine Learning Approach*. Cambridge, Mass.: MIT Press.

Shannon, C. E. (1948). "A mathematical theory of communication," *Bell System Technical Journal* 27(July and October): 379–423 and 623–56.

Shannon, C. E. (1951). "Prediction and Entropy of Printed English," *Bell System Technical Journal* 30:50–64.

11   Agent-Based Software

In this chapter, we'll investigate the topic of agent computing. We'll discuss the broad range of software agents in terms of their applications as well as introduce their various attributes and models. To demonstrate some agent capabilities, we'll build a news-filtering agent that uses two standard Internet protocols to present targeted information to a user.

WHAT IS AN AGENT?

Alan Kay, an original proponent of agency, defined an agent as a software robot that given a goal could act in the place of a user within the domain of the computer's world. If the agent became stuck, it could ask for advice from its user to continue to act on the user's behalf [Kay 1984]. Recently, this concept has been adopted for the development of "Bots," which exist within the Internet to provide capabilities to their user's.

Agents are also called intelligent agents, as intelligence is a key component of agency. While agents can take a variety of forms, some consider agents to be surrogates on a network or the Internet that could fulfill some activity useful to their user in the real world [King 1995]. The agent would be endowed with the wishes of its user and then make any necessary decisions while communicating with other agents (possibly representing other users). An example selling agent of this type may find other buying agents at specially created auction hosts to sell goods for their user. These agents could also deceptively act as buyers, in order to identify the costs of a similar good for sale and adjust their prices accordingly.

These concepts can open the definition of agency to a large variety of programs. Therefore, rather than specify exactly what an agent is, we'll discuss some of the attributes of agents initially and then return to provide a taxonomy of agents.

Agent Attributes

Agents can have one or more attributes, as defined in Table 11.1. This section discusses each of these attributes.

TABLE 11.1   Common Attributes for Software Agents.

Attribute	Definition
Autonomous	Operate independently from its user
Adaptive	Learns while it operates
Communicative	Communicates with its user or other agents
Collaborative	Works with other agents to reach its goal
Personal	Exhibit believable character behavior (emotion)
Mobile	Can move around its environment

One of the primary attributes that is associated with software agents is *autonomy*. An agent is autonomous if it operates without the constant direction of a human. Being autonomous implies that the agent has one or more goals that can be achieved. While goal-orientedness can be viewed as a separate attribute, it is a necessary element of autonomy and therefore covered as a subordinate. Having goals can also imply that the agent has the ability to plan; this brings us to the adaptive characteristic.

An agent is *adaptive* if it can change its behavior based upon its experience. Being adaptive means that the agent has the ability to learn and reason about its environment and own knowledge. While this is the most intriguing aspect of agency, it is also the most difficult and therefore is commonly found only in very domain-specific agents.

The ability to *communicate* is also a very important characteristic of agents. The agent must be able to communicate with its user to identify its goals or initial information as well as communicate within its environment. For example, a search agent that identifies Web pages of interest must be able to communicate using the HTTP (HyperText Transfer Protocol) in order to connect to Web sites and gather Web pages. A related attribute is the ability to communicate with other agents.

An agent is *collaborative* if it communicates with other agents in order to achieve its goals. For example, agents that act on behalf of their users in auction environments can communicate to broker deals given information by their users. Collaborative agents are commonly studied under the name *multiagent systems*, as multiple agents are required for collaboration. This attribute is very important for software agents and is therefore a widely studied and researched characteristic.

For some special agents, the ability to exhibit a *personality* can be important. Such agents are commonly found in entertainment, but research in the domain of emotion has found that intelligence and emotion are linked. Therefore, allowing an interface agent to exhibit a personality that changes with the information to be portrayed can simplify our ability to understand what the agent is trying to communicate. For example, if we try to communicate information without changing our expression, it can be difficult for the receiver to understand exactly what we're trying to get across. The information encoded within our expression represents meta-data for our actual message and therefore providing this ability to certain classes of agents can be important.

Finally, some agents are provided with *mobility*, or the ability to move within their environment. This may seem like an odd attribute but can be important in some circumstances. For example, consider an agent that communicates with a remote database to gather information. In the traditional case, the host communicates with the remote database, gathers the defined information, and then filters this information for the user based upon the specific criteria. Given mobility, an agent could be dispatched to the remote database to automatically filter the results and then return only what was required by the end user. This provides both network-bandwidth savings and a simpler architecture, especially when the two hosts can be disconnected from one another for durations.

To be classified as an agent, not all of the attributes must be demonstrated. In most cases, only two or more are used. In our simple application, to be discussed later, the autonomous and communicative attributes will be applied to a news-filtering agent.

Agent Taxonomy

Let's now return to a broader scope of agents and identify some of the higher-level types that exist using the previously defined attributes (see Figure 11.1).

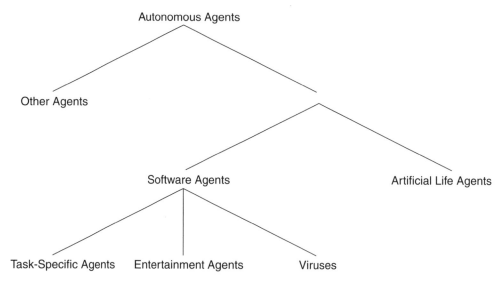

FIGURE 11.1 Franklin and Graesser's agent taxonomy.

As we're interested only in agents that operate autonomously, we'll use Franklin and Graesser's 1996 taxonomy [Franklin and Graesser 1996]. While there are many other classifications, we'll focus specifically on the software-agents variety from Franklin and Graesser's taxonomy.

Task-Specific Agents

A task-specific agent is one that is deployed to solve a specific problem. An example of a task-specific agent is a Web search agent. In addition to performing searches given the user's constraints, a Web search agent also monitors which of the returned links the user follows. This provides a weighting scheme for searches to help better sort the results with the hope of providing the user what they want more quickly. The Web search agent could also operate in the background, doing earlier searches to see if new information has become available, and then presenting this to the user.

In addition to being autonomous, the Web search agent is adaptive as it learns what the user is most interested in based upon his behavior (i.e., what links they actually follow).

Another example of a task-specific agent is an auction agent. An auction agent could act on a user's behalf to purchase goods on the Internet with the goal of paying the lowest price possible. It could do this through collaboration with other auction agents. In trying to find other users that are attempting to purchase similar items, a cooperative bulk purchase could be made with the intent that a lower overall price would be paid.

Entertainment Agents

Entertainment agents are a new type of agent that exist for creating a socially intelligent agent. This type of agent is useful for acting in a social capacity, interacting in virtual worlds, or presenting a persona as a user interface to disseminate information. For example, the Ananova agent from Ananova Ltd. is a talking head that reads news using graphical lip-syncing. The Ananova agent also exhibits natural-looking head motion to make the character more believable.

The Ananova agent has personal and communicative characteristics. By its nature, the Ananova agent exhibits something of a personality, though it has difficulty exhibiting emotion while it provides the news. Ananova is also communicative, it lip-syncs with its text-to-speech interface to look like a newscaster reading the news.

Viruses

A virus could be called instead a malicious mobile software agent. While a virus may not be adaptive, it is autonomous and, more importantly, mobile. Instead of using a specific agent-based protocol to migrate around a network, the virus utilizes standard protocols to distribute itself. The most common protocol used is the mail transport protocol, SMTP (Simple Mail Transport Protocol).

Giving mobility to less malicious agents can also be provided through a mobile agent framework. One such framework is IBM's Aglet framework that is freely downloadable from the Internet (see the Resources section).

GIVING AGENTS INTELLIGENCE

While making an agent intelligent is not a simple task, there are a variety of methods that can be used to endow an agent with reasonable decision-making capabilities. Some of these methods are discussed within this book (see Figure 11.2).

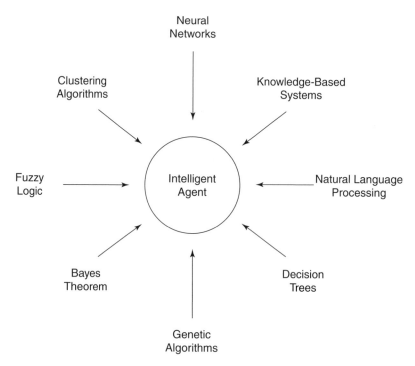

FIGURE 11.2 Providing agents with decision-making capabilities.

The creation of game AI characters is discussed in Chapter 5 using the backpropagation neural network model. One key characteristic of neural networks is that they're not only capable of generalizing (making good decisions for unforeseen circumstances); they also can adaptively modify their behavior given changes in their environment.

The use of forward-chaining, rules-based systems is discussed in Chapter 8. The rules-based system permits an agent to reason about its environment given a set of rules and facts that describe its environment. An important characteristic of rules-based systems is that they can describe their line of reasoning (what facts lead to a particular decision).

Clustering algorithms (such as adaptive resonance theory, described in Chapter 3) are another useful technique for agent intelligence. These algorithms permit agents to identify relationships within their environment. This can help an agent learn patterns without any instruction (unsupervised learning).

Numerous other methods can be used, some of which were described in prior chapters. Fuzzy logic is also useful as an element for intelligent agents (described in Chapter 9), as is simulated annealing (described in Chapter 2) for constraint satisfaction.

SAMPLE APPLICATION

Let's now look at a very simple example of an agent that provides a service to a user under the classification of a filtering agent. The purpose of the agent is to communicate with news services on the Internet and to collect information of interest to the user based upon the user's predefined criteria. The filtering agent will then provide the information back to the user in the order most applicable to the user's request (information that scores best based upon the search terms).

WebAgent Design

The WebAgent is constructed using a variety of standard protocols, and utilizes the standard Web browser to report results back to the user. The WebAgent utilizes a HyperText Transfer Protocol (HTTP) server to communicate with a user, an HTTP client to communicate with external servers, and a Network News Transfer Protocol (NNTP) client to communicate with external news sources (see Figure 11.3).

The WebAgent will serve as an application that mediates between the user and the Internet for news reading. The user configures the WebAgent through a simple configuration file (to be detailed later). In this configuration file, the user defines Web pages to monitor (report if they change) and newsgroups to monitor for specific search criteria. When news items are found that match a given criteria, the item is saved and delivered to the user through a simple Web page in order of most search terms matched. The user can then click on the link for the particular monitored Web site or news item and be taken directly to that content.

The goal of the agent is to simplify news reading for a user, filtering out content that may not be of interest and presenting first what should be of most interest to the user.

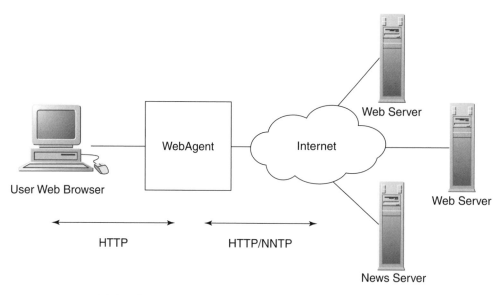

FIGURE 11.3 High-level architecture for the WebAgent.

WebAgent Characteristics

The WebAgent represents a very simple agent and includes no learning ability. Its characteristics include autonomy (it works in the background without user direction) and its communicative ability with external servers for data collection.

The WebAgent's sensors are the standard application layer protocols that allow it to gather the information that it needs for its user based upon predefined search criteria. The HTTP Web protocol is also used to communicate results back to the user. The user then connects to the WebAgent just as it would any other Web server.

The source code for the WebAgent application can be found on the CD-ROM at ./software/ch11.

SOURCE DISCUSSION

Let's now walk through the source for the WebAgent. To more easily understand the overall structure of the WebAgent, consider the data flow in Figure 11.4.

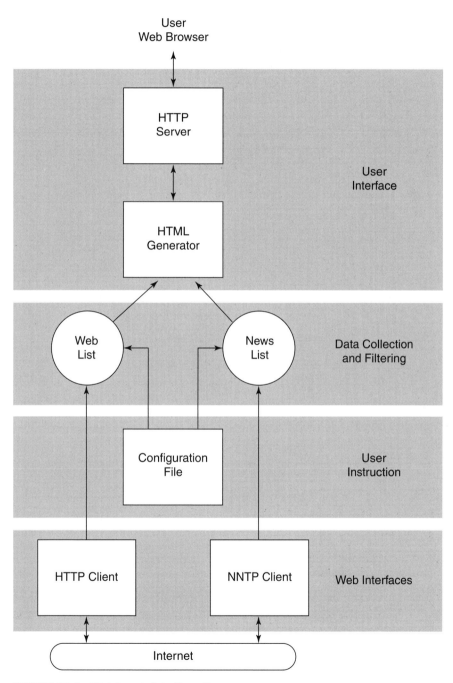

FIGURE 11.4 WebAgent data flow diagram.

Data collection occurs on a timed basis (every 10 minutes), which feeds data up to the data repositories. Using the search criteria stored in the configuration file (predefined by the user), the data is pruned. When the user requests the current information via the Web page, the HTML generator constructs a dynamic Web page that is served back through the HTTP server (see Figure 11.5).

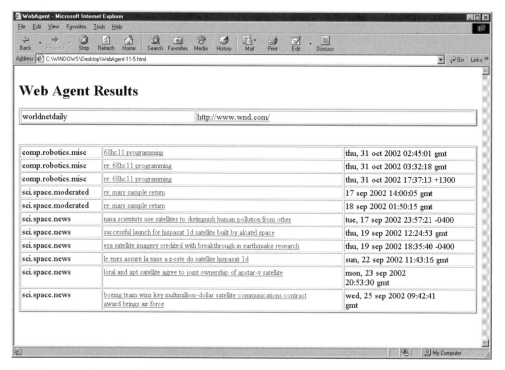

FIGURE 11.5   Sample view of the WebAgent Web page.

The user can then view specific news items by clicking on the links (see Figure 11.6).

When the user completes reading the articles of interest, the "Mark Read" button can be depressed to clear the current news set. This is saved at the WebAgent so that these news items will not be seen again.

While the configuration is defined in a file outside of the WebAgent, the user can review the configuration settings through the WebAgent. The cur-

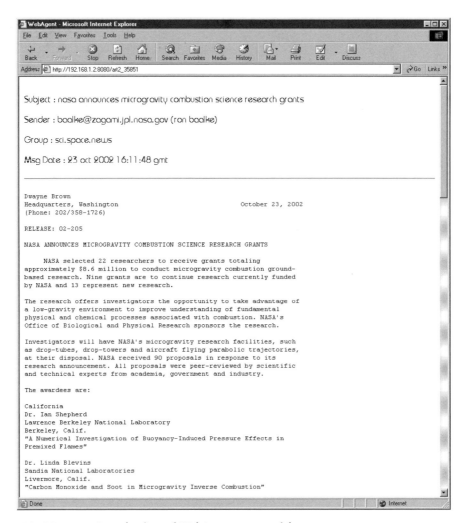

FIGURE 11.6 Sample view of WebAgent news article.

rent configuration settings are presented by requesting the file config.html (see Figure 11.7).

The following sections will describe the WebAgent software in the layers as defined by Figure 11.4. The Web interfaces layer provides the ability to communicate with external data servers using standard protocols. User instruction layer defines how a user will instill the agent its knowledge of the user's search constraints. The data collection and filtering layer performs

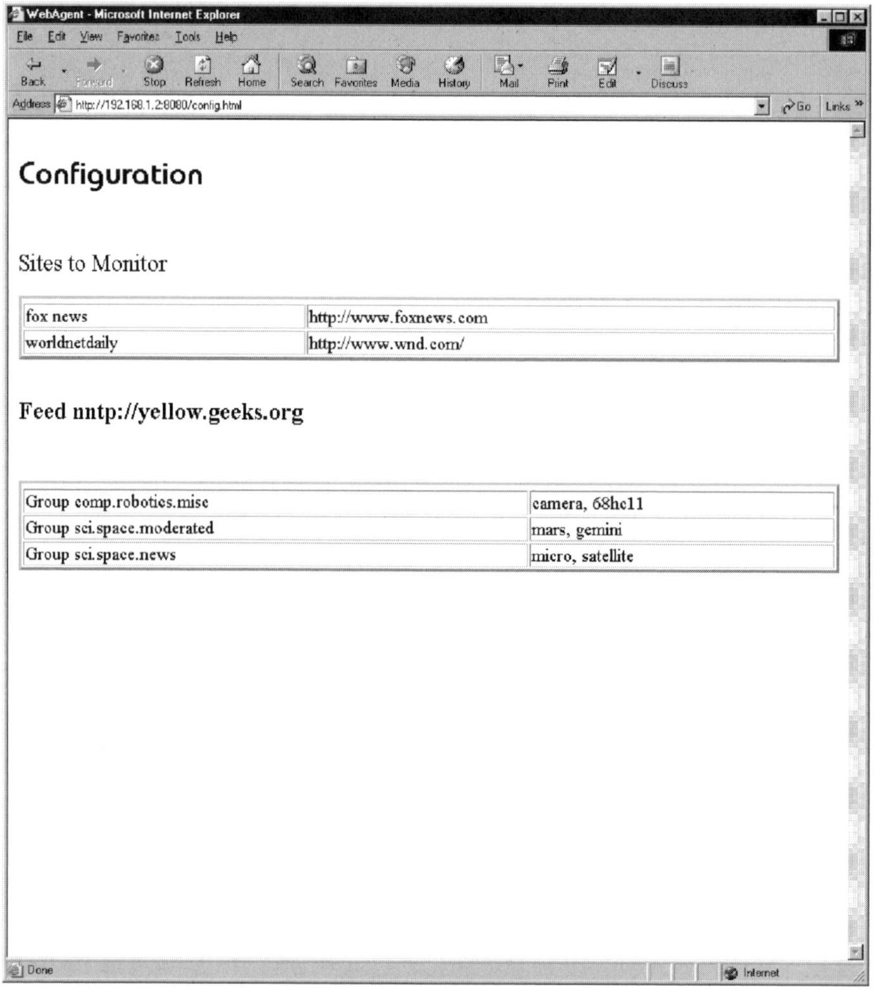

FIGURE 11.7 Viewing the configuration of the WebAgent.

the actual filtering of incoming data per the user's instruction. Finally, the user interface layer provides the HTTP server for viewing of filtered news.

Web Interfaces

The WebAgent implements simple versions of the NNTP client interface and HTTP client interface. A simple HTTP server is also implemented, which will be covered in the user interface section.

Simple HTTP Client

The HTTP client's purpose is site monitoring. We want to know when a Web site has changed, so that the user can be notified. To do this, the HTTP client interface implements a simple version of the GET request. The purpose of the GET request is to specify a file on the remote server and then to collect the file through the socket. We're interested only in the header, specifically the "Content-Length" header element. This element tells us the size of the actual content (the size of the file). We use the file size as an indication of whether the file has changed. It's not perfect, but unfortunately, not all servers send the modified header element.

The monitorSite function utilizes the monitor's structure array to know which sites to monitor (this structure initialization will be discussed later). Function monitorSite is shown in Listing 11.1.

Listing 11.1   Simple HTTP Client Interface.

```
typedef struct {
  int   active;
  char url[MAX_URL_SIZE];
  char urlName[MAX_SEARCH_ITEM_SIZE+1];
  int   length;
  int   changed;
  int   shown;
} monitorEntryType;


int monitorSite( int siteIndex )
{
  int ret=0, sock, result, len;
  struct sockaddr_in servaddr;
  char buffer[MAX_BUFFER+1];
  char fqdn[80];

  extern monitorEntryType monitors[];

  /* Create a new client socket */
  sock = socket(AF_INET, SOCK_STREAM, 0);

  prune( monitors[siteIndex].url, fqdn );

  memset(&servaddr, 0, sizeof(servaddr));
```

```
        servaddr.sin_family = AF_INET;
        servaddr.sin_port = htons( 80 );

        /* Try and resolve the address */
        servaddr.sin_addr.s_addr = inet_addr( fqdn );

        /* If the target was not an IP address, then it must be a fully
         * qualified domain name. Try to use the DNS resolver to resolve
         * the name to an address.
         */
        if ( servaddr.sin_addr.s_addr == 0xffffffff ) {
          struct hostent *hptr =
            (struct hostent *)gethostbyname( fqdn );
          if ( hptr == NULL ) {
            close(sock);
            return -1;
          } else {
            struct in_addr **addrs;
            addrs = (struct in_addr **)hptr->h_addr_list;
            memcpy( &servaddr.sin_addr, *addrs, sizeof(struct in_addr)
);
          }
        }

        /* Connect to the defined HTTP server */
        result = connect(sock,
                      (struct sockaddr_in *)&servaddr,
sizeof(servaddr));

        if (result == 0) {

          /* Perform a simple HTTP GET command */
          strcpy(buffer, "GET / HTTP/1.0\n\n");

          len = write(sock, buffer, strlen(buffer) );

          if ( len == strlen(buffer) ) {
            char *cur;

            len = grabResponse( sock, buffer );

            cur = strstr(buffer, "Content-Length:");

            if (cur != NULL) {
```

```
        int curLen;

        sscanf(buffer, "Content-Length: %d", &curLen);

        if (len != monitors[siteIndex].length) {
          monitors[siteIndex].shown = 0;
          monitors[siteIndex].changed = 1;
          monitors[siteIndex].length = len;
          ret = 1;
        }

      }

    }

  }

  close(sock);

  return(ret);
}
```

The monitorEntryType structure includes an URL (Uniform Resource Locator), otherwise known as the Web address. The urlName is a simple textual description (the name of the Web site being monitored). The length field holds the cached length of the Web site, used to determine if the site has changed.

The monitorSite function implements a very simple client socket application. A socket is created using the socket function. The URL is pruned using the prune function to take an address in the form *http://www.mtjones.com/* and translate it to *www.mtjones.com* (not shown in text, see CD-ROM).

ON THE CD

The final address (called a fully-qualified domain name) can then be resolved using a client resolver (resolve from an FQDN to an IP address). Using the IP address, we can connect to the remote site. Note that our address could be an FQDN or a simple IP address. Therefore, we try the inet_addr function first to convert a string IP address to a numeric IP address. If this doesn't work, the resolver (interfaced via the gethostbyname function) will convert the name into an IP address using an external domain name server (DNS).

Once we have a numeric IP address (within the servaddr structure), we try to connect to the remote server using the connect function. This function creates a bidirectional connection between the two endpoints that can be used for communication. Since we're connecting to the HTTP port on the remote server (port 80), we know that the application layer protocol used on this socket is HTTP. We issue the GET command and then await the response from the server with the `grabResponse` function (see Listing 11.2). Using the response, returned in buffer, we search for the "`Content-Length:`" header element, and store the value associated with it. If there's a change in the length (from the stored length), we mark this as changed so that it will show up in the filtering layer.

Listing 11.2 Retrieving an HTTP Response.

```
int grabResponse( int sock, char *buf )
{
  int i, len, stop, state, bufIdx;

  if (buf == NULL) return -1;

  len = bufIdx = state = stop = 0;

  while (!stop) {

    if (bufIdx+len > MAX_BUFFER - 80) break;

    len = read( sock, &buf[bufIdx], (MAX_BUFFER-bufIdx) );

    /* Search for the end-of-mail indicator in the current buffer
     */
    for ( i = bufIdx ; i < bufIdx+len ; i++ ) {
      if       ( (state == 0) && (buf[i] == 0x0d) ) state = 1;
      else if ( (state == 1) && (buf[i] == 0x0a) ) state = 2;
      else if ( (state == 2) && (buf[i] == 0x0d) ) state = 3;
      else if ( (state == 3) && (buf[i] == 0x0a) ) { stop = 1;
        break; }
      else state = 0;
    }

    bufIdx += len;

  }

  bufIdx -= 3;
  buf[bufIdx] = 0;
```

```
    return bufIdx;
}
```

The HTTP response is terminated (as the request) with two carriage-return/line-feed pairs. A simple state machine (shown in Listing 11.2) reads data from the socket until this pattern is found. Once found, the loop is terminated and a NULL is added to the end of the buffer.

This is the basis for a simple HTTP client. For each site that's monitored, a socket is created to the site and an HTTP request sent. The response is then captured to parse the length of the resulting content. This value is used to determine if the site has changed since the last check.

Simple NTTP Client

The NNTP client provides a simple API to communicate with news servers. The API allows an application to connect to a news server (nntpConnect), set the group of interest (nntpSetGroup), peek at the header of a news message (nntpPeek), retrieve the entire news message (nntpRetrieve), parse the news message (nntpParse), skip the current news message (nntpSkip), and close the connection to the news server (nntpClose).

NNTP is an interactive command-response protocol that is entirely ASCII-text based. By opening a simple telnet session to port 119 of the NNTP server (see Listing 11.3) we can carry out a dialog with the server. User input is shown in bold.

Listing 11.3   Sample Interaction with an NNTP Server.

```
root@plato /root]# telnet localhost 119
S: 201 plato.mtjones.com DNEWS Version 5.5d1, SO, posting OK
C: list
S: 215 list of newsgroups follows
S: control 2 3 y
S: control.cancel 2 3 y
S: my.group 10 3 y
S: new.group 6 3 y
S: .
C: group my.group
S: 211 8 3 10 my.group selected
C: article 3
S: 220 3 <3C36AF8E.1BD3047E@mtjones.com> article retrieved
S: Message-ID: <3C36AF8E.1BD3047E@mtjones.com>
```

```
S: Date: Sat, 05 Jan 2002 00:47:27 -0700
S: From: "M. Tim Jones" <mtj@mtjones.com>
S: X-Mailer: Mozilla 4.74 [en] (Win98; U)
S: X-Accept-Language: en
S: MIME-Version: 1.0
S: Newsgroups: my.group
S: Subject: this is my post
S: Content-Type: text/plain; charset=us-ascii
S: Content-Transfer-Encoding: 7bit
S: NNTP-Posting-Host: sartre.mtjones.com
S: X-Trace: plato.mtjones.com 1010328764 sartre.mtjones.com (6 Jan
2002 07:52:44 -0700)
S: Lines: 6
S: Path: plato.mtjones.com
S: Xref: plato.mtjones.com my.group:3
S:
S:
S: Hello
S:
S: This is my post.
S:
S:
S: .
C: date
S: 111 20020112122419
C: quit
S: 205 closing connection - goodbye!
```

From Listing 11.3, we see that the NNTP server connection is created
using a telnet client. The NNTP server responds with a salutation (the server
type, etc.). We can now issue commands through the connection. There are
two basic types of responses that are expected from the server, single-line responses and multi-line responses. A single-line response is simple (see the
date command above). The multi-line response is similarly easy to deal with
given the universal termination symbol. NNTP follows the Simple Mail
Transport Protocol (SMTP) by using a single '.' on a line by itself to identify
the end of response (see the **list** and **article** commands, for example).

Now that we have a basic understanding of NNTP, let's now look at the
API that will be used to communicate with the news server.

The basic type that is used within the NNTP API is the news_t type. This
type defines the message unit that is communicated by the NNTP API functions (see Listing 11.4).

Listing 11.4   The Basic Message Structure, news_t.

```
typedef struct {
  char *msg;
  int  msgLen;
  int  msgId;
  char subject[MAX_LG_STRING+1];
  char sender[MAX_SM_STRING+1];
  char msgDate[MAX_SM_STRING+1];
  char *bodyStart;
} news_t;
```

The news_t structure includes the unparsed buffer (msg), length of the unparsed message (msgLen) and the numeric identifier for the message (msgId). Also parsed out of the message header are the subject, sender, and msgDate. Finally, the bodyStart field points to the body of the news message.

The first function that must be used when starting a new NNTP session is the nntpConnect function. This function establishes a connection to an NNTP server given the address of an NNTP server (either an IP address or a fully-qualified domain name). The nntpConnect function is shown in Listing 11.5.

Listing 11.5   nntpConnect API Function.

```
int nntpConnect ( char *nntpServer )
{
  int result = -1;
  struct sockaddr_in servaddr;

  if (!nntpServer) return -1;

  sock = socket( AF_INET, SOCK_STREAM, 0 );

  bzero( &servaddr, sizeof(servaddr) );
  servaddr.sin_family = AF_INET;
  servaddr.sin_port = htons( 119 );

  servaddr.sin_addr.s_addr = inet_addr( nntpServer );

  if ( servaddr.sin_addr.s_addr == 0xffffffff ) {
    struct hostent *hptr =
            (struct hostent *)gethostbyname( nntpServer );
    if ( hptr == NULL ) {
      return -1;
```

```
      } else {
        struct in_addr **addrs;
        addrs = (struct in_addr **)hptr->h_addr_list;
        memcpy( &servaddr.sin_addr, *addrs, sizeof(struct in_addr)
);
    }
  }

  result = connect( sock,
                  (struct sockaddr *)&servaddr, sizeof(servaddr)
                  );

  if ( result >= 0 ) {

    buffer[0] = 0;
    result = dialog( sock, buffer, "201", 3 );

    if (result < 0) nntpDisconnect();

  }

  return ( result );
}
```

The nntpConnect function first resolves the address passed in from the user (nntpServer). As with the monitorSite function, this can be a string IP address or a fully-qualified domain name, so each case is handled (see the monitorSite function discussion for a more detailed analysis of this function). The connect function is then used to connect to the remote server. As with all NNTP responses, a numeric ID is returned to identify the status of the response (through the dialog function). With an initial connect, the NNTP server should respond with a code 201 (successful connect). This is illustrated in the interactive NNTP session in Listing 11.3. If this code is found, success is returned to the caller, otherwise the NNTP session is disconnected and a failure code is returned (-1).

The dialog function is used by all NNTP API functions to validate the server's response (see Listing 11.6). We pass in the socket descriptor ID, a buffer that will be used to grab the response, our expected status response, and its length. We pass in our own buffer because of TCP re-packetization. Even though the server may emit one string containing the status line and another string with data, the network stack may combine these two before sending them out. Therefore, we provide the buffer to use to gather the response because it may have extra data within it that we'll need to parse later.

Listing 11.6   The NNTP `dialog` Support Function.

```
int dialog( int sd, char *buffer, char *resp, int rlen )
{
  int ret, len;

  if ((sd == -1) || (!buffer)) return -1;

  if (strlen(buffer) > 0) {
    len = strlen( buffer );
    if ( write( sd, buffer, len ) != len ) return -1;
  }

  if (resp != NULL) {
    ret = read( sd, buffer, MAX_LINE );
    if (ret >= 0) {
      buffer[ret] = 0;
      if (strncmp( buffer, resp, rlen )) return -1;
    } else {
      return -1;
    }
  }

  return 0;
}
```

Since we may not always want to send a command to the server, the `buffer` argument is checked to see if it contains a command (using `strlen`). If it does, we'll send this through the socket using the `write` function. Likewise, a response is not always desired. If the caller passes a buffer for the response string, we'll read some amount of data through the socket and check our status code against it. If it matches, a success code is returned (0); otherwise a failure code is returned (-1).

Once connected to a news server, a group must be set in order to look at any messages available. This is accomplished through the `nntpSetGroup` API function. The caller passes in the group name to be subscribed (such as "comp.ai.alife") and the last message read from the group. At initialization, the caller would pass in −1 for `lastRead` which indicates that no messages have been read. When messages are finally read through nntpPeek or nntp-Retrieve, the first message available will be read. Otherwise, the caller may specify the last message read, allowing the NNTP client to ignore previously read messages (see Listing 11.7).

Listing 11.7   nntpSetGroup API Function.

```
int nntpSetGroup( char *group, int lastRead )
{
  int result = -1;
  int numMessages = -1;

  if ((!group) || (sock == -1)) return -1;

  snprintf( buffer, 80, "group %s\n", group );

  result = dialog( sock, buffer, "211", 3 );

  if (result == 0) {
    sscanf( buffer, "211 %d %d %d ",
            &numMessages, &firstMessage, &lastMessage );

    if (lastRead == -1) {
      curMessage = firstMessage;
    } else {
      curMessage = lastRead+1;
      numMessages = lastMessage - lastRead;
    }

    printf("Set news group to %s\n", group);

  }

  return( numMessages );
}
```

Within the NNTP protocol, the group command is used to specify the group for subscription. The response will be a 211 (success) code, three numbers representing the number of messages available to read, and the first message and last message identifiers. These are stored internally on the NNTP client, and used on subsequent calls to NNTP API functions. The function returns the number of messages that are available to read.

Once subscribed to a group, the user may retrieve messages from the server using the message identifier attached to the message. Two API functions are available to read messages from the server, nntpPeek and nntpRetrieve.

The nntpPeek function reads only the header of the message, while nntpRetrieve reads the entire message (header and message body). The nntpPeek function is shown in Listing 11.8.

Listing 11.8   nntpPeek API Function.

```
int nntpPeek ( news_t *news, int totalLen )
{
  int result = -1, i, len=0, stop, state, bufIdx=0;

  if ((!news) || (sock == -1)) return -1;

  if ((curMessage == -1) || (curMessage > lastMessage)) return -2;

  /* Save the message id for this particular message */
  news->msgId = curMessage;

  snprintf( buffer, 80, "head %d\n", curMessage );

  result = dialog( sock, buffer, "221", 3 );

  if (result < 0) return -3;

  /* Skip the +OK response string and grab any data (end with
    CRLF) */
  len = strlen( buffer );
  for ( i = 0 ; i < len-1 ; i++ ) {
    if ( (buffer[i] == 0x0d) && (buffer[i+1] == 0x0a) ) {
      len -= i-2;
      memmove( news->msg, &buffer[i+2], len );
      bufIdx = len;
      break;
    }
  }

  state = stop = 0;

  while (!stop) {
```

```
        if (bufIdx+len > totalLen - 80) break;

        len = read( sock, &news->msg[bufIdx], (totalLen-bufIdx) );

        /* Search for the end-of-mail indicator in the current buffer
*/
        for ( i = bufIdx ; i < bufIdx+len ; i++ ) {
          if      ( (state == 0) && (news->msg[i] == 0x0d) ) state =
            1;
          else if ( (state == 1) && (news->msg[i] == 0x0a) ) state =
            2;
          else if ( (state == 2) && (news->msg[i] == 0x0d) ) state =
            1;
          else if ( (state == 2) && (news->msg[i] ==  '.') ) state =
            3;
          else if ( (state == 3) && (news->msg[i] == 0x0d) ) state =
            4;
          else if ( (state == 4) && (news->msg[i] == 0x0a) ) {
            stop = 1; break;
          } else state = 0;
        }

        bufIdx += len;

      }

      bufIdx -= 3;
      news->msg[bufIdx] = 0;
      news->msgLen = bufIdx;

      return bufIdx;
    }
```

The first task of nntpPeek is to emit the head command through the socket to the NNTP server. The NNTP server should respond with a '221' status code indicating that the head command succeeded. We then copy any other data that may have accompanied the status command from the NNTP server to our news message (news->msg). Finally, we read additional data from the socket until the end-of-mail indicator is found (a '.' on a line by itself). At this point, our message (stored in news->msg) contains only the message header and can be parsed accordingly (see nntpParse discussion).

The nntpRetrieve function is very similar to nntpPeek, except that the entire message is downloaded instead of the header alone (see Listing 11.9).

Listing 11.9   nntpRetrieve API Function.

```
int nntpRetrieve ( news_t *news, int totalLen )
{
  int result = -1, i, len=0, stop, state, bufIdx=0;

  if ((!news) || (sock == -1)) return -1;

  if ((curMessage == -1) || (curMessage > lastMessage)) return -1;

  /* Save the message id for this particular message */
  news->msgId = curMessage;

  snprintf( buffer, 80, "article %d\n", curMessage++ );

  result = dialog( sock, buffer, "220", 3 );

  if (result < 0) return -1;

  len = strlen(buffer);
  for ( i = 0 ; i < len-1 ; i++ ) {
    if ( (buffer[i] == 0x0d) && (buffer[i+1] == 0x0a) ) {
      len -= i-2;
      memmove( news->msg, &buffer[i+2], len );
      break;
    }
  }

  state = stop = 0;

  while (!stop) {

    if (bufIdx+len > totalLen - 80) break;

    /* Search for the end-of-mail indicator in the current buffer
*/
    for ( i = bufIdx ; i < bufIdx+len ; i++ ) {
      if      ( (state == 0) && (news->msg[i] == 0x0d) ) state =
        1;
      else if ( (state == 1) && (news->msg[i] == 0x0a) ) state =
        2;
      else if ( (state == 2) && (news->msg[i] == 0x0d) ) state =
        1;
      else if ( (state == 2) && (news->msg[i] ==  '.') ) state =
        3;
```

```
      else if ( (state == 3) && (news->msg[i] == 0x0d) ) state =
        4;
      else if ( (state == 4) && (news->msg[i] == 0x0a) ) {
        stop = 1; break;
      } else state = 0;
    }

  bufIdx += (i-bufIdx);

  if (!stop) {

    len = read( sock, &news->msg[bufIdx], (totalLen-bufIdx) );

    if ( (len <= 0) || (bufIdx+len > totalLen) ) {
      break;
    }

  }

  }

  bufIdx -= 3;
  news->msg[bufIdx] = 0;
  news->msgLen = bufIdx;

  return bufIdx;
}
```

The nntpRetrieve function uses the article NNTP command to request the entire message. Recall that nntpPeek used the head command to request the headers. NNTP returns the header and full message in the same way, a sequence of characters with a single '.' on a line by itself as an end-of-message indicator. Therefore, the nntpPeek and nntpRetrieve commands server similar purposes, but result in differing amounts of data. One additional difference between the two functions is the advancement of the current message identifier. The nntpPeek function does not advance the current message, while the nntpRetrieve function does. This is primarily because the nntpPeek function is used to look at the message to know if the entire message should be downloaded. If the user does not wish to download the message, the nntpSkip function can be used to advance the message identifier (see Listing 11.10).

Listing 11.10 `nntpSkip` API Function.

```
void nntpSkip( void )
{
  curMessage++;
}
```

Recall that `curMessage` is a static variable within the NNTP client that is initialized when the `nntpSetGroup` command is called.

Once the message (or header) has been downloaded from the NNTP server, it is contained within the `news_t` structure (see Listing 11.4). This structure can then be passed to the `nntpParse` function to parse out the subject, date, and sender of the news posting. Additionally, the start of the message body (message excluding the NNTP headers) is found and loaded into the `bodyStart` field. The `nntpParse` function can be found in Listing 11.11.

Listing 11.11 `nntpParse` API Function.

```
int nntpParse( news_t *news, unsigned int flags )
{
  int result;

  if (!news) return -1;

  result = parseEntry( news, "Subject:", news->subject );
  if (result < 0) return -1;

  result = parseEntry( news, "Date:", news->msgDate );
  if (result < 0) return -2;

  result = parseEntry( news, "From:", news->sender );
  if (result < 0) return -3;
  fixAddress( news->sender );

  if (flags == FULL_PARSE) {
    result = findBody( news );
  }

  return result;
}
```

The caller must define whether a header-only parse is required or if an entire message parse should be performed. A header-only parse is defined by passing in flags equal to HEADER_PARSE. For a full parse (includes identifying where the message body exists), flags should be equal to FULL_PARSE. The nntpParse function uses support functions parseEntry and findBody.

ON THE CD

While not discussed in this text, they can be found on the CD-ROM.

The parseEntry function simply parses the value associated with the header element as passed into parseEntry. Function findBody finds where the body of the message begins within the full message (header and body).

The final API function for NNTP is the nntpDisconnect function. This closes the session with the NNTP server (see Listing 11.12).

Listing 11.12   nntpDisconnect **API Function.**

```
int nntpDisconnect ( void )
{
  if (sock == -1) return -1;
  close(sock);
  sock = curMessage = firstMessage = lastMessage = -1;
  return 0;
}
```

In addition to closing the socket associated with the NNTP session, the function also initializes the internal state variables that will be reset when a new session is opened.

These seven API functions provide the ability for the WebAgent to retrieve news from an NNTP server and further filter this news based upon a user's criteria.

User Instruction

The user provides their filtering knowledge to the WebAgent through a simple configuration text file. This file has a very simple format, as illustrated by Listing 11.13.

Listing 11.13   WebAgent Configuration File Example.

```
#
# Sample config file
#
[monitor]
```

```
http://www.foxnews.com;Fox News
http://www.wnd.com/;WorldNetDaily
[feeds]
nntp://yellow.geeks.org
[groups]
comp.robotics.misc;camera;68HC11
sci.space.moderated;mars;gemini
sci.space.news;micro;satellite
```

The configuration file is made up of three sections, each of which is optional. The first section identifies the Web sites that are to be monitored (under the heading [monitor]). The Web sites must be specified in full URL format, including the http:// protocol specification. After the URL, a semicolon is used to separate the text name of the site (used for display purposes only).

A single feed is supported by the WebAgent, which defines where the agent may collect news items (under the heading [feeds]). The single feed is defined in URL format, including the protocol specification (in this case nntp://, specifying that the Network News Transfer Protocol). This is the site for which the WebAgent has the authority to connect. In this case, a freely available (and reliable) news server is illustrated.

Given the definition of a news feed, one or more groups may be defined (specified by the [groups] heading). Each line may contain a news-group definition that is terminated by a semicolon. Each word following the group specification is a search keyword that the WebAgent will use to determine if a given news article should be presented to the user. The more words that are found within the subject of the news article, the higher it is rated and the higher on the list it will be presented.

Let's now look at how the file is parsed. Recall that in Listing 11.1, we presented the monitorEntryType structure, which is used to represent the Web sites to monitor. In Listing 11.14, we present the feedEntryType structure that represents the news feed and news groups to monitor within that feed.

Listing 11.14   Types feedEntryType and groupEntryType.

```
#define MAX_URL_SIZE            80
#define MAX_SEARCH_ITEM_SIZE    40
#define MAX_SEARCH_STRINGS      10

#define MAX_GROUPS        20
```

```
typedef struct {
  int   active;
  char  groupName[MAX_URL_SIZE+1];
  int   lastMessageRead;
  char  searchString[MAX_SEARCH_STRINGS][MAX_SEARCH_ITEM_SIZE+1];
  int   numSearchStrings;
} groupEntryType;


typedef struct {
  char            url[MAX_URL_SIZE];
  groupEntryType  groups[MAX_GROUPS];
} feedEntryType;
```

The feedEntryType includes the URL of the feed itself (as parsed from the configuration file) and one or more group elements. A group structure maps to each line under the [groups] heading. This includes the name of the group, the last message that was read from the group and a set of search strings (as parsed after the group name). These two linked structures define the working state of the news-monitoring aspect of the WebAgent.

The first step to parsing the configuration file is a call to the parseConfig-File function. This is the main function for parsing and includes support for parsing each of the three elements from the configuration file (see Listing 11.15).

Listing 11.15   Main Configuration File Parsing Function.

```
int parseConfigFile( char *filename )
{
  FILE *fp;
  char line[MAX_LINE+1], *cur;
  int parse, i;

  bzero( &feed, sizeof(feed) );
  bzero( monitors, sizeof(monitors) );

  fp = fopen(filename, "r");

  if (fp == NULL) return -1;

  while( !feof(fp) ) {
```

```
fgets( line, MAX_LINE, fp );

if (feof(fp)) break;

if      (line[0] == '#') continue;
else if (line[0] == 0x0a) continue;

if        (!strncmp(line, "[monitor]", 9)) {
  parse = MONITOR_PARSE;
} else if (!strncmp(line, "[feeds]", 7)) {
  parse = FEEDS_PARSE;
} else if (!strncmp(line, "[groups]", 8)) {
  parse = GROUPS_PARSE;
} else {

  if (parse == MONITOR_PARSE) {

    if (!strncmp(line, "http://", 7)) {
      cur = parseURLorGroup( line, monitors[curMonitor].url );
      parseString( cur, monitors[curMonitor].urlName );
      monitors[curMonitor].active = 1;
      curMonitor++;
    } else return -1;

  } else if (parse == FEEDS_PARSE) {

    if (!strncmp(line, "nntp://", 7)) {
      cur = parseURLorGroup( line, feed.url );
    } else return -1;

  } else if (parse == GROUPS_PARSE) {

    cur = parseURLorGroup( line,
                           feed.groups[curGroup].groupName );

    i = 0;
    while (*cur) {
      cur = parseString(
              cur, feed.groups[curGroup].searchString[i] );

      if (strlen(feed.groups[curGroup].searchString[i])) i++;
      if (i == MAX_SEARCH_STRINGS) break;
    }
```

```
                feed.groups[curGroup].numSearchStrings = i;
                feed.groups[curGroup].active = 1;

                curGroup++;

            }

        }

    }

    readGroupStatus();

    return 0;
}
```

After initializing the WebAgent base structures, the configuration file is opened and each line is read from the file in the while loop. If a line starts with a '#' sign or with a line-feed (0x0a, an empty line), the line is ignored and the loop continues to read the next line. Otherwise, we test the line to see if it labels a new section (for monitor, feed, or groups). If so, we set our local parse variable to the appropriate state to know how to parse subsequent lines of the file.

If the line does not contain a label, we parse the line according to the current parse state (as defined by the parse variable).

For monitor state parsing, we first test the line to see if it contains a hypertext protocol URL. If it does, we call the parseURLorGroup function to parse the URL from the line. We then call the parseString function to parse the text name of the Web site that represents the URL. These two functions can be seen in Listing 11.16. Finally, we set the current monitor row to active (contains an URL to monitor) and increment the curMonitor variable for the next parse.

For feeds parsing, we look for a single line that defines the NNTP server to use. We use the parseURLorGroup function to parse the URL from the line and store this within the feed.url. The WebAgent will later connect to this URL to gather news.

Parsing a group is very similar to monitor state parsing, except for the fact that search strings follow the news-group name. As shown in Listing 11.14, up to 10 search strings may be present. If more are provided in the configuration file, they are simply ignored. The number of search strings is stored within the numSearchStrings field and it is activated by setting the active field to one.

Listing 11.16   Functions `parseURLorGroup` and `parseString`.

```c
char *parseURLorGroup( char *line, char *url )
{
  int i = 0;

  /* Search for the ';' or ' ' seperator */
  while ((*line != ' ') && (*line != ';') && (*line != 0x0a)) {
    url[i++] = *line++;
    if (i == MAX_URL_SIZE-1) break;
  }
  url[i] = 0;

  while ((*line != ';') && (*line != 0) && (*line != 0x0a)) i++;

  return( line );
}


char *parseString( char *line, char *string )
{
  int j=0;

  if (*line != ';') {
    *line = 0;
    return line;
  }
  line++;

  while (*line == ' ') line++;

  while ((*line != ';') && (*line != 0x0a)) {
    string[j++] = tolower(*line++);
    if (j == MAX_SEARCH_ITEM_SIZE-1) break;
  }
  string[j] = 0;

  while ((*line != ';') && (*line != 0)) line++;

  return( line );
}
```

The `parseURLorGroup` function is used to parse an URL or group from a line. The URL or group is the same to this function, as it simply looks for a separator (space, semicolon, or line-feed). Each of the characters that do not exist in the separator set is copied into the url character array passed by the user. When the separator is found, we skip any blank space found to prepare for the next parsing function.

The parseString function is similar to parseURLorGroup in that we copy the string found until a separator is found or line-feed, but convert each character to lowercase as we copy. In this way, search strings are case independent and simpler to match. When the separator is found, the new string is null-terminated and white space is skipped in preparation for another potential call to parseString.

Continuing from Listing 11.15, the parsing process continues until the end of the file is reached (no additional configuration entries found). At this point, a special function called readGroupStatus is called (see Listing 11.17). The purpose of this function is to read the archived information about the last message read for the news groups read from the configuration file.

Listing 11.17   Function readGroupStatus to Read the News Group State.

```
void readGroupStatus( void )
{
  FILE *fp;
  int  i, curMsg;
  char line[80];

  for (i = 0 ; i < MAX_MONITORS ; i++) {
    feed.groups[i].lastMessageRead = -1;
  }

  fp = fopen(GRPSTS_FILE, "r");
  if (fp == NULL) return;

  while (!feof(fp)) {

    fscanf( fp, "%s : %d\n", line, &curMsg );

    for (i = 0 ; i < MAX_MONITORS ; i++) {

      if (feed.groups[i].active) {

        if (!strcmp(feed.groups[i].groupName, line)) {

          feed.groups[i].lastMessageRead = curMsg;
```

```
        break;

      }

    }

  }

}

  return;
}
```

The purpose of readGroupStatus is to read the last message read for each of the configuration news groups (if available). If the group was just added to the configuration file, no first message is available and the WebAgent will read the first available message (as gathered by the nntpSetGroup function). Listing 11.18 shows the format of the file.

Listing 11.18   Format of the Group Status File Read by readGroupStatus.

```
comp.robotics.misc : 96000
sci.space.history : 135501
```

The format of the group status file (named group.sts within the file-system) provides a group on each line. The first element is the news-group name, a ':' separator, and the last message read for that group.

The first step in reading the group status is clearing out the lastMessageRead field for each of the groups within the feed structure. We then walk through each element of the group status file and try to parse each line to a group name and a message number. Upon reading a line, we search the feed groups to see if the group name exists (since the user could have removed it). If the group is found, we update the lastMessageRead field for that group with the message number (curMsg) read from the file. We'll look later at how and when this file is generated.

That completes the configuration process for the WebAgent. We'll now look at the meat of the WebAgent, data collection and filtering.

News Gathering and Filtering

Let's now focus on the process of gathering news and filtering it according to the user's specification. The process of gathering and filtering news is performed by a call to the checkNewsSources function (see Listing 11.19). This function very simply walks through the active groups in the feed structure and calls the checkGroup function to check the specific group.

Listing 11.19 Function checkNewsSources.

```
void checkNewsSources( void )
{
  int i;

  extern feedEntryType feed;

  for (i = 0 ; i < MAX_GROUPS ; i++) {

    if ( feed.groups[i].active ) {

      checkGroup( i );

    }

  }

  return;
}
```

The checkGroup function utilizes the previously discussed NNTP API to gather news based upon the user's specification (see Listing 11.20).

Listing 11.20 Function checkGroup.

```
void checkGroup( int group )
{
  int result, count, index = 0;
  char fqdn[80];
  news_t news;

  news.msg = (char *)malloc(MAX_NEWS_MSG+1);
  bzero( news.msg, MAX_NEWS_MSG+1 );
  news.msgLen = MAX_NEWS_MSG;

  prune( feed.url, fqdn );

  /* Connect to the defined NNTP server */
```

```
count = nntpConnect( fqdn );

if (count == 0) {

  /* Set to the defined group */
  count = nntpSetGroup( feed.groups[group].groupName,
                        feed.groups[group].lastMessageRead );

  index = 0;

  if (count > 200) count = 200;

  while (count-- > 0) {

    result = nntpPeek( &news, MAX_NEWS_MSG );

    if (result > 0) {

      result = nntpParse( &news, HEADER_PARSE );

      if (result == 0) {

        testNewsItem( group, &news );

      }

    }

    feed.groups[group].lastMessageRead = news.msgId;
    nntpSkip();

  }

}

free( news.msg );

nntpDisconnect();

return;
}
```

Function checkGroup first prunes the NNTP server name using the prune function. Recall that this function removes the initial protocol specification from the URL (nntp://) and any trailing '/' if it exists. Next, the news message is constructed. The NNTP API requires the user to define the actual buffer to be used to collect news (since it could be arbitrarily large to download certain messages). We allocate a buffer here of 64K for the buffer, and then load this into the msg field of the news structure. The size of this buffer is also loaded into the msgLen field so that the NNTP API does not overwrite the bounds of the buffer.

A session is constructed to the named NNTP server through the nntpConnect API function. If the return value indicates connection success, the group is set. Note that the group is set here based upon the user specification of the group argument. This is the index for the particular group of interest. This function returns the number of messages that are available to read. To avoid spending an inordinate amount of time working through all of the available messages, we cap the value at 200.

A loop is then performed to read the computed number of messages for the current group. We use the nntpPeek function since we're only interested in getting the message header information, specifically the subject field to test whether it matches the group's search criteria. The nntpParse function is called to parse the subject (and other fields) from the header and into the news structure. Given successful returns from nntpPeek and nntpParse, we pass the news item to testNewsItem to see if the search criteria match.

After the news item is tested, we update the lastMessageRead field to account for the current message and then skip the message. Recall that when only the nntpPeek function is used, we must also call nntpSkip to step to the next available message.

Upon completion of the loop, we free our previously malloc'd news buffer (news.msg) and disconnect from the NNTP server using nntpDisconnect.

Testing the news message, based upon the current news group's search criteria is a very simple process as shown in Listing 11.21.

Listing 11.21   Function testNewsItem.

```
void testNewsItem( int group, news_t *news )
{
  int i, count=0;
  char *cur;

  if (feed.groups[group].numSearchStrings > 0) {
```

```
    for ( i = 0 ; i < feed.groups[group].numSearchStrings ; i++ ) {

      cur = strstr( news->subject,
                         feed.groups[group].searchString[i] );

      if (cur) count++;

    }

  } else {

    count = -1;

  }

  if (count) {

    insertNewsItem( group, count, news );

  }

  return;
}
```

We use a very simple threshold to define whether a message matches the search criteria. If any of the search strings defined for the group are found within the subject of the message, we keep the news item to later present to the user. The search is performed using the strstr function, which identifies whether one string is found in another. For each of the search strings of the current group, we search the subject using strstr. If the return is non-NULL, a match was found and we increment a count variable. The count variable represents the number of matched search strings and is used as a 'goodness' indicator of the message (the higher the count, the higher the item will appear on the news list). If the count is non-zero (or no search strings were presented by the user), then we add this to the list of news items for later presentation.

The news list is a list of elements that act as containers for news data. The elementType is provided in Listing 11.22. This structure contains all the necessary information to describe a news message so that if the user desires to view the full message later, the relevant information can be used to retrieve the message.

Listing 11.22   Structure `elementType` for Storing Interesting News Items.

```
typedef struct elementStruct *elemPtr;

typedef struct elementStruct {
  int  group;
  int  rank;
  int  msgId;
  char subject[MAX_LG_STRING+1];
  char msgDate[MAX_SM_STRING+1];
  char link[MAX_SM_STRING+1];
  int  shown;
  struct elementStruct *next;
} elementType;
```

While many of these items are self-explanatory, the rest will be discussed within the context of the `insertNewsItem` function (see Listing 11.23).

Listing 11.23   Function `insertNewsItem`.

```
// Define the head of the news list.
elementType head;
void insertNewsItem( int group, int count, news_t *news )
{
  elementType *walker = &head;
  elementType *newElement;

  newElement = (elementType *)malloc(sizeof(elementType));

  newElement->group = group;
  newElement->rank = count;
  newElement->msgId = news->msgId;
  strncpy( newElement->subject, news->subject, MAX_LG_STRING );
  strncpy( newElement->msgDate, news->msgDate, MAX_SM_STRING );
  newElement->shown = 0;
  sprintf(newElement->link, "art%d_%d", group, news->msgId);
  newElement->next = (elementType *)NULL;

  while (walker) {
```

```
  /* If no next element, add new element to the end */
  if (walker->next == NULL) {
    walker->next = newElement;
    break;
  }

  /* Otherwise, insert in rank order (descending) */
  if (walker->next->rank < newElement->rank) {
    newElement->next = walker->next;
    walker->next = newElement;
    break;
  }

  walker = walker->next;

}

  return;
}
```

The first step of adding a news item to the list is to create a new news element (of type elementType). The element is created by mallocing a block of memory, and casting the memory to type elementType. The group for which the item was found is then loaded into group and the count is loaded as the rank (relative position based upon other news items in the list). The message identifier is stored as msgId (the unique ID of the message within the group) and the subject and msgDate are copied.

The shown field represents an indication of whether the particular items have been shown to the user. This is important because the user has the ability to clear the list of currently-viewed news items. When the clearing process occurs, it is performed only on those items that the user has seen (not items that may have been collected but not yet seen). When the item is displayed, the shown flag is set to one. It's initialized to zero here representing a new item not yet seen.

The link field is a special field used by the WebAgent to uniquely identify the article. The link is presented to the user as part of an HTML link tag. When the WebAgent's HTTP server receives a request for this link, it understands how to identify which particular message the user has requested to see. For example, if the group of the message is seven and the message ID is 20999, then the link will be defined as 'art7_20999'. The WebAgent understands how to parse this link to retrieve the article (identifier 20999) from the group (index 7 in the groups table of the feed structure).

Finally, the `next` field is the next element in the list. We initialize this to NULL (end of list) until we figure out where this particular item should be inserted).

At this point, we have a new `elementType` structure with the fields initialized based upon the news argument passed by the caller. The task is now simply to insert the item into the list based upon the rank. The higher the rank, the higher it will appear in the list. Recall that at the beginning of the function we set a walker variable to the header of the list. The head is a dummy element that contains no data, but exists only to simplify the management of the linked list (see Figure 11.8).

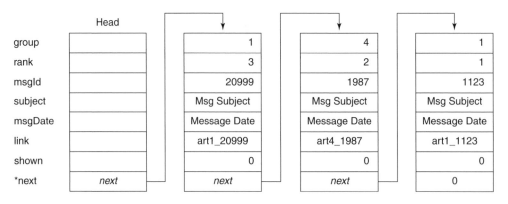

FIGURE 11.8   News list example.

From Listing 11.23, it's clear that the algorithm walks down the list of elements by sitting on one element and looking forward to the next. This is the only way to insert into a singly linked-list, as you can manipulate the next pointer on the current item, as well as the item to be inserted.

The first case to be handled is where there's no element next on the list. In this case, we simply add our current element to the tail (point the tail of our current element to the element to be added). We then break from the loop and return. Otherwise, we test the rank of the next element against the rank of the element to be inserted. If our element to be inserted has a rank greater than the element next on the list, then the element should be inserted here (between the current element on which we sit, and the next element to which it points). To insert the item, we set the next pointer of our element to be inserted to the next element in the list, and then point the next pointer of our current element to our element to be inserted. This completes the chain with the newly inserted element.

If the rank test was not satisfied, then we walk to the next element in the list (set our current element to the next element), and repeat the test as discussed above. This process creates a linked-list of news items that are to be presented to the user, in rank descending order. We'll look at the presentation of this data in the next section.

User Interface

The user interface presented by the WebAgent is an HTTP server accessible through a simple Web browser. In this section, we'll describe the HTTP server and how it operates to present dynamic data collected through the NNTP API.

The HTTP server must be initialized through a call to `initHttpServer`. This function is called once by the main application to create the HTTP server and socket to which clients may connect (see Listing 11.24).

Listing 11.24   Function `initHttpServer`.

```
int initHttpServer( void )
{
  int on=1, ret;
  struct sockaddr_in servaddr;

  if (listenfd != -1) close( listenfd );

  listenfd = socket( AF_INET, SOCK_STREAM, 0 );

  /* Make the port immediately reusable */
  ret = setsockopt( listenfd, SOL_SOCKET,
                    SO_REUSEADDR, &on, sizeof(on) );
  if (ret < 0) return -1;

  /* Set up the server socket to accept connections from any
   * address at port 8080.
   */
  bzero( (void *)&servaddr, sizeof(servaddr) );
  servaddr.sin_family = AF_INET;
```

```
        servaddr.sin_addr.s_addr = htonl( INADDR_ANY );
        servaddr.sin_port = htons( 8080 );

        /* Bind the socket with the prior servaddr structure */
        ret = bind( listenfd,
                    (struct sockaddr *)&servaddr, sizeof(servaddr) );

        if (ret < 0) return -1;

        listen(listenfd, 1);

        return 0;
    }
```

The `initHttpServer` function simply creates the server socket for which another function will check to see if clients have connected. This server will be non-traditional in that we won't sit blocked on the accept call awaiting client connections. Instead, we'll make use of the select call to know when a client has connected.

Upon creating the socket (in Listing 11.24), we enable the `SO_REUSEADDR` socket option to allow us to bind quickly to port 8080. If this option were not used, we would be required to wait two minutes between stopping and starting the WebAgent (due to the socket being in a time wait state). We then bind to port 8080, and allow any interface to permit connections (if the host happens to be multi-homed) using the `INADDRY_ANY` symbol. Once `bind` succeeds, we call `listen` to put the socket into the listening state (and allow clients to connect).

Since the WebAgent is required to multi-task (collect news, monitor Web sites, and gather news), we must support the ability to periodically perform tasks while awaiting user interaction through the HTTP server. We accomplish this through the WebAgent by checking for client connections, and at timeout intervals, check to see if any data collection is necessary. The timeout is provided by the `select` function (see Listing 11.25).

Listing 11.25 Function `checkHttpServer`.

```
    void checkHttpServer( void )
    {
      fd_set rfds;
      struct timeval tv;
      int ret = -1;
```

```
int connfd;
socklen_t clilen;
struct sockaddr_in cliaddr;

FD_ZERO( &rfds );
FD_SET( listenfd, &rfds );

tv.tv_sec = 1;
tv.tv_usec = 0;

ret = select( listenfd+1, &rfds, NULL, NULL, &tv );

if (ret > 0) {

  if (FD_ISSET(listenfd, &rfds)) {

    clilen = sizeof(cliaddr);
    connfd = accept( listenfd,
                     (struct sockaddr *)&cliaddr, &clilen );
    if (connfd > 0) {
      handleConnection( connfd );
      close( connfd );
    }

  } else {

    /* Some kind of error, reinitialize... */
    initHttpServer();

  }

} else if (ret < 0) {

    /* Some kind of error, reinitialize... */
    initHttpServer();

} else {

  // timeout -- no action.

}

return;
}
```

Recall from Listing 11.24 that `listenfd` represents the sock descriptor for the HTTP server. This descriptor is used with the select call to notify us when a client connection is available. The select call also provides a timeout feature, so that if a client connection does not occur within some period of time, the timeout forces the select call to unblock and notify the caller. The caller can then perform other processing. This is the basis for the WebAgent's ability to perform data collection on a periodic basis. Once data collection is complete, WebAgent returns to `checkHttpServer` to see if a client has connected to gather data. A full discussion of the `select` call is outside of the scope of this book, but a few useful references are provided in the resources section.

The `rfds` structure is used by the `select` call to create a bitmap of the sockets to monitor. We have only one, `listenfd`, and use the `FD_SET` macro to enable this socket within the `rfds` structure. We also initialize our `timeval` structure, specifying that the timeout is one second. The call to `select` is then made, specifying that we're awaiting a read event (for which a client connect is covered) in addition to a timeout event. The caller will be notified of the first occurrence of either event.

Once `select` returns, we check the return value. If the return is less than zero, then some type of error has occurred and we reinitialize the HTTP server through a call to `initHttpServer`. A return of zero indicates that the call timed-out (based upon the caller's predefined timeout value). In this case, we take no action and simply return. Data collection may then occur, if the time has come to do this. Finally, if the return value is greater than zero, a socket event occurred. We use the `FD_ISSET` macro to identify which socket caused the event (which should be our `listenfd`, since no other sockets were configured). If the `FD_ISSET` function confirms to us that the `listenfd` indeed has a client waiting, we accept the connection using the `accept` call and invoke `handleConnection` to service this request. Otherwise, an internal error has occurred and we reinitialize using `initHttpServer`.

The `handleConnection` function handles a single HTTP transaction. The HTTP request is first parsed to identify what the client is asking us to do. Based upon this request, a handler function is called to generate an HTTP response (see Listing 11.26).

Listing 11.26   Function `handleConnection`.

```
void handleConnection( int connfd )
{
  int len, max, loop;
```

```
char buffer[MAX_BUFFER+1];
char filename[80+1];

/* Read in the HTTP request message */
max = 0; loop = 1;
while (loop) {
  len = read(connfd, &buffer[max], 255); buffer[max+len] = 0;
  if (len <= 0) return;
  max += len;
  if ((buffer[max-4] == 0x0d) && (buffer[max-3] == 0x0a) &&
      (buffer[max-2] == 0x0d) && (buffer[max-1] == 0x0a)) {
        loop = 0;
  }
}

/* Determine the HTTP request */
if (!strncmp(buffer, "GET", 3)) {

  getFilename(buffer, filename, 4);

  /* Within this tiny HTTP server, the filename parsed from the
   * request determines the function to call to emit an HTTP
   * response.
   */
  if      (!strncmp(filename, "/index.html", 11))
    emitNews( connfd );
  else if (!strncmp(filename, "/config.html", 12))
    emitConfig( connfd );
  else if (!strncmp(filename, "/art", 3))
    emitArticle( connfd, filename );
  else
    write(connfd, notfound, strlen(notfound));

} else if (!strncmp(buffer, "POST", 4)) {

  getFilename(buffer, filename, 5);

  /* Ditto for the POST request (as above for GET). The POST
   * filename determines what to do -- the only case though
   * is the "Mark Read" button which clears the shown entries.
   */
  if (!strncmp(filename, "/clear", 6)) {
    clearEntries();
    emitHTTPResponseHeader( connfd );
```

```
        strcpy(buffer, "<P><H1>Click Back and Reload to "
                       "refresh page.</H1><P>\n\n");
      write(connfd, buffer, strlen(buffer));
    } else {
      write(connfd, notfound, strlen(notfound));
    }

  } else {

    strcpy(buffer, "HTTP/1.1 501 Not Implemented\n\n");
    write(connfd, buffer, strlen(buffer));

  }

  return;
}
```

The first step in handling a new HTTP connection is to read the HTTP request. The initial loop reads in the request, looking for an empty line. The empty line that follows the request is HTTP's way of terminating the request. Once we have our buffer with the completed request, we test it to see if the browser client sent us a GET request or a POST request. The GET request is used to request a file from the HTTP server; in our case, all files are dynamically generated based upon the filename that was requested. The POST request specifies that the user clicked a button within the served page, and is accompanied by a filename (traditionally a CGI filename, or Common Gateway Interface). CGI provides the means to interface the HTTP server with scripts to allow the server to perform actions. We simply look at the filename that the client POSTed, and use this to determine which action to perform.

For GET requests, the server knows how to serve three filenames. The '/index.html' is the default file and represents the main page for news browsing and Web site monitoring (recall Figure 11.5). When the client browser requests this file, the function emitNews is called to serve the news page. File '/config.html' represents the WebAgent configuration page (displays the current configuration). This was shown in Figure 11.7. If the filename begins with '/art' then the client browser has requested a particular piece of news (recall Figure 11.6). We'll see in the emitNews function how articles are linked within the news page. Function emitArticle is used to satisfy this request. Finally, if the HTTP server does not recognize the filename requested, an HTTP error response is generated (HTTP error code 404, file not found).

For POST requests, the associated filename is parsed from the HTTP request message. If the requested file was '/clear', then the client has requested that we clear the news that has already been viewed (as invoked through a button-click on the news page). We clear the viewed news items using clearEntries and then emit the HTTP response message header using emitHTTPResponseHeader. Finally, we write a short message to the user (which is displayed in the browser) to hit the back button and refresh to view the current news. If '/clear' was not the requested file, then an error has occurred and the error response is generated.

One final error leg in the handleConnection function exists for an unknown request. If the HTTP request message was not of type GET or POST, then we emit an error response that specifies that the feature is unimplemented.

Let's now look at some of the support functions used by handleConnection. The first, getFilename (Listing 11.27) is used to parse the filename from the HTTP request message. It parses the filename by skipping the HTTP request type and then copying any characters present until a space is found. One special case for getFilename is if the file requested was simply '/'. This is automatically converted to '/index.html', our news presentation page.

Listing 11.27 Support Function getFilename.

```
void getFilename(char *inbuf, char *out, int start)
{
  int i=start, j=0;

  /*
   * Skip any initial spaces
   */
  while (inbuf[i] == ' ') i++;

  for ( ; i < strlen(inbuf) ; i++) {
    if (inbuf[i] == ' ') {
      out[j] = 0;
      break;
    }
    out[j++] = inbuf[i];
  }

  if (!strcmp(out, "/")) strcpy(out, "/index.html");
```

```
        return;
    }
```

The next support function is emitHTTPResponseHeader, and is used to generate a simple HTTP response header (see Listing 11.28). This response instructs the client browser that the request was understood and that the response will be in HTML format (through the Content-Type header element).

Listing 11.28 Support Function emitHTTPResponseHeader.

```
void emitHTTPResponseHeader( int connfd )
{
  char line[80];

  strcpy( line, "HTTP/1.1 200 OK\n" );
  write( connfd, line, strlen(line) );

  strcpy( line, "Server: tinyHttp\n" );
  write( connfd, line, strlen(line) );

  strcpy( line, "Connection: close\n" );
  write( connfd, line, strlen(line) );

  strcpy( line, "Content-Type: text/html\n\n" );
  write( connfd, line, strlen(line) );

  return;
}
```

The caller passes in the socket descriptor for the current HTTP connection, which the emitHTTPResponseHeader function uses to send back the response.

The final support function for handleConnection is clearEntries (see Listing 11.29). This function is used to clear any news elements that have already been viewed by the client. We initialize the shown variable of the news element to zero, representing not yet viewed. This flag is set to one after the news page is served that contains those news elements. When the user clicks the "Mark Read" button on the news page, this function is called to clear the previously viewed items.

Listing 11.29   Support Function `clearEntries`.

```
void clearEntries( void )
{
  elementType *walker = &head;
  elementType *temp;
  int i;

  extern monitorEntryType monitors[];

  /* Clear the news chain (for items that have been viewed) */
  while (walker->next) {

    if (walker->next->shown) {
      temp = walker->next;
      walker->next = walker->next->next;
      free(temp);
    } else {
      walker = walker->next;
    }

  }

  /* Clear sites to be monitored (that have been seen) */
  for (i = 0 ; i < MAX_MONITORS ; i++) {

    if ((monitors[i].active) && (monitors[i].shown)) {
      monitors[i].changed = 0;
      monitors[i].shown = 0;
    }

  }

  emitGroupStatus();

}
```

The `clearEntries` function works similarly to `insertNewsItem` (shown in Listing 11.23). The function walks through the list of news items looking for an item that has the `shown` flag set. Note that we look forward from the current element, as this is the only way to remove an element. This is because we must set the `next` pointer of the current element to the `next` pointer of the next element. This effectively removes the item from the chain. We store the item to the `temp elementType`, so that we can free it once the chain is updated.

Function `clearEntries` also clears the shown flag for Web sites that are monitored. If the Web site has been noted as changed and shown, these flags are cleared so that it will not show up on the next request of the news page. Finally, the `clearEntries` function calls the function `emitGroupStatus` to write the group status file. This file identifies the last message read for each of the current news groups (see Listing 11.30).

Listing 11.30   Function `emitGroupStatus`.

```
void emitGroupStatus( void )
{
  FILE *fp;
  int  i;

  fp = fopen(GRPSTS_FILE, "w");

  for (i = 0 ; i < MAX_MONITORS ; i++) {

    if (feed.groups[i].active) {

      fprintf( fp, "%s : %d\n",
                   feed.groups[i].groupName,
                   feed.groups[i].lastMessageRead );

    }

  }

  fclose(fp);

  return;
}
```

Function `emitGroupStatus` simply emits the group name and last message read for each active group in the feed structure. If the WebAgent were stopped after this function, it could be restarted without missing any new messages or reintroducing older messages.

We continue with the user interface functionality by analyzing the three functions that generate the content served through the HTTP server. Recall from Listing 11.26, once the HTTP GET request was identified, the filename was parsed to route the request to the function to provide the required content.

The first content delivery function that we'll investigate is `emitConfig` (see Listing 11.31). This function displays the current configuration of the WebAgent for user review. The configuration cannot be changed through the Web page, but must instead be modified by editing the configuration file.

Listing 11.31   Function `emitConfig`.

```
const char *prologue={
  "<HTML><HEAD><TITLE>WebAgent</TITLE></HEAD>"
  "<BODY TEXT=\"#000000\" bgcolor=\"#FFFFFF\" link=\"#0000EE\""
  "vlink=\"#551A8B\" alink=\"#FF0000\">"
  "<BR><font face=\"Bauhaus Md BT\"><font color=\"#000000\">"
};


const char *epilogue={
  "</BODY></HTML>\n"
};


void emitConfig( int connfd )
{
char line[MAX_LINE+1];
  int i, j;

  extern monitorEntryType monitors[];
  extern feedEntryType feed;

  emitHTTPResponseHeader( connfd );

  write( connfd, prologue, strlen(prologue));

  strcpy(line, "@h1:Configuration</H1></font></font><BR><BR>");
  write( connfd, line, strlen(line));

  strcpy(line, "<font size=+2>Sites to Monitor</font><BR><BR>");
  write( connfd, line, strlen(line));

  strcpy(line, "<center><table BORDER=3 WIDTH=100%
NOSAVE><tr>\n");
```

```
   write( connfd, line, strlen(line));

  for (i = 0 ; i < MAX_MONITORS ; i++) {

    if (monitors[i].active) {

      sprintf(line, "<tr><td><font size=+1>%s</font></td><td>"
                    "<font size=+1>%s<font></td></tr>\n",
              monitors[i].urlName, monitors[i].url);
      write( connfd, line, strlen(line));

    }

  }

  strcpy(line, "</tr></table></center><BR><BR>\n");
  write( connfd, line, strlen(line));

  sprintf(line,
    "<H2>Feed %s</H2><BR><BR>\n", feed.url);
  write( connfd, line, strlen(line));

  strcpy(line, "<center><table BORDER=3 WIDTH=100%
NOSAVE><tr>\n");
  write( connfd, line, strlen(line));

  for (i = 0 ; i < MAX_GROUPS ; i++) {

    if (feed.groups[i].active) {

      sprintf(line, "<tr><td><font size=+1>Group
%s</font></td>\n",
              feed.groups[i].groupName);
      write( connfd, line, strlen(line));

      strcpy(line, "\n<td><font size=+1>");
      if (feed.groups[i].numSearchStrings > 0) {
        for (j = 0 ; j < feed.groups[i].numSearchStrings ; j++) {
          if (j > 0) strcat(line, ", ");
          strcat(line, feed.groups[i].searchString[j]);
        }
      } else {
        strcat(line, "[*]");
      }
```

```
        strcat(line, "</font></td></tr>\n");
        write( connfd, line, strlen(line) );

    }

  }

  strcpy(line, "</tr></table></center><BR><BR>\n");
  write( connfd, line, strlen(line));

  write( connfd, epilogue, strlen(epilogue));

  return;
}
```

The first item to notice is the construction of two constant character arrays that contain the HTML header and trailer information. The prologue sets up the color scheme, font size, and page title. The epilogue serves to complete the HTML page.

The first step in serving an HTML page through the server is emitting the HTTP response header (using the previously discussed emitHTTPResponse-Header). Emitting the prologue follows next along with some captions for the page. All of these elements use the connfd socket descriptor passed into the function. This is our conduit to the client browser; anything we send through this socket will be received and interpreted by the client.

Prior to emitting our Web site monitoring information, an HTML is created using the <table> HTML tag. Each of the elements within the table is then encapsulated within the row tag <tr>. We walk through the monitors table looking for active elements. Once found, we emit them with the appropriate tags to create the row with two columns. The columns represent the URL name (textual name for the Web site) and the actual URL. After we've exhausted the elements of the table, we close out the table using the </table> tag.

Next, we emit the feed URL as a single write through the socket. The line is constructed as one element using sprintf, and then emitted through the socket using the standard write call.

Emitting the group's information is very similar to the method used to emit the monitors. A new table is defined and each of the rows is emitted. Two columns are present per row, one for the news-group name and the other for the search strings applied to that group. The group name is defined as one element but the search strings are independent elements. Therefore, a loop is performed to construct a single string from each of the independent search strings, along with ', ' separators. If no search strings were present, we emit the '[*]' symbol to represent no search strings. Note that without any search strings; all messages are presented to the user. Once the outer loop has completed, the table is terminated with the </table> tag.

Finally, the epilogue is emitted to close out the HTML page. This tells the client browser that it can render the page and present it to the user.

The next function (emitNews, shown in Listing 11.32) is very similar to emitConfig except for a couple of minor points. We'll illustrate these, and ignore the duplicate elements that were discussed for emitConfig.

Listing 11.32 Function emitNews.

```
void emitNews( int connfd )
{
  int  i;
  char line[MAX_LINE+1];
  elementType *walker;

  extern monitorEntryType monitors[];
  extern feedEntryType feed;
  extern elementType head;

  emitHTTPResponseHeader( connfd );

  write( connfd, prologue, strlen(prologue));

  strcpy(line,
         "<H1>Web Agent Results</H1></font></font><BR><BR>");
  write( connfd, line, strlen(line));

  strcpy(line, "<center><table BORDER=3 WIDTH=100%
NOSAVE><tr>\n");
  write( connfd, line, strlen(line));

  for (i = 0 ; i < MAX_MONITORS ; i++) {

    if ((monitors[i].active) && (monitors[i].changed)) {

      sprintf(line, "<tr><td><font size=+1>%s</font></td>\n"
```

```
                    "<td><font size=+1><a href=\"%s\">%s</a>"
                    "</font></td></tr>\n",
             monitors[i].urlName, monitors[i].url,
             monitors[i].url);

    write( connfd, line, strlen(line));

    monitors[i].shown = 1;

  }

}

strcpy(line, "</tr></table></center><BR><BR>\n");
write( connfd, line, strlen(line));

walker = head.next;

if (walker) {

  strcpy(line,
        "<center><table BORDER=3 WIDTH=100% NOSAVE><tr>\n");
  write( connfd, line, strlen(line));

  while (walker) {

    sprintf(line, "<tr><td><font size=+1>%s</font></td>\n"
                  "<td><font size=+1><a href=\"%s\">"
                  "%s</a></font></td>"
                  "<td><font size=+1>%s</font></td></tr>",
                  feed.groups[walker->group].groupName,
                  walker->link,
                  walker->subject,
                  walker->msgDate );
    write( connfd, line, strlen(line));

    walker->shown = 1;
    walker = walker->next;

  }

  strcpy(line, "</tr></table></center>\n");
  write( connfd, line, strlen(line));
```

```
   }

   strcpy(line, "<FORM METHOD=\"POST\" ACTION=/clear\">");
   write( connfd, line, strlen(line));

   strcpy(line, "<BR><BR><INPUT TYPE=\"submit\" "
                "VALUE=\"Mark Read\"><BR>\n");
   write( connfd, line, strlen(line));

   write( connfd, epilogue, strlen(epilogue));

   return;
 }
```

The first item to note is in the section emitting the monitors (monitors loop). Only those rows that are `active`, and have previously been defined as `changed` are emitted. Once the item is displayed, the `shown` flag is set. Recall from the discussion of Listing 11.29 (`clearEntries`), that the `shown` flag is the indicator that when the client requests a clear of the previously displayed items, the item can be safely deleted. Similarly, the `shown` flag is also set in the news items that are displayed.

The final item to note in Listing 11.32 is the use of a link reference to permit the client browser to click the subject of a news item to view that actual news item. The HTML `<a href>` tag is used when displaying the subject to create this reference. The link field of the `elementType` is used to create this string reference (recall the discussion of the `link` field with Listing 11.23).

The final content generation function is `emitArticle`. This function is slightly more complicated in that it must communicate with the NNTP server to gather the body of the news item. Recall that only the head of the news message was initially extracted. This was done for time and space savings. When the user requests to view the article, a connection is created to the NNTP server to extract the entire article (see Listing 11.33).

Listing 11.33 Function `emitArticle`.

```
   void emitArticle( int connfd, char *filename )
   {
     int group, article, count, result;
     news_t news;
     char line[MAX_LINE+1];
```

```
extern feedEntryType feed;

sscanf(filename, "/art%d_%d", &group, &article);

news.msg = (char *)malloc(MAX_NEWS_MSG+1);
bzero( news.msg, MAX_NEWS_MSG+1 );
news.msgLen = MAX_NEWS_MSG;

emitHTTPResponseHeader( connfd );

write( connfd, prologue, strlen(prologue));

prune( feed.url, line );

count = nntpConnect( line );

if (count == 0) {

  count = nntpSetGroup( feed.groups[group].groupName,
                        article-1 );

  if (count > 0) {

    result = nntpRetrieve( &news, MAX_NEWS_MSG );

    if (result > 0) {

      result = nntpParse( &news, FULL_PARSE );

      if (result == 0) {

        /* Write to http */
        sprintf( line,
            "<font size=+1>Subject  : %s\n</font><BR><BR>",
                news.subject );
        write( connfd, line, strlen(line) );

        sprintf( line,
            "<font size=+1>Sender   : %s\n</font><BR><BR>",
                news.sender );
        write( connfd, line, strlen(line) );

        sprintf( line,
            "<font size=+1>Group    : %s\n</font><BR><BR>",
```

```
                        feed.groups[group].groupName );
            write( connfd, line, strlen(line) );

            sprintf( line, "<font size=+1>Msg Date : %s\n</font>"
                           "<BR><BR><hr><PRE>",
                     news.msgDate );
            write( connfd, line, strlen(line) );

            write( connfd,
                   news.bodyStart, strlen(news.bodyStart) );
            sprintf(line,
                "</PRE><BR><BR>End of Message\n<BR><BR>");
            write( connfd, line, strlen(line) );

          } else {

            /* Write error */
            printf("Parse error\n");

          }

        }

      }

    }

    write( connfd, epilogue, strlen(epilogue));

    free( news.msg );

    nntpDisconnect();

    return;
  }
```

The first step in emitting an article is identifying which article the client browser has requested. The filename argument (parsed from the HTTP get request in handleConnection) specifies this. We parse the filename to extract the group and article number. Recall that the group number is the index into the groups array of the feed structure. The article number is the actual numeric identifier of the article from the NNTP server.

Next, we create our news message that will be used to retrieve the full news message. The URL of the news feed is parsed and used to connect to the NNTP server with the `nntpConnect` function. If successful, we set the group to the group parsed from the "`/art`" filename (as `feed.groups[group]`). Note that we set the last message read to "`article-1`." This means that once the `nntpSetGroup` has completed, the first message to retrieve will be the article of interest. We then call `nntpRetrieve` and parse the results using `nntpParse`. One difference here is that we pass the `FULL_PARSE` symbolic to `nntpParse` so that the body of the message is identified.

What remains is to emit the retrieved information to the user through the passed socket descriptor `connfd`. We've seen most of the data that's being emitted. The new item is `bodyStart`, which represents the start of the message body of the article. Function `emitArticle` completes by writing the `epilogue`, freeing the buffers allocated for the `news` message and disconnecting from the NNTP server using `nntpDisconnect`.

Main Function

Let's now put it all together with the `main` function for WebAgent. This function provides the basic loop for the WebAgent functionality (see Listing 11.34).

Listing 11.34   The WebAgent `main()` Function.

```
int main()
{
  int timer=0, ret, i;

  extern monitorEntryType monitors[];

  /* Parse the configuration file */
  ret = parseConfigFile( "config" );

  if (ret != 0) {
    printf("Error reading configuration file\n");
    exit(0);
  }

  /* Start the HTTP server */
  initHttpServer();
```

```
      while (1) {

        /* Check the news and monitor sites every 10 minutes */
        if ((timer % 600) == 0) {

          /* Check news from the defined net news server */
          checkNewsSources();

          /* Check to see if any defined Web-sites have been
           * updated.
           */
          for (i = 0 ; i < MAX_MONITORS ; i++) {
            if (monitors[i].active) monitorSite( i );
          }

        }

        /* Check to see if a client has made a request */
        checkHttpServer();

        timer++;

      }

    }
```

WebAgent is first initialized by reading and parsing the configuration file using parseConfigFile and then starting the HTTP server with initHttpServer. We then start an infinite loop that performs two basic functions. The first is data collection and the second is checking for HTTP client connections.

Data collection is performed every 10 minutes (as defined by (timer % 600)). Function checkNewsSources is used to check if any news is available that matches the user's search criteria. The monitorSite function is used to check to see if any Web sites have changed, using an inner loop.

At the end of the loop, the HTTP server is checked for incoming client connections using checkHttpServer. The checkHttpServer function blocks for one second awaiting client connections. If no connection arrives in that time, the function returns and we check to see if data collection occurs. If a connection arrives during the time that we're collecting data, the connection is blocked and we pick it up at the next call to checkHttpServer.

OTHER APPLICATIONS

The applications of agent technology are quite large. Agents offer another paradigm for the development of distributed software outside of the development of intelligent applications. A very good resource for agent applications is the UMBC Agent Web page and the BotSpot Web page (see the Resources section). Table 11.2 provides a small sample of current agent applications.

TABLE 11.2 Current Agent Applications.

Agent Type	Description
Search Agents	Search and Filter the Web, Newsgroups, Databases, etc
Scheduling Agents	Schedule Resources Given Dynamic Constraints
Planning Agents	Create a Plan Given Resources, a Timeline, and Constraints
Auction Agents	Efficiently Trade Resources
Personal Agents	Work on a User's Behalf as an Intermediary

SUMMARY

In this chapter, we've looked at the field of intelligent agents. Intelligent agents are an interesting subfield of AI, as they exist to give applications some form of intelligence. After looking at the attributes commonly found in software agents, we looked at a common taxonomy of agents. We then looked at a variety of ways that intelligence could be given to agents, some of which are detailed in this book. Finally, we looked at an implementation of a very simple Web-filtering agent, discussing the variety of network interfaces that were utilized.

REFERENCES

[Franklin and Graesser 1996] Franklin, S., and A. Graesser. (1996). *Is It an Agent or Just a Program? A Taxonomy for Autonomous Agents.* Proceedings of the Third International Workshiop on Agent Theories, Architectures, and Languages. New York: Springer Verlag.

[Kay 1984] Kay, Alan, (1994). "Computer Software," *Scientific American* 251(3): 53–59, September.

[King 1995] King, J. (1995). "Intelligent Agents: Bringing Good Things to Life," *AI Expert*: 17–19 (February), available online at *http://coqui.lce.org/cedu5100/Intelligent_Agents.htm* (accessed January 17, 2003)

RESOURCES

Ananova Ltd. "Ananova Agent," available online at *http://www.ananova.com/video* (accessed January 18, 2003)

BotSpot. *http://www.botspot.com*

Bradshaw, J. (1997). *Software Agents*. AAAI Press / MIT Press.

SourceForge. "Aglet Software Development Kit," available online at *http://sourceforge.net/projects/aglets/* (accessed January 18, 2003)

University of Maryland Baltimore Count. "Agent Web," available online at *http://agents.umbc.edu/* (accessed January 18, 2003)

12 ▪ AI Today

In this final chapter, we'll look at where research is going for AI today. AI is a classic example of a technology that seemed initially so solvable, and then, on closer examination, so thorny and difficult. The early promises of AI didn't work out, which make predicting its future ambitious at best. This section will provide some of the interesting developments that are changing AI today.

TOP DOWN TO BOTTOM UP

The methods to achieve artificial intelligence can be divided into two broad categories; top down and bottom up. The top-down category is synonymous with traditional symbolic AI where cognition is a high-level concept and is independent of the lower-level details that implement it. The bottom-up category is synonymous with connectionist AI (neural networks); following closely the model of our own mammalian brains. Cognition, from the bottom-up perspective, is hoped to emerge from the operation of many simple elements. Also included in the bottom-up approach are the evolutionary algorithms and artificial life.

Consider our own brains. We have yet to define plausible structures that exist within the brain that yield what we consider intelligence or consciousness. Yet, the firing of millions of neurons somehow provides intelligence at the global level. The simple process of a neuron firing at the micro level gives rise to something much greater at the macro level.

AI began in the top-down camp with only minor amounts of research in connectionism. Research in neural networks was almost halted completely after Marvin Minsky and Seymour Papert published the book *Perceptrons*, but it didn't take long for the research community to realize that the problems identified in the book were easily solved. As it stands now, the bottom-up camp has the edge for the future of AI. An interesting question for AI is whether we can program an AI that mimics human intelligence, or build the basic needs and allow the AI to learn and evolve into human intelligence. The results in both camps show the bottom-up camp moving ahead.

BUILDING ARTIFICIAL ANIMALS

Alan Turing first proposed the idea of a "Child Machine," with the premise that an intelligent machine would not be turned on and immediately be intelligent, but would learn as do children. The desire to learn would be programmed, but the knowledge contained with the machine would be learned over time.

Others have proposed that building artificial animals is the right approach. Could we build an artificial insect, for example, that could mimic the behavior and learning abilities of the physical insect? This is a much smaller step than building an artificial human, but it's very likely that the lessons learned along the way will help us in this endeavor.

The logical progression of artificial insects, animals, and humans are their physical embodiments in robots. This will require innovations in the development and construction of micro sensors and actuators in addition to software-based cognitive structures that permit unbounded learning.

COMMONSENSE REASONING AND CYC

Marvin Minsky identified one of the primary problems of expert systems today—while they include a large mass of knowledge about a particular domain, they lack commonsense [Minsky 1992]. Consider the example of an expert system and a chess-playing program. Both are reasonably intelligent within the tiny domain for which they exist, but the expert system knows nothing about chess, and the chess-playing program is unable to reason about anything but selecting a chess move. In other words, these intelligent programs are useless outside of their particular expertise. Perhaps if these systems were endowed with some kind of commonsense, they could communicate with each other and perhaps even cooperate?

One of the most visible commonsense reasoning projects today is the CYC project at Cycorp. This project is led by Doug Lenat (we'll see this name again in the domain of scientific discovery). The original goal of CYC was to develop a knowledge base containing a massive amount of commonsense knowledge. In addition to simple facts, the knowledge base also includes assertions (rules) that relate facts. CYC includes "microtheories" that bundle assertions together for a particular domain of knowledge to support and optimize the inference process. The inference engine supports reasoning about the facts in the knowledge base.

Cycorp has recently released OpenCyc, which is an open source version of the CYC technology. This includes a knowledge base (6,000 concepts with 60,000 assertions), the CYC inference engine and a number of language bindings and APIs to support software development with the knowledge base.

AUTONOMIC COMPUTING

At Artificial Life IV workshop in 1994, Jeffrey O. Kephart of IBM presented the paper "A Biologically Inspired Immune System for Computers." In this paper, Jeffrey described an antivirus architecture that modeled an immune system for computers and computer networks. Other biologically motivated ideas in this paper include the use of self-replication to fight virus self-replication.

IBM has since moved forward with a very aggressive strategy of building self-managing computer systems based upon autonomic principles. The four key areas they identify for their self-managing systems are:

- Self-Configuring, adapting to dynamic environments
- Self-Healing, diagnosing and preventing problems
- Self-Optimizing, automatically tuning and balancing
- Self-Protecting, detecting and protecting against attacks

The goals of this effort are manifold, and include a reduction in computing complexity of future systems, decreasing demand for IT specialists, cost savings, and providing the ability for systems and humans to collaborate to solve complex problems.

While it's not entirely clear how autonomic computing will be built and used in practice, it's an intriguing idea that may help in the development of robust and reliable software systems.

AI AND SCIENTIFIC DISCOVERY

Imagine using a computer to augment a human's creativity, or to assist in the discovery of interesting new theories in a variety of fields. This area of study is not new, but continues to receive attention. The benefits are twofold: understanding the creative process in humans, and the result of discovery in computers, both of which produce new theories and ideas.

Some of the original discovery programs were developed to discover new concepts and conjectures in elementary mathematics, set theory, and graph theory. Doug Lenat's Automatic Mathematician (AM) and his later Eurisko rediscovered some fundamental mathematical axioms in addition to some new conjectures.

Artificial scientific discovery methods have also been applied to other domains of science including chemistry, particle physics, and orbital mechanics. The BACON.3 system (developed by P. Langley) rediscovered Kepler's third law (the squares of the periods of the planets are proportional to the cubes of their semimajor axes). While rediscovery may not add to new knowledge, it does illustrate that computers can discover complex theories and shows hope for future discovery.

AFFECTIVE COMPUTING

Recently, momentum is increasing in the belief that emotion is a critical part of intelligence. Further, some believe that true intelligence may not be possible without also including emotion into the model. The Affective Computing group at MIT, under the direction of Rosalind Picard, has been at the forefront of research in this area. Rosalind's group focuses on a wide spectrum of research areas, from computers sensing affect in humans to synthesizing emotions in computers.

Sensing emotions in users is an important aspect of future user interfaces. For example, if a computer could sense that its user was getting frustrated, it could change the way in which information was being presented. A vehicle equipped with affect sensing equipment might be able to detect if a driver was falling asleep, or impaired due to alcohol or drugs. The group uses a variety of sensors to evaluate the user's affective state. For example, a galvanic skin response sensor (GSR) for measuring skin conductance can identify the user's anxiety or a startle response. A respiration sensor can measure the rate and depth of a user's breathing, which can be used to identify the user's state of alertness. Finally, an electromyogram sensor can measure the electromygraphic activity of muscles, detecting muscle contraction. The affective computing group has successfully measure jaw clenching with this device that could be used to identify states of anger in the user.

Sensing the external effects of emotion is one task, but identifying what they represent for an individual user is another. The group also researches recognizing (and learning) emotive states based upon a set of externally visible markers. Since these can be different for each person, the recognition task must including learning so that physical measurements properly map to defined states of emotion.

The ability to synthesize emotions in intelligent machines is another interesting area of research within MIT's group. They focus on not only synthesizing emotions that are externally understood, but also modeling true emotions as an internal mechanism. Consider a spacecraft subsystem that modeled varying types of emotion. If the spacecraft had lost pointing to a ground station on the Earth, it could integrate emotions of fear and raised state of awareness about its position. Consider also that while in this state, its lack of pointing causes it to decrease its available store of power in its onboard batteries. In this scenario, the spacecraft's pointing becomes even more critical as complete loss of power can lead to the loss (death) of the spacecraft. The incremental fear "experienced" by the spacecraft would lead to progressively more drastic measures in order to gain control, leading to decreased degrees of fear and an increasing state of happiness. While the spacecraft is in a state of fear, it would concentrate less on tasks that don't affect the survival of the spacecraft (such as onboard science experiments) and more on those aspects that decrease the fear and lead to happiness. While this scenario is imaginative, affective states can offer new ways to think about fault management and recovery, in addition to dealing with combinations of failures that may or may not have similar mechanisms for recovery.

SEMANTIC WEB

While the Internet is a huge mass of information, its primary representation is HTML and is useful only to humans. The Semantic Web was created to change this by making the information useful also to machines. This process will not only make Web searches more specific, but will permit the representation of Internet information as knowledge that can then be tapped on a global scale.

The Semantic Web is still in its infancy, but is growing quickly since it will be a very important development. It was created by Tim Berners-Lee, the originator of the World Wide Web and the protocol on which it exists, HTTP. The Semantic Web is built upon two basic technologies, also relatively new. The first is XML (eXtensible Markup Language), which is an encoding scheme that permits wrapping information with tags that identify what the information represents. For example, if a Web page included the following information:

```
<BR>
Part Number: 2N2222
<BR>
Type: Transistor
<BR>
Leads: 3
<BR>
Cost: $0.25
```

This could be represented in XML as:

```
<discrete-part>
    <part-number>2N2222</part-number>
    <type>Transistor</part-type>
    <lead-count>3</part-lead-count>
    <price-usd>0.25<price-usd>
</discrete-part>
```

In this case, there's no ambiguity about what the information represents. The information is easily parsed from the XML using the tags as markers for what is being represented. From the initial HTML representation, if a manufacturer used the term "Pins" instead of "Leads," then the meaning would break down. Additionally, in HTML, is the price U.S. dollars or Australian dollars? The XML tag makes this very unambiguous. Therefore, from this simple example it's clear that having an information schema can lead to more globally useful information. XML provides the ability to build up schemas so that a transistor could be represented by its own set of tags, which further simplifies this process.

The second technology that provides the basis for the Semantic Web is RDF, or Resource Description Framework. RDF is an XML-based language that permits information on the Web to be machine-processable, unambiguous, and meaningful. RDF is coded in triplets where each element of the triplet is an URI, or Uniform Resource Identifier. A URL (Uniform Resource Locator), of which a link on a Web page is the most common use, is a URI. The elements in an RDF triplet can take the form subject, verb, and object. Therefore, we can tie information together on the Web to draw similarities or associations.

Recall from the discussion of XML that schemas can be defined so that terms have a common meaning. With RDF, a corresponding ontology is used. An ontology is a document (referenced by RDF triplets) that defines the classes of objects and relations among them. Ontologies provide the mechanism for understanding data in a particular domain, in addition to drawing inferences about the data. This allows new knowledge to be created about existing knowledge within the Semantic Web. There are many challenges in this space, but the Semantic Web could be one of the most useful developments for AI.

REFERENCES

[Minsky 1992] Minsky, Marvin. (1992). "Future of AI Technology," *Toshiba Review* 47, no. 7 (July). Available online at *http://web.media.mit.edu/~minsky/papers/CausalDiversity.html* (accessed January 18, 2003)

RESOURCES

Affective Computing Group at MIT. *http://affect.media.mit.edu/*

Berners-Lee, T., Hendler, J., Lassila, O. (2001). "The Semantic Web," *Scientific American*, May. Available online at *http://www.sciam.com/article.cfm?articleID=00048144-10D2-1C70-84A9809EC588EF21* (accessed January 18, 2003)

Cycorp Web site. http://www.cyc.com

IBM's Autonomic Computing Web site. *http://www-3.ibm.com/autonomic/index.shtml*

Kephart, Jeffrey. "A Biologically Inspired Immune Systems for Computers," in *Artificial Life IV:Proceedings of the Fourth International Workshop on the Synthesis and Simulation of Living Systems*. Cambridge, Mass: MIT Press.

OpenCyc. *http://www.opencyc.org*

Scientific Discovery. *http://www.aaai.org/AITopics/html/discovery.html*

Semantic Web Community Portal. *http://www.semanticweb.org/*

Wagman, Morton, (2000). *Scientific Discovery Processes in Humans and Computers: Theory and Research in Psychology and Artificial Intelligence*. Praeger Publishers.

About the CD-ROM

T he CD-ROM contains a number of useful applications that demonstrate the properties of AI algorithmic techniques and methods. The methods and applications that demonstrate them are noted in this section.

SIMULATED ANNEALING

Simulated annealing, or modeling of systematic cooling of a molten metal to a solid, is described in Chapter 2. The theoretical N-Queens problem is used to demonstrate the constraint satisfaction properties of the algorithm. The algorithm and application can be found on the CD-ROM at `./software/ch2`.

ADAPTIVE RESONANCE THEORY

Adaptive resonance theory, also called ART1, is a clustering algorithm that provides the ability to separate (or cluster) elements in a data set into independent data sets based upon properties of the individual data items. The algorithm does this in an unsupervised manner, allowing the algorithm to find patterns in the data that a user may not notice. In chapter 3, the practical problem of personalization is used to demonstrate ART1 in the context of a recommender system. The algorithm and application can be found on the CD-ROM at `./software/ch3`.

ANT ALGORITHMS

Ant algorithms are a relatively new method that can be used to identify optimal paths through a graph. This method is described in Chapter 4. Ant algorithms model the movement of ants within an environment and use simulated pheromone to communicate with other ants (the process of stigmergy). The theoretical problem of the Traveling Salesman Problem (or TSP) is used to demonstrate the ant algorithm. The algorithm and application can be found on the CD-ROM at ./software/ch4.

BACKPROPAGATION ALGORITHM

The backpropagation algorithm, discussed in Chapter 5, is one of the primary methods used to train multi-layer neural networks given a training set and a set of desired outputs. Backpropagation propagates errors back through the nodes of a network, altering the weights of the connections based upon the error of the actual and desired outputs. The interesting problem of training game neurocontrollers (game AI) is used to demonstrate backpropagation. Given a simple neural network, a set of environmental inputs and a set of allowable actions (otherwise known as the training set), the algorithm trains the network to perform the desired action for the current environment. It is then demonstrated that the neurocontroller is able to generalize and perform useful behaviors for unforeseen environments. The backpropagation algorithm and neurocontroller application can be found on the CD-ROM at ./software/ch5.

GENETIC ALGORITHMS / GENETIC PROGRAMMING

Genetic algorithms, described in Chapter 6, provide a novel optimization technique that can be applied to both numerical and symbolic problems. The subfield of genetic programming is further used to illustrate the creation of instruction sequences to solve problems in code generation. Sequences of instructions are evolved to solve mathematical functions, and it is demonstrated how these sequences can find novel strings that are both interesting and optimal given a simple virtual machine. The genetic programming algorithm and application can be found on the CD-ROM at `./software/ch6`.

ARTIFICIAL LIFE / EVOLVING NEURAL NETWORKS

Artificial life, described in Chapter 7, is studied here in the context of neural networks through evolution of simple organisms in a synthetic environment. Organisms survive through successfully existing within their environment, avoiding prey and foraging for food. Organisms are permitted to reproduce once they reach a high enough level of internal energy. Therefore, reproduction is only permitted if organisms can survive within the environment, which should lead to more fit organisms. The organisms are provided with multi-layer, neural networks as their neurocontrollers. Two different types of organisms illustrate simple food-web organizations. The artificial life application can be found on the CD-ROM at `./software/ch7`.

EXPERT SYSTEMS

Rules-based systems are the topic of Chapter 8, which emphasizes the implementation of a forward-chaining system. Varieties of examples are provided, in the form of rules and initial facts, with a final example of embedded the rules-based system into an embedded system and utilizing it for sensor fault-tolerance. The forward-chaining, rules-based system and application files can be found on the CD-ROM at `./software/ch8`.

FUZZY LOGIC

In Chapter 9, fuzzy logic and fuzzy control are described including an implementation of a fuzzy API for inclusion into other applications. The API provides not only the standard fuzzy operators, but also helper functions that support the simple creation of fuzzy membership functions. The fuzzy logic API and a simple battery charger example is provided on the CD-ROM at `./software/ch9`.

HIDDEN MARKOV MODELS

Bigram models (a type of Hidden Markov Model) are the topic of Chapter 10, which are networks that include states and transitions with associated probabilities. The outcome, or observation, of a state is generated based upon the associated probability distribution. The action is performed and made visible, though the internal state is hidden, thus the hidden aspect of the Markov model. Hidden Markov models have a variety of applications; in Chapter 10 we look at the generation of meaningful text based upon training by a corpus. The HMM and a text generation example is provided on the CD-ROM at `./software/ch10`.

INTELLIGENT AGENTS

Intelligent agents are the final topic in Chapter 11, with emphasis on search and filtering agents. Intelligent agents are applied in a number of different ways; the application chosen for this chapter is a filtering agent that acts as an intermediary to UseNet sites on the Internet. The WebAgent is configured through a simple configuration file. It then autonomously gathers news using the NNTP protocol and presents it to the user with the HTTP protocol (acting as a simple Web server). The WebAgent is provided on the CD-ROM at `./software/ch11`.

SYSTEM REQUIREMENTS

Applications on this CD-ROM require a PC with Windows 95, 98, 2000, Me, or XP using the Cygwin UNIX environment (freely downloadable at *www.cygwin.com*) or Linux (Red Hat 6.1 or later, or comparable Linux distribution); 486 or higher CPU; 64MB RAM; 60MB disk space; CD-ROM drive; Internet access and Web browser (for the WebAgent example).

Index

X

Z